WHERE TO WATCH BIRDS IN
BRITAIN & IRELAND

DAVID TIPLING

NEW HOLLAND

This edition first published in 2006 by New Holland Publishers (UK) Ltd
London • Cape Town • Sydney • Auckland
www.newhollandpublishers.com

Garfield House, 86–88 Edgware Road, London W2 2EA
80 McKenzie Street, Cape Town 8001, South Africa
14 Aquatic Drive, Frenchs Forest, NSW 2086, Australia
218 Lake Road, Northcote, Auckland, New Zealand

10 9 8 7 6 5 4 3 2 1

ISBN 1 84537 459 2

Publishing Manager: Jo Hemmings
Cover Design: Gülen Shevki-Taylor
Cartographer: William Smuts
Design and Editorial: Warrender Grant Publications
Production: Joan Woodroffe

Reproduction by Modern Age Repro Co., Hong Kong
Printed and bound in Singapore by Kyodo Printing Co (Singapore) Pte Ltd

AUTHOR'S ACKNOWLEDGEMENTS

It would be impossible to write such a guide without the help of many people along the way. Since I last made a similar
undertaking, so much has changed. New reserves have been born, some sites once prominent for their attraction to birds
have faded away, while others have risen to prominence.
    Perhaps most marked to me have been the shifts in bird populations around the country in just eight years. For
example, in Kent, Wood Warblers have just about disappeared in the county, Redstarts have disappeared from many sites,
and a whole tern colony has moved across the English Channel to France. Yet on the plus side, Little Egrets have
colonized, and Buzzards are once more nesting annually in the county. In Shetland Kittiwake colonies with their
distinctive sound, no longer haunt many cliffs, Black Grouse and Capercaillie have continued to decline, yet Bitterns are
bouncing back, and Ospreys now nest in England after an absence of many generations.
    It is for these reasons that I have relied upon a number of experts around the country to check and comment on my
text. I do of course take full responsibility for any errors or omissions within this book. My grateful thanks go to Robin
Chittenden, Angus Murray, Hugh Harrop, Tom Ennis, Judd Hunt, Paul Rogers, Phil Newton, Steve Young, John North,
Barry Wright and Tim Melville for checking and commenting on drafts of text. My thanks, too, to the many reserve staff
from organizations such as the RSPB, WWT and various Wildlife Trusts who answered my queries.

THE WILDLIFE TRUSTS

The Wildlife Trusts partnership is the UK's leading voluntary organization working, since 1912, in all areas of nature conservation. We are fortunate to have the support of more than 450,000 members, including some famous household names.

The Wildlife Trusts protect wildlife for the future by managing in excess of 2,500 nature reserves, ranging from woodlands and peat bogs, to heathlands, coastal habitats and wild flower meadows. We campaign tirelessly on behalf of wildlife, including of course the multitude of bird species.

We run thousands of events, including dawn chorus walks and birdwatching activities, and projects for adults and children across the UK. Leicestershire and Rutland Wildlife Trust organizes the British Birdwatching Fair at Rutland Water – now also home to Osprey. The Wildlife Trusts work to influence industry and government and also advise landowners.

As numbers of formerly common species plummet, we are urging people from all walks of life to take action, whether supporting conservation organisations in their work for birds, or taking a few small steps in their own lives.

For many birders exploring every corner of the British Isles, and beyond, is a great way to see a wide variety of species that are not likely to be encountered in the local park or back garden, and perhaps take their birding one step further.

And it is for all those birdwatchers who wish to go further afield that *Where to Watch Birds in Britain and Ireland* is such an excellent guide. David Tipling covers a varied selection of sites, including not only the most popular, but also some of the most interesting areas and habitats regardless of size. The book includes details on how to get to each site, the habitat that is predominant and the birds most likely to be witnessed, providing a valuable resource to those birding hot spots around Britain and Ireland. David also notes in his acknowledgements the species and their decline or increase in numbers at a given site from previous years.

A recent survey conducted by The Wildlife Trusts, in association with the *Daily Telegraph* and BBC's *Tomorrow's World*, asked people to tick off the wildlife they had seen in their garden over the previous year. The list included Robin, Blackbird, Wren and House Sparrow. More than 66,000 people responded, confirming what experts had warned, for example that the House Sparrow had declined dramatically. Results also told us just how much people love watching wildlife, especially birds.

The Wildlife Trusts is a registered charity (number 207238). For membership and other details, please phone The Wildlife Trusts on 0870 0367711, log on to www.wildlifetrusts.org, or complete the form on the inside back cover.

CONTENTS

CONTENTS

Scale

m   0 10 20 30 40 50 60 70 80 90 100

km   0   20   40   60   80   100

SHETLAND

ORKNEY

SCOTLAND

GLASGOW   EDINBURGH

LONDONDERRY

NORTHERN IRELAND

BELFAST

NEWCASTLE UPON TYNE

SUNDERLAND

NORTHERN ENGLAND

REPUBLIC OF IRELAND (EIRE)

DUBLIN

BRADFORD   LEEDS   HULL

MANCHESTER

LIVERPOOL   SHEFFIELD

STOKE-ON-TRENT   DERBY   NOTTINGHAM

LIMERICK

WATERFORD

CORK

WOLVERHAMPTON   LEICESTER

BIRMINGHAM   COVENTRY

EAST ANGLIA

WALES

THE MIDLANDS

LONDON

CARDIFF   BRISTOL

SOUTH-EAST ENGLAND

SOUTHAMPTON

SOUTH-WEST ENGLAND

PLYMOUTH

N

INTRODUCTION

Birdwatching entered my life almost 30 years ago. From my first memories of being distracted in class by a Nuthatch visiting the school bird table, I was soon exploring the fields and woods close to home in Kent. By my teens Bough Beech Reservoir some 12 miles away was within pedalling distance. My only experience of reserves away from the vicinity of home was from Young Ornithologists Club field trips, and family holidays. But I knew great discoveries lay further afield. There was just one site guide available, from which I gleaned this information.

How times have changed. Today, information on birding sites and reserves is available from a myriad sources, yet much of this information is spread through a variety of books, magazines and on the internet. My aim in writing this book has been to give an overview, in a single volume, of Britain and Ireland's best birdwatching sites. The choice of sites is a personal one, and one that not everyone may agree with – such is the difficulty of choosing just over 300 sites from the whole of the region.

HOW THIS BOOK WORKS
Each entry has a brief introduction, outlining habitat, special birds and, where appropriate, information on locations within the site. The size and status are also provided, where applicable, with the names of most organizations given in full. However, the following are abbreviated:

LNR   Local Nature Reserve
NNR   National Nature Reserve
RSPB   Royal Society for the Protection of Birds
WWT   Wildfowl & Wetlands Trust

The information is then divided into the following sections:

KEY BIRDS
A listing of seasonal birds is provided. I have attempted to list only species that regularly occur, or can be expected on a typical visit. Of course, no visit is likely to yield all the birds listed for that season – if birding was so predictable, then where would be the fun? However, during the course of a number of visits to a given site in season, you would expect to see most of the birds listed.

Inevitably, the seasons do overlap. For the purposes of this book, I have separated them as follows: winter is from November to mid-March; spring is from mid-March to late May; summer is from late May to mid-July, and autumn is from mid-July to late October.

Naturally, some species of breeding wader may be migrating south again by mid-June, while many species are on the move in what would normally be described as summer, hence, why in this book autumn begins so early. Birds do not keep to a strict timetable. For example, Red-necked Grebes are considered a winter visitor to Britain, but by August – a month that most people would consider as summer – they can be found in the Firth of Forth. Many wintering species often stay late into spring as they await the thawing of their Arctic breeding grounds, while many other wintering species may well be returning to their winter quarters during late summer and autumn.

⬛ ACCESS

OS MAP: **203** REF: **SW 520 413**

Access information on reserves is listed. Where no opening times are mentioned, you can assume the reserve is open during all daylight hours. Some reserves charge admission for non-members, but because these charges change, they have not been listed. However, a phone call or look on the relevant website should reveal exactly how much you will be expected to pay. Detailed instructions are given on how to find the site.

Most British site – and some Irish ones – have a six figure grid reference and number for the relevant Ordnance Survey 1:50,000 Landranger map covering the area. The Landranger series of maps are excellent, all-purpose maps with a scale of 2 cm to 1 km (1¼ inches to 1 mile). There are 204 maps in the series, covering the whole of the British Isles. For Britain, the grid reference starts with two letters that signify a 100 km square, so for example, the square covering most of Kent is TQ. These letters are then followed by numbers, which relate to 1 km squares within the map. The lines making these squares are numbered along the margins, the sides being northings and the horizontal being eastings.

The first three figures relate to the easting, so if the first three numbers are 545, then you go to the horizontal line on which 54 is written and go half way across the square, as it is five-tenths. You then take the last three numbers, for example, 662, so you take the line on the northing for 66 and go up two-tenths for the two in the square and then move across the map until the square at coordinates 545662 is found. The easy way of remembering the sequence in which to read a reference is to memorize the line 'in the hall then up the stairs' so starting along the bottom then up the side. In some cases, sites are so large or linear that only a map number or a four figure grid reference, which simply refers to the square as a whole, has been given.

⬛ FACILITIES

Facilities include details of hides, trails and visitor centres, and this information frequently changes, too. Nevertheless, I have listed them where relevant. Toilet facilities have not been included, but you will find that most of the larger reserves, if they have a visitor centre, are likely to have washrooms, too. Finally, in this section, disabled facilities have been detailed. The definition of disabled for the sake of this guide means accessible by a wheelchair.

Finally, I hope you enjoy discovering our wonderful islands with the aid of this book. I have been lucky enough to travel the length and breadth of Britain and Ireland experiencing for myself the spectacular sights and diverse array of birdlife on offer, and I hope the pages that follow encourage you to do the same.

KEY TO MAPS

M5 (interchange 35a)	Motorway	BRISTOL □	City	℗	Parking
A5	Primary road	Bath □	Major town	⬛	Hide
A86	Main road	Frome □	Small town	⬛	Viewpoint
B6681	Secondary road	Cheddar ○	Large village	■	Building
==========	Path	Manton ○	Village	✈	Small airfield
	Railway		Built-up	⬛	Ferry
lake / river / marsh	Water features	●	Place of interest	▲	Mountain peak

SOUTH-WEST ENGLAND

A mild climate, great beaches and stunning landscapes are all factors that attract mass tourism to the south-west each year. Yet, just a stone's throw from bustling tourist centres such as Poole and Torquay, there are wonderful nature reserves, coastlines of outstanding beauty, rugged uplands, forests, marshes and estuaries – all great habitats for birds.

Some of our best-known birding locations are found in the region. The almost sub-tropical Isles of Scilly complete with palm trees and long sandy beaches are invaded each October by hundreds of birders on the trail of rarities. Along the south coast there are estuaries, such as the Fal and Exe, that swarm with wildfowl and waders from autumn through to spring. Inland, Dartmoor and Exmoor possess magical oak woods, which are home to three western specialities: Redstart, Pied Flycatcher and Wood Warbler. Then there are the lowland heaths such as Aylesbeare, lakes such as Chew Valley, and bird-filled islands such as Lundy and Steep Holm.

The climate lends itself to helping colonists from continental Europe get a foothold. Little Egrets, which recently bred for the first time on Brownsea Island, are now colonizing Britain at an impressive rate. Cetti's Warbler thrives in scrub and reed beds throughout much of the region. The last stronghold of the Cirl Bunting – a common bird in many European countries – can be found in Devon. Honey Buzzards nest here and numbers of its Dartford Warblers have boomed due to the changing climate. With such sought-after birds and the sheer variety of sites, the south-west has year-round appeal.

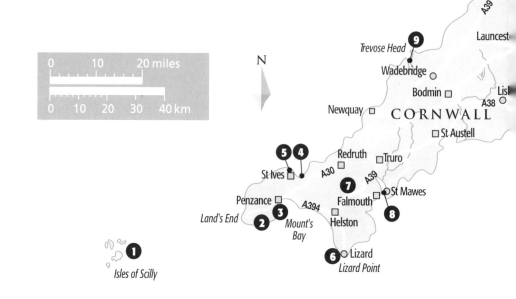

Lundy **31**

0   10   20 miles

0   10   20   30   40 km

N

Bude

A39

Trevose Head **9**

Launcest

Wadebridge

Bodmin

Lis

A38

Newquay   CORNWALL

St Austell

5 4

Redruth   Truro

St Ives   A30

7   A39

Penzance   A394   St Mawes

Land's End   **2**   **3**   Falmouth

Mount's   Helston   **8**
Bay

1

Isles of Scilly

6 Lizard
Lizard Point

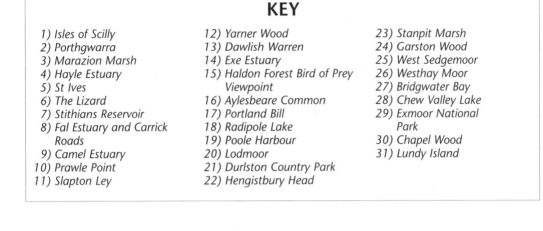

KEY

1) Isles of Scilly
2) Porthgwarra
3) Marazion Marsh
4) Hayle Estuary
5) St Ives
6) The Lizard
7) Stithians Reservoir
8) Fal Estuary and Carrick Roads
9) Camel Estuary
10) Prawle Point
11) Slapton Ley

12) Yarner Wood
13) Dawlish Warren
14) Exe Estuary
15) Haldon Forest Bird of Prey Viewpoint
16) Aylesbeare Common
17) Portland Bill
18) Radipole Lake
19) Poole Harbour
20) Lodmoor
21) Durlston Country Park
22) Hengistbury Head

23) Stanpit Marsh
24) Garston Wood
25) West Sedgemoor
26) Westhay Moor
27) Bridgwater Bay
28) Chew Valley Lake
29) Exmoor National Park
30) Chapel Wood
31) Lundy Island

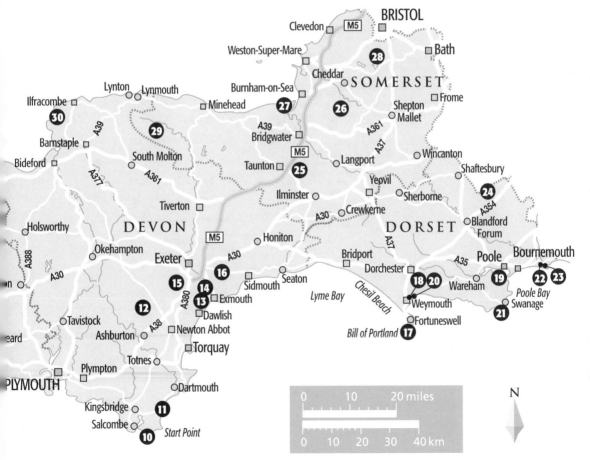

ISLES OF SCILLY
THE WILDLIFE TRUSTS

Long sandy beaches, deserted cliff tops and quiet country lanes – there are few more tranquil places in Britain than the Scillies, that is, until the month of October. Lying 45 km (28 miles) off Land's End, the islands are legendary for rare birds and, come the magical month when anything might turn up and often does, they are invaded by an army of twitchers. If you enjoy rare birds and don't mind watching them with a few kindred spirits, then there is nowhere quite like it. The islands can be buzzing with excitement.

Rarities arrive from all points on the compass. After westerly blows, usually fast-moving depressions originating off the eastern seaboard of the United States, American vagrants are likely. Favourable weather can also bring vagrants from the east.

The spring can be exciting, with both plentiful numbers of common migrants and rarities that annually include continental visitors such as Hoopoe and Golden Oriole.

St Mary's and Tresco both boast a variety of habitats. Freshwater lakes such as the Great Pool on Tresco, and marshy pools and reed beds such as Lower Moors on St Mary's provide habitats for resident and migrant wildfowl, waders, crakes, rails and warblers. Woodland and scrub abound, with passerine migrants likely to turn up anywhere.

The Isles have seabird colonies, which can be enjoyed by taking boat excursions from St Mary's. Early autumn can be productive for seawatching, with petrels, shearwaters and skuas passing off the islands. The crossing from Penzance is a good way of seeing these. During August occasional trips are arranged from St Mary's to track down Wilson's Petrel – good 'sea legs' are recommended for this!

🦆 KEY BIRDS

ALL YEAR: Shag, Oystercatcher, Ringed Plover, Rock Pipit, Stonechat.
SPRING: Passage waders include Greenshank and Whimbrel. Garganey, Ring Ouzel, Wheatear, Whinchat, Grasshopper and Wood Warblers, plus most other common migrants. Scarce species include Hoopoe, Golden Oriole and often Woodchat Shrike.
SUMMER: Breeding seabirds include Manx Shearwater, European Storm Petrel, Fulmar, Kittiwake, Common Tern, Puffin, Guillemot and Razorbill. Cuckoo and some warblers breed.
AUTUMN: Seabirds include Sooty, Great and Cory's Shearwaters, European Storm Petrel and skuas. Scarce migrants include Spotted Crake, Jack Snipe, Dotterel, Buff-breasted Sandpiper (September), Red-breasted Flycatcher, Yellow-browed, Icterine, Melodious and Barred Warblers, Firecrest, Tawny and Richard's Pipits, Rose-coloured Starling, Red-backed Shrike, Snow and Lapland Buntings. In October, European, Asian and American vagrants. It is *the* place in Britain for American landbird vagrants, with Red-eyed Vireo and Blackpoll Warbler being two of the most frequently recorded.
WINTER: Great Northern Diver, wildfowl, Merlin, Water Rail; waders include Purple Sandpiper.

🚣 ACCESS
OS MAP: 203 REF: SV 915 115
There are five main inhabited islands. The off islands – as Tresco, Bryher, St Agnes and St Martin's are known – are easily accessible by boat, daily from St Mary's quay. A helicopter service from Penzance serves Tresco. St Mary's can be reached by sea, or plane and helicopter from Penzance; the latter is the more reliable during autumn, when sea crossings and light-aircraft flights can occasionally be disrupted by stormy weather.

📷 FACILITIES
Hides overlook the Great Pool on Tresco. On St Mary's there are hides and nature trails at Porth Hellick and Lower Moors. Boats to the off islands go twice daily from St Mary's quay.

Yellow-browed Warbler
Phylloscopus inornatus

Small and beautifully patterned, the Yellow-browed Warbler is an annual migrant visitor from its breeding grounds in West Siberia and Central Asia. During October, the Scillies is the easiest place to see this rarity, often giving its presence away with a distinctive 'chu-wee' call.

Yellow-browed Warblers can turn up just about anywhere on Scilly where there is suitable cover. However, favoured locations include Holy Vale, Porth Hellick, Lower Moors and the Garrison on St Mary's, the Parsonage on St Agnes and along the sallows by the Great Pool on Tresco.

2 PORTHGWARRA

Porthgwarra is Britain's most south-westerly valley. During passage periods the scrub and gardens in the valley bottom often hold migrants, with rarities being a feature. Gwennap Head is the best place on Land's End for seawatching.

KEY BIRDS

SPRING AND AUTUMN: Summer migrants in spring, and rarities, including Hoopoe and Serin. Autumn migrants include all the commoner warblers, chats and flycatchers. Melodious Warbler is possible; other scarce migrants include Wryneck and Firecrest. Asian and American vagrants are annual. Seawatching in spring will produce divers, grebes, scoters, terns, Whimbrel, Manx Shearwater and, in May, Pomarine Skua. In autumn expect European Storm Petrel, Great, Sooty and Balearic Shearwaters, and from late July into August, Cory's Shearwater.

ACCESS
OS MAP: 203 REF: SW 372 218
On the A30 from Penzance to Land's End, turn on to the B3283 to St Buryan. Drive through the village, past the junction with the B3315 heading towards Sennen. Where the road turns sharply to the right, take the turn off to the left, down a narrow lane to the car park at the bottom of the valley. Gwennap Head can be reached by walking west along the cliff top from the car park.

3 MARAZION MARSH

RSPB RESERVE
52.5 ha (130 acres)
From early August to mid-September, this small wetland is the best place in Britain to see the rare Aquatic Warbler. The other autumn speciality here is Spotted Crake. Nearby Mount's Bay attracts waders. Mediterranean Gulls are regularly recorded on the beach.

KEY BIRDS
ALL YEAR: Cetti's Warbler.
SPRING: Possible Garganey, a good variety of summer migrants.
SUMMER: Breeding birds include Reed and Sedge Warblers.
AUTUMN: Passage waders, including Green and Wood Sandpipers. Annual rarities include

Aquatic Warbler and Spotted Crake.
WINTER: Wildfowl. In Mount's Bay, Great Northern Diver, often Black-throated Diver, grebes and seaduck. Waders such as Sanderling, and Mediterranean Gull, on shore line.

ACCESS
OS MAP: 203 REF: SW 510 315
On the A30 from Penzance to Hayle, turn off for St Michael's Mount. Pass over the railway line and turn left; a little further on the left is the car park.

FACILITIES
One hide and limited wheelchair access.

4 HAYLE ESTUARY

RSPB RESERVE
90 ha (220 acres)
Salt marsh and tidal creeks attract wildfowl and waders, with autumn and winter being the ideal time to visit. There are various vantage points, some of the best being from the vicinity of the Old Quay House Inn at the head of the estuary, Carnsew Pool and Copperhouse Creek.

Autumn annually produces rare American waders and sometimes ducks, such as American Wigeon.

KEY BIRDS
ALL YEAR: Little Egret.
SPRING: Sandwich Tern, possible Black Tern, migrants such as Whimbrel and Wood Sandpiper.
SUMMER: Shelduck breed, a few lingering waders.
AUTUMN: Passage and wintering waders that include Little Stint, various sandpipers, godwits, Spotted Redshank, Greenshank, and American vagrant waders. Little, Mediterranean and possible Ring-billed Gulls.
WINTER: Great Northern Diver, Brent Goose, Wigeon, Teal, Peregrine, Kingfisher, estuarine waders; Ring-billed Gull a possibility.

ACCESS
OS MAP: 203 REF: SW 550 370
To view the head of the estuary around the Old Quay House, leave the A30 just before the Hayle bypass. Carnsew Pool is reached along the road on the east side of the estuary, not far from the pub. Take a path by some industrial units. Copperhouse Creek can be viewed from a car park as you enter Hayle.

5 ST IVES

This picturesque fishing port is one of the best seawatching sites in Britain. Autumn is the time to visit, and in the right conditions spectacular seabird movements can be enjoyed.

The weather is the vital ingredient to success – the perfect scenario is for a deep Atlantic depression to move across from the south-west with associated gale force south-westerly winds. Once these winds go round to a west-north-west to north-westerly, then thousands of birds can get pushed close in, often into St Ives Bay and stream out past the Coastguard Tower on St Ives Island, the best place to watch from. A sewage outfall in the bay often persuades species such as European Storm Petrel to linger.

KEY BIRDS

AUTUMN: Divers, grebes, seaduck, Manx and Balearic Shearwaters, Sooty, Great and more rarely Cory's Shearwaters, European Storm Petrel, Leach's Petrel, Arctic, Great, Pomarine and Long-tailed Skuas, Sabine's Gull, Grey Phalarope, auks, including Little Auk.
WINTER: Check bay for Great Northern Diver, Black-throated Diver, Slavonian Grebe, Eider and occasional wind-blown Grey Phalarope.

ACCESS
OS MAP: 203 REF: SW 520 413
From the car park at the northern end of the town walk to the top of St Ives Island and watch from the coastguard's lookout.

6 THE LIZARD

As the southernmost point on the British mainland, it stands to reason that the Lizard should produce migrants and rarities in spring and autumn.

The coves around the point and any other suitable-looking habitat are worth checking for migrants. Notable vagrants discovered on the Lizard have included Little Bustard and Upland Sandpiper in recent years. While spring produces migrants in small numbers, along with overshooting continental rarities, such as Serin, it is the autumn that provides most interest.

KEY BIRDS
SPRING AND AUTUMN: Migrants can include chats, flycatchers, warblers, and in early spring, Ring Ouzel, Black Redstart and Firecrest. Late spring sees more chance of a rarity, with overshoots possible. Autumn migrants are similar but in much larger numbers. Late autumn sees the arrival of buntings, finches and winter thrushes. Rarities are annual. Offshore, seabirds can include Cory's, Great, Sooty and Balearic Shearwaters.

ACCESS
OS MAP: 203 REF: SW 430 290
Kynance Cove is reached via a private toll road, and has a car park. For Church Cove, take the road that forks left just before Lizard Town and immediately past the road for Kynance Cove. At Church Cove, check the elms and the vicinity around the church before birding along the National Trust footpath and valley that leads back to the church.

7 STITHIANS RESERVOIR

CORNWALL BIRDWATCHING AND PRESERVATION SOCIETY
111 ha (274 acres)
Viewable from the road, this shallow reservoir is at its best during the autumn season. At this time waders, and often American vagrants are attracted to feed along its muddy margins, when these are present.

KEY BIRDS
ALL YEAR: Little Grebe.
SPRING: Sprinkling of passage waders.
AUTUMN: Passage waders include Dunlin, Ringed Plover and Little-ringed Plover, Wood Sandpiper, Common Sandpiper, Green Sandpiper and Curlew Sandpipers, Little Stint, Ruff, Greenshank, Spotted Redshank, Golden Plover, Little Gull and Black Tern and, almost annually, American vagrants, such as Pectoral Sandpiper and Lesser Yellowlegs.
WINTER: Wigeon, Teal, Gadwall, Pochard, Tufted Duck, Goldeneye, Peregrine, Merlin, Golden Plover, Lapwing, Snipe and Ruff.

ACCESS
OS MAP: 203 REF: SW 710 350
From Redruth, take the A393 and then the B3297, before turning left to the reservoir. Both ends can be viewed from the road.

8 FAL ESTUARY AND CARRICK ROADS

263 ha (649 acres)

Of most interest in autumn and winter, the sheltered Fal Estuary attracts wildfowl and waders. The Fal leads into the Carrick Roads, a deep waterway also served by the River Truro.

The wide upper reaches of the Fal at Ruan Lanihorne are favoured by waders, and dabbling ducks.

KEY BIRDS

ALL YEAR: Little Egret, Kingfisher.
SPRING: Passage waders, including Whimbrel.
SUMMER: Mid-July for return of passage waders.
AUTUMN: Passage waders include Spotted Redshank, Greenshank, Common Sandpiper, Little Stint and Curlew Sandpiper.
WINTER: On Carrick Roads, Great Northern Diver, Black-throated Diver (more frequent in late winter), Slavonian and less reliably Black-necked and Red-necked Grebes, Goldeneye, Red-breasted Merganser; other seaducks might include scoters and Long-tailed Duck. In Fal Estuary, wildfowl, estuarine waders, Avocet and gulls.

ACCESS

OS MAP: 204 REF: SW 830 360

For Carrick Roads, leave the A39 Truro to Falmouth Road at St Gluvias and park at Mylor village. Walk along the beach on the southern side of creek to Pencarrow Point. For Ruan Lanihorne, leave the A3078 Truro to St Mawes road at Ruan High Lanes.

9 CAMEL ESTUARY

The upper reaches at Amble are where most bird interest lies, with waders congregating to feed at low tide on the exposed mud. The surrounding marshes attract wildfowl. At the mouth of the estuary gulls and terns feed and loaf on the sandbanks.

KEY BIRDS

ALL YEAR: Grey Heron, Shelduck, Kingfisher.
SPRING: Terns, including Sandwich and Black. Greenshank, Ruff and Whimbrel.
AUTUMN: Passage waders, including Greenshank, Spotted Redshank, Curlew Sandpiper, Little

Stint, Green Sandpiper; possible Osprey.
WINTER: Little Egret, Great Northern Diver at the estuary mouth, Slavonian Grebe, wildfowl and estuarine waders, Spotted Redshank, gulls.

ACCESS

OS MAP: 200 REF: SW 980 740

The best place for viewing the head of the estuary is at the Amble Dam outflow. Take the A39 north out of Wadebridge, then the B3314 to the left. Park at Trewornan Bridge. Check the marshes here, then go through the gate just before the bridge – the footpath leads to a hide. The lower estuary can be viewed from the car park at Rock.

10 PRAWLE POINT

THE NATIONAL TRUST

Tucked away at the end of one of Devon's typically high-hedged lanes, Prawle is arguably the easiest site in Britain to find Cirl Bunting. Prawle Point's other claim to fame are the rarities it has attracted, particularly American autumn vagrants. One reason for this is its position as the southernmost point in Devon, which makes it good for seawatching, too.

KEY BIRDS

ALL YEAR: Stonechat, Cirl Bunting, Raven.
SPRING: Offshore, Manx Shearwater, divers, scoters, skuas including Pomarine (late April / early May), Whimbrel. Black Redstart, Wheatear, Firecrest, various warblers, chats, Hobby; possible rarities may include Hoopoe or Serin.
AUTUMN: Offshore, Manx, Balearic and possible Sooty Shearwaters, migrants as for spring plus a possibility of American vagrants in October.
WINTER: Offshore, Great Northern Diver, scoter, auks, Gannet; Peregrine and possible Purple Sandpiper on rocks.

ACCESS

OS MAP: 202 REF: SX 770 350

Take the A379 from Kingsbridge, turning off down minor roads for East Prawle Village, and go through the village to The National Trust car park at the end. The coastal path, leading west, will take you to Pig's Nose Valley, which is good for migrants. Cirl Buntings are best looked for in the vicinity of the car park. There is seawatching from Prawle Point, west of the car park.

11 SLAPTON LEY

NNR

200 ha (494 acres)

These two pools, separated from the sea by a narrow shingle bank on which the A379 sits, stretch for 2.4 km (1.5 miles).

Attracting migrants in spring and autumn, coupled with a good variety of breeding species and wintering wildfowl, a visit at any time of year can be recommended. Start Bay opposite attracts divers, grebes and seaduck in winter.

KEY BIRDS

ALL YEAR: Water Rail, Cetti's Warbler, Buzzard, Stonechat.
SPRING: Garganey, Marsh Harrier, terns, Yellow Wagtail, Whinchat, Wheatear, hirundines and warblers.
SUMMER: Offshore in Start Bay, Manx Shearwater, Reed and Sedge Warblers.
AUTUMN: Black Tern, Little Gull, Common Sandpiper, Greenshank, Hobby and large numbers of hirundines, especially Swallows, which roost. Warblers and chats.
WINTER: Offshore in Start Bay, Great Northern Diver, Slavonian Grebe, scoters and often Long-tailed Duck, Eider. On the ley, Gadwall, Teal, Shoveler, Tufted Duck, Pochard, Goldeneye and occasional sawbills. Bearded Tit in reed bed, Chiffchaff, Blackcap and Firecrest in scrub areas.

ACCESS

OS MAP: **202** REF: **SX 820 430**

The Ley lies alongside the A379 south of Dartmouth.

FACILITIES

A public hide by the Tank Monument in Torcross, allows wheelchair access. There is a second hide on the opposite bank reached from the A379. The Field Studies Council (FSC) runs a centre here; details from FSC.

12 YARNER WOOD

NNR

150 ha (370 acres)

Sessile oak and birch dominate this woodland on the edge of Dartmoor, which is very productive for woodland birds. Visit in May or June as most species will be singing and are easier to see.

KEY BIRDS

ALL YEAR: Mandarin, Buzzard, Sparrowhawk, Tawny Owl, Green, Great Spotted and Lesser Spotted Woodpeckers, Marsh Tit, Grey Wagtail, Raven.
SPRING AND SUMMER: Tree Pipit, Whitethroat, Wood Warbler, Redstart, Spotted and Pied Flycatchers.
AUTUMN AND WINTER: Woodcock, Redpoll, Siskin.

ACCESS

OS MAP: **191** REF: **SX 778 787**

From Bovey Tracey take the B3344 to Manaton. The reserve is 3 km (2 miles) along on the left. Open from 8.30am to 7pm, or dusk if earlier.

FACILITIES

Self-guided trails, a hide and an interpretation display.

13 DAWLISH WARREN

NNR

202 ha (500 acres)

A sand spit jutting out into the mouth of the Exe Estuary, Dawlish Warren is ideal for viewing wildfowl and waders. The hide at the end of the point provides good views of waders on a rising tide.

A few pools and scrub amongst the dunes attract migrants, while in winter, offshore, divers, grebes and seaduck congregate.

KEY BIRDS

ALL YEAR: Shag, Eider, Red-breasted Merganser, Ringed Plover.
SPRING: Arctic Skua, Sandwich, Little, Common and Black Terns, Whimbrel, Wheatear, Cuckoo, warblers and a chance of rarities.
SUMMER: Returning waders, Sandwich and Common Terns.
AUTUMN: Peregrine, Little Stint, Whimbrel, Ruff, Curlew Sandpiper, Spotted Redshank, Green Sandpiper, Greenshank, plus estuarine waders. Arctic Skua and terns offshore.
WINTER: Red-throated and Great Northern Divers, Slavonian Grebe, Brent Goose, Shelduck, Goldeneye, Common and possible Velvet Scoters, Long-tailed Duck, Peregrine, Merlin, Short-eared Owl, Avocet, Greenshank and common estuarine waders, Mediterranean Gull, Chiffchaff, possible Snow Bunting.

ACCESS

OS MAP: 192 REF: SX 983 788

On the A379 road from Dawlish to Exeter, turn off to Dawlish Warren and into the car park by Lee Cliff Holiday Park. Proceed under the railway bridge at the far end. A gate leads to the reserve.

FACILITIES

A hide overlooks the wader roost. A visitor centre is open most weekends throughout the year and during most weekdays in summer.

14 EXE ESTUARY

RSPB RESERVE

Apart from Dawlish Warren (featured as a separate site), there are two other protected areas on the Exe Estuary worthy of a visit.

Bowling Green Marsh lies on the east side of the river, while Exminster Marshes nestles on the opposite bank. Both are marsh and coastal grazing land ideal for breeding and passage waders and wildfowl. There is year round interest at both sites, although a winter visit is likely to be most productive.

KEY BIRDS

ALL YEAR: Grey Heron, Buzzard, possible Barn Owl, Cetti's Warbler.
SPRING AND AUTUMN: Passage waders may include Whimbrel and Green Sandpiper.
SUMMER: Wader roosts; breeding waders include Lapwing and Redshank.
WINTER: Wigeon, Shoveler, Teal, Pintail, Black-tailed Godwit, Golden Plover, Avocet, Short-eared Owl, Water Rail.

ACCESS

OS MAP: 192 REF: SX 972 876

Bowling Green Marsh is on the outskirts of Topsham, and signposted from the Holman Way car park in Topsham.

OS MAP: 192 REF: SX 954 872

Exminster Marshes lies east of Exminster village. It is reached by taking the lane towards Swan's Nest Inn at the southern end of the village, and going over the humpback bridge.

FACILITIES

A hide and roadside viewing at Bowling Green Marsh. Footpaths across Exminster Marshes.

15 HALDON FOREST BIRD OF PREY VIEWPOINT

FOREST ENTERPRISE

This has traditionally been a good site for watching Honey Buzzard and Goshawk. In recent times both have become less reliable, due to shifting breeding territories. If these two species are your main quarry then check as to the frequency of sightings before a visit.

KEY BIRDS

ALL YEAR: Sprrowhawk, Buzzard.
SPRING AND SUMMER: Honey Buzzard, Goshawk, Hobby, other migrant raptors (particularly in May), Redstart, Nightjar, Tree Pipit, Whinchat.
AUTUMN AND WINTER: Hawfinch a possibility.

ACCESS

OS MAP: 192 REF: SX 870 850

From Exeter take the A38 towards Plymouth. Near the crest of the steep hill, turn off left just before the racecourse, follow the road round, going under the A38 – the viewpoint is a little way along here on the left.

16 AYLESBEARE COMMON

RSPB RESERVE

218.5 ha (540 acres)

A heathland reserve, Aylesbeare has a good variety of lowland heath birds. With woodland, pools and streams, this is also an excellent place for insects, especially butterflies and dragonflies. Spring and summer are the peak seasons for a visit. Winter on the heath can be very quiet.

KEY BIRDS

ALL YEAR: Woodcock, Sparrowhawk, Buzzard, Woodlark, Stonechat, Dartford Warbler, possible Crossbill.
SPRING AND SUMMER: Hobby, Cuckoo, Tree Pipit, possible Wood and Grasshopper Warblers, Redstart, Whinchat. Nightjar from mid-May.
AUTUMN AND WINTER: Late autumn, a chance of Hen Harrier, Merlin and Great Grey Shrike.

ACCESS

OS MAP: 192 REF: SY 058 897

From Newton Poppleford take the A3052 Lyme Regis to Exeter road. The reserve is 1.6 km (1 mile) along here on the right.

Above: Birders wandering down a wooded lane on St Mary's, Isles of Scilly in October.

Above: Cryptically camouflaged, the Wryneck is an annual but scarce migrant to many coastal sites in Britain.

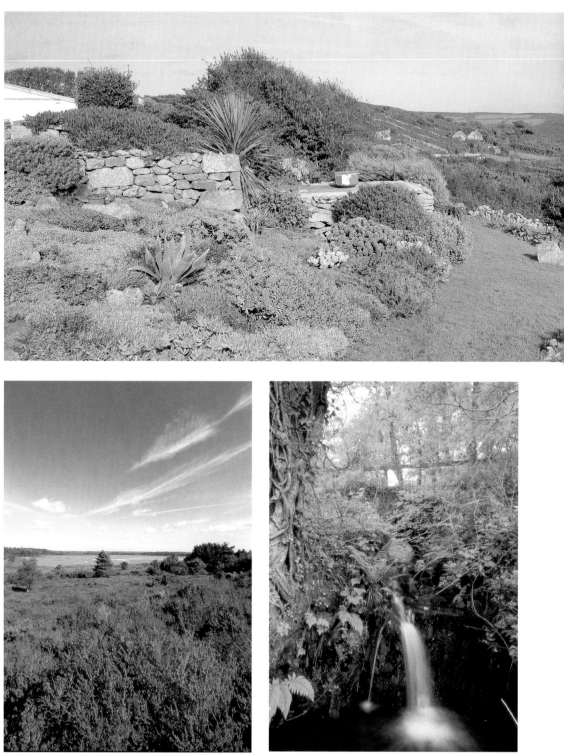

Above: Looking towards Poole Harbour from the picturesque Arne RSPB reserve.

Above: Yarner Wood in spring.

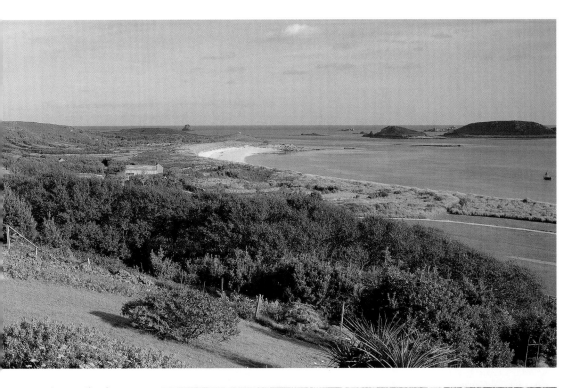

Above: Like the other Scilly Isles, St Martin's has a subtropical feel, and often has exotic avian visitors to match!

Right: Redstarts (such as this male) are one of Yarner Wood's specialities.

Above: The New Forest is home to some of Britain's rarest breeding birds.

Above: Wood Warblers emit their distinctive trilling song on many reserves in spring.

Above: Thursley Common in Surrey is easily explored through its network of trails and boardwalks.

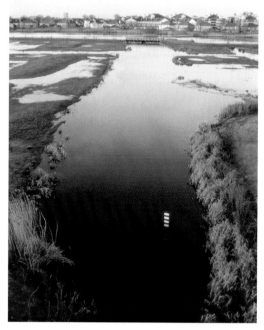

Above: More often heard than seen, Water Rails are resident to many wetland sites.

Above: Barn Elms in London.

Above: The vast shingle spit of Dungeness juts out into the English Channel making it an arrival and departure lounge for migrants.

Above: Since re-colonizing Britain nearly 60 years ago, Avocets continue to spread across the country.

Above: The spectacular gathering of wildfowl at Welney in winter can be enjoyed from a heated observatory!

Above: The scrape at Minsmere is the centrepiece to a reserve that contains more habitats within its boundaries than any other.

Above: Lekking Ruffs in their characteristic breeding plumage. The Ouse Washes in spring is one of the best places to observe this unique behaviour.

17 PORTLAND BILL

PORTLAND BIRD OBSERVATORY

Portland, renowned as a migration watch-point, juts 9.3 km (6 miles) out into the English Channel. Attached to the mainland by Chesil Beach, the harbour on one side of the road and The Fleet extending for 13 km (8 miles) to the west on the other are also great birding sites.

Portland Bill boasts a bird observatory and most birds tend to be found around here. Passerine migrants and seawatching are of main interest, with spring and autumn the key times. Like all migration hotspots, weather is usually crucial. A south or south-easterly wind is best, and an early-morning visit in spring is likely to be productive.

A well-timed visit is less important in autumn, as migrants are usually in greater numbers and tend to linger, sometimes for days. Any patch of cover at the Bill is worth investigating. Always check the latest news at the observatory.

Seawatching is often best in spring, with southerly onshore winds ideal. Both the harbour and fleet attract birds throughout the year, however, the harbour is best in winter for seaduck, divers and grebes, and often the odd auk seeking shelter.

The Fleet, a brackish lagoon separated from the sea by the 29km (18 mile) long Chesil Beach, enters Portland Harbour at Ferry Bridge. The latter site can be good for waders, and is easily viewed from the road. The Fleet itself has various access points and is of most interest in winter.

KEY BIRDS

ALL YEAR: Fulmar, Cormorant.
SPRING AND AUTUMN: Passage waders on the Fleet. Offshore, Manx Shearwater, Gannet, Common Scoter, skuas, including Pomarine in April / May, terns, Whimbrel, Bar-tailed Godwit, Little Gull, Kittiwake. Passerine migrants at Portland Bill include Black Redstart, Ring Ouzel, Wheatear, warblers, wagtails, Tree Pipit, Whinchat, Spotted and Pied Flycatchers (the latter in autumn), Wryneck, plus rarities with spring overshoots, including Hoopoe, Serin and Quail. In autumn, a chance of Melodious and Icterine Warblers, Richard's and Tawny Pipits. Vagrants recorded annually.
WINTER: Most interest in the harbour, with divers, grebes and seaduck, plus a good chance of auks, such as Black Guillemot.

ACCESS

OS MAP: 194 REF: SY 681 690

Portland Bill is reached by taking the A354 south from Weymouth, and following the signs once on Portland. The Fleet and harbour are either side of the A354 before reaching Portland. Various vantage points can be used for both. However, The Fleet at Ferry Bridge (overlooked by a car park), is accessed from the A354 as it cuts between here and the harbour.

FACILITIES

Accommodation is available by advance booking, from the Portland Bird Observatory, Old Lower Light, Portland Bill, Dorset DT5 2JT.

18 RADIPOLE LAKE

RSPB RESERVE
89 ha (220 acres)

Lying in the heart of Weymouth, Radipole is a mosaic of pools, reed bed and scrub. This is one of the easiest places in Britain to see the often elusive Cetti's Warbler.

Migrants, particularly warblers, pass through, while wagtails and swallows use the reed beds as roost sites. Wildfowl, a few waders and gulls are the other main attractions.

KEY BIRDS

ALL YEAR: Water Rail, Kingfisher, Cetti's Warbler, Bearded Tit.
SPRING: Garganey, terns, passage waders, Yellow Wagtail, Grasshopper Warbler, Nightingale.
SUMMER: Reed and Sedge Warblers breed, Nightingale, Cuckoo.
AUTUMN: Garganey, Hobby, Spotted Crake (regular), passage waders, terns, gulls including Mediterranean; Swallow and Yellow Wagtail roost in reed bed.
WINTER: Possible Bittern, Teal, Shoveler, Tufted Duck, Pochard, Snipe, Mediterranean Gull and chance of a white-winged gull.

ACCESS

OS MAP: 194 REF: SY 677 796

Radipole lies just north of the King's Roundabout in the centre of Weymouth.

FACILITIES

All hides are accessible to wheelchairs, and a visitor centre is open daily from 9am to 5pm.

POOLE HARBOUR

NNR, RSPB RESERVE, THE NATIONAL TRUST AND DORSET WILDLIFE TRUST

The extensive heaths, woodlands, mud flats, salt marsh and open water provide a diversity of habitats that make the reserve one of Britain's top birding sites. The heaths on the southern and western shores encompass reserves such as Arne and are important for the wildlife they support – our scarcest reptiles such as the Smooth Snake and Sand Lizard live here. Arne has wonderful stretches of heath, which, in spring, come alive with the scratchy song of Dartford Warblers. A walk around the reserve takes in all its habitats, from oak woodland to open heath and a wader-rich salt marsh overlooked by hides. Nearby, Studland shares many of the same species and although there is not the mosaic of habitats here, it encompasses fine stretches of heath and a large freshwater lake attractive to waterfowl.

Brownsea Island is the largest of a number of islands in Poole Harbour. Pine woods, rhododendron thickets and scrub cloak the island, supporting a range of woodland birds.

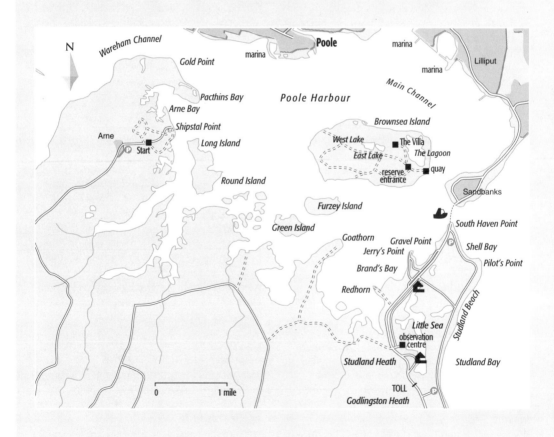

It is also the UK's last southern stronghold of the Red Squirrel. Of main interest is the Lagoon to the east of the island, leased to the Dorset Wildlife Trust by the islands' owner, the National Trust. This area of brackish water and mud is a magnet for waders throughout the year. In summer, terns use artificial rafts to breed, while nearby, Little Egrets now nest with the Grey Herons in the heronry. This was their first breeding site in the UK back in 1996.

KEY BIRDS
ALL YEAR: Little Egret, Golden Pheasant (Brownsea), Black-tailed Godwit, Water Rail, Stonechat, Dartford Warbler, Woodlark.
SPRING: Passage waders include Whimbrel, Common Sandpiper, Greenshank, Spotted Redshank. Terns and passerine migrants such as Wheatear and Whinchat.
SUMMER: Sandwich and Common Terns breed on the Lagoon on Brownsea. On the heaths, Nightjar, Hobby, Wood Warbler, and Crossbill (mainly Brownsea). Returning waders.
AUTUMN: Passage waders as for spring, plus Little Stint, Curlew Sandpiper, Ruff, Green and occasional Wood Sandpipers (Brownsea). Black and Little Terns and passerine migrants such as Pied Flycatcher.
WINTER: In the harbour on open water, divers and Slavonian and Black-necked Grebes are regular, also wildfowl such as Brent Geese, Common Scoter, Red-breasted Merganser, Long-tailed Duck. On Studland, dabbling and diving ducks on Little Sea (a freshwater lake). Hunting over heaths, a chance of Hen Harrier, Merlin and Peregrine. Wintering waders include large numbers of Avocets and Black-tailed Godwits on Brownsea. Also, Curlew, Bar-tailed Godwit, Knot, Grey Plover, Sanderling, Dunlin, Oystercatcher, Ringed Plover, Turnstone and a few wintering Spotted Redshank.

ACCESS
OS MAP: 195 REF: SY 973 882
Arne is south-east of Wareham off the A351. Park at the car park in Arne Village.
OS MAP: 195 REF: SZ 030 846
Studland Heath is reached by taking the B3351 to Studland village, then taking the toll road to the peninsula, or alternatively, taking the ferry from Sandbanks. In summer, the ferry is very busy, and long delays are not uncommon.
OS MAP: 195 REF: SZ 035 875
Brownsea Island is reached by boat from Poole Quay and Sandbanks every half hour from 10am to 5pm (6pm in July and August). The island is open from April to September. Note that at weekends and in the height of summer, the island can become very crowded. Non-members of the Dorset Wildlife Trust can access the Lagoon for a fee, except in July and August, when access is by afternoon guided tour only.

FACILITIES
There are hides, nature trails and information points. There is no disabled access, except for Brownsea, where paths are good and hides accessible to wheelchairs.

Dartford Warbler
Sylvia undata

Benefiting from mild winters, the Dartford Warbler is thriving. This is our only true resident warbler and it is confined to lowland heaths in southern Britain. The heaths on the edge of Poole Harbour are one of the easiest spots in the country to track this colourful warbler down. Arne RSPB reserve is one of the best sites, with a visit in spring the best time.

Dartford Warblers have a scratchy song, often delivered from the top of a gorse clump, where they are most likely to be located. Although resident, they can be tricky to find outside the breeding season.

20 LODMOOR

RSPB RESERVE
89 ha (220 acres)
Close to the sea and Weymouth, this marsh with shallow pools, reeds and scrub attracts a similar range of species to nearby Radipole.

KEY BIRDS
ALL YEAR: Water Rail, Cetti's Warbler, Bearded Tit.
SPRING: Garganey, Hobby, Common Tern, Little Tern, Black Tern. Passage waders including Whimbrel, Green and Common Sandpipers, godwits, Greenshank, Spotted Redshank. Yellow Wagtail, Water Pipit.
SUMMER: Reed, Sedge and Grasshopper Warblers, Yellow Wagtail, gulls and returning waders.
AUTUMN: Passage waders as for spring, plus Ruff, Little Stint, Curlew Sandpiper, Wood Sandpiper, Mediterranean Gull, Little Gull, terns.
WINTER: Teal, Wigeon, possible Merlin, Peregrine, Jack Snipe, Snipe, Mediterranean Gull, possible Glaucous or Iceland Gulls; over-wintering Blackcap, Chiffchaff and Firecrest.

ACCESS
OS MAP: 194 REF: SY 686 807
Travel east out of Weymouth – the reserve is on the left off the A353 coast road.

FACILITIES
Disabled access on good paths.

21 DURLSTON COUNTRY PARK

DORSET COUNTY COUNCIL
100 ha (247 acres)
Perched above the seaside resort of Swanage, Durlston is best visited between spring and autumn. The cliffs at Durlston Head support breeding seabirds, and the head itself is a good seawatching point.
   Dotted across the downland, woods, hedgerows and scrub act as a refuge for migrants.

KEY BIRDS
SPRING: Offshore in early spring, divers, grebes, scoters and waders. In April/May, terns and skuas. Breeding on the cliffs are Shag, Fulmar, Kittiwake, Guillemot and Razorbill. Passerine migrants include hirundines, chats, flycatchers and warblers. Good chance of rarities.

SUMMER: Breeding seabirds as above. Manx Shearwater offshore.
AUTUMN: Passerine migrants as for spring, with scarce migrants such as Wryneck likely. Arrival of winter thrushes. Offshore, a chance of Little Gull, Little Auk and petrels.
WINTER: Offshore, seaduck, divers and grebes.

ACCESS
OS MAP: 195 REF: SZ 032 774
The country park is well signposted from the centre of Swanage, and is only a 15-minute, uphill walk from the town.

FACILITIES
A visitor centre, viewing platform and trails.

22 HENGISTBURY HEAD

BOURNEMOUTH BOROUGH COUNCIL
Dominating the southern side of Christchurch Harbour, woodland and scrub act as a refuge for arriving and departing migrants, and for occasional rarities.

KEY BIRDS
SPRING AND AUTUMN: Passerine migrants including chats, flycatchers, warblers and crests. Scarce migrants are regular; chance of a rarity.

ACCESS
OS MAP: 195 REF: SZ 184 904
Reached by roads from Southbourne – park at the car park at the head.

FACILITIES
Wheelchair access possible on good path.

23 STANPIT MARSH

CHRISTCHURCH BOROUGH COUNCIL
51 ha (126 acres)
Bordering the River Avon in Christchurch Harbour, salt marsh, brackish marsh and mud flats attract passage and wintering wildfowl and waders. The site enjoys public access, and there are a number of paths leading on to the periphery of the marsh.

KEY BIRDS
ALL YEAR: Shelduck, Water Rail, Bearded Tit, Cetti's Warbler, Kingfisher.

SPRING: Passage waders.
SUMMER: Breeding Sedge and Reed Warblers, a few non-breeding wildfowl; waders.
AUTUMN: Passage waders. Arrival of wintering estuarine waders; terns and gulls; potential for rarities.
WINTER: Wintering waders, plus wildfowl such as Brent Geese and dabbling ducks. In a hard winter, grey geese and wild swans.

ACCESS
OS MAP: 195 REF: SZ 167 924
Most easily reached from the recreation ground car park off Stanpit Lane just south of the Ship in Distress pub. Stanpit Lane is off the A3059.

24 GARSTON WOOD

RSPB RESERVE
This ancient coppiced woodland on the chalk downs of Cranborne Chase is at its best in spring.

KEY BIRDS
ALL YEAR: Common woodland species, including Great Spotted Woodpecker, Nuthatch, Sparrowhawk and Buzzard.
SPRING AND SUMMER: Turtle Dove, Garden Warbler, Blackcap, Nightingale.

ACCESS
OS MAP: 184 REF: SU 004 194
From the A354 Salisbury to Blandford Forum road, take the B3081 at the roundabout, then a minor road to Broad Chalke. Reserve is on the left.

25 WEST SEDGEMOOR

RSPB RESERVE
1,016 ha (2,510 acres)
As a part of the Somerset Levels, this reserve attracts breeding waders and waterfowl, and in winter acts as an important refuge. A wooded escarpment at the reserve entrance gives added interest, with one of the largest heronries in the UK and a good variety of woodland birds.

KEY BIRDS
ALL YEAR: Grey Heron, Buzzard, Lapwing, Snipe, Curlew, Redshank, Barn Owl, woodpeckers, Willow and Marsh Tits.
SPRING: Staging post for migrant Whimbrel. Hobby, Marsh Harrier, passage waders.

SUMMER: Hobby, breeding waders include Black-tailed Godwit. Nightingale, Whinchat, Yellow Wagtail, Sedge and Reed Warblers.
AUTUMN: Passage waders.
WINTER: Bewick's Swan, Wigeon, Teal, Pintail, Shoveler, Goldeneye, Hen Harrier, Merlin, Peregrine, Water Rail, Golden Plover, Jack Snipe.

ACCESS
OS MAP: 193 REF: ST 361 238
The reserve is signposted off the A378, 1.6 km (1 mile) east of Fivehead.

FACILITIES
There are two hides, one overlooking the meadows, the other in woodland – the latter is accessible by wheelchair.

26 WESTHAY MOOR

NNR/SOMERSET WILDLIFE TRUST
513 ha (1,269 acres)
This reserve is an example of what can be achieved on land that was once harvested for its peat. Hides overlook reed-fringed pools. Two Droves cut across the reserve, which is bordered by scrub and grassland. The surrounding fields and peat workings should not be ignored, being reclaimed for wildlife as the peat industry contracts.

KEY BIRDS
ALL YEAR: Little Grebe, Water Rail, Buzzard, Marsh Harrier, Snipe, Barn Owl, Lesser Spotted Woodpecker, Cetti's Warbler.
SPRING: Garganey, possible calling Quail, a few passage waders.
SUMMER: Reed and Sedge Warblers, Tree Pipit, hunting Hobby in evenings.
AUTUMN Passage waders such as Green Sandpiper.
WINTER Wigeon, Pintail, Teal, Shoveler, occasional Peregrine, Merlin, Short-eared Owl and Jack Snipe.

ACCESS
OS MAP: 182 REF: ST 458 438
From the A39 east of Bridgwater, take the B3151 north through Shapwick (another good birding site), past Westhay – the reserve is approximately 1.6 km (1 mile) north-west of Westhay.

FACILITIES
Hides with disabled access.

27 BRIDGWATER BAY

NNR
2,510 ha (6,202 acres)
Mud flats, salt marsh, grazing marsh and reed beds provide refuge for the many wildfowl and waders that use this estuary throughout the year.

Waders are of most interest, with autumn and winter being the best seasons for a visit. To get the most out of a visit, it is necessary to arrive on a rising tide: only then are the waders pushed close enough to the shore for decent views.

While there are a number of viewing points, Steart offers the best vantage with hides and a patchwork of habitats that should provide a range of species on a typical visit.

KEY BIRDS
ALL YEAR: Little Egret, Shelduck, Oystercatcher.
SPRING: Passage waders include Greenshank and Whimbrel. Terns, Arctic Skua, Wheatear, Whinchat, Yellow Wagtail, hirundines.
SUMMER: Moulting Shelduck, Yellow Wagtail, Reed and Sedge Warblers; wader passage starts.
AUTUMN: Passage waders include Greenshank, Spotted Redshank, Curlew Sandpiper, Little Stint; possibility of storm-driven seabirds, such as Manx Shearwater, petrels and skuas in bad weather. Passerines as for spring (Aquatic Warblers have been trapped on occasion).
WINTER: Wigeon, Teal, Hen Harrier, Peregrine, Merlin, Short-eared Owl, Golden Plover, typical estuarine waders, including both godwits and Spotted Redshank.

ACCESS
OS MAP: 182 REF: ST 270 470
From Bridgwater, take the A39 towards Minehead, turn right at Cannington and follow the signs to Combwich and Hinkley Point. After Combwich, turn right to Otterhampton, then after 1.6 km (1 mile), take the right again to Steart Village. There is a car park on the left. A path leads past the farmhouse out across the fields to the hides.

FACILITIES
Hides overlook the bay.

28 CHEW VALLEY LAKE

AVON WILDLIFE TRUST/BRISTOL WATER PLC
486 ha (1,200 acres)
Quiet in summer, Chew is at its best in autumn and winter. Once the muddy margins are exposed, passage waders are able to linger and feed. Wildfowl abound in winter when there is an impressive gull roost, too.

Chew is a popular recreational centre 13 km (8 miles) from Bristol, so the quieter spots designated as nature reserves should be sought for birds. Herriot's Bridge is one such area where large numbers of wildfowl congregate.

KEY BIRDS
ALL YEAR: Great Crested and Little Grebes, Shoveler, Pochard, Ruddy Duck, Kingfisher, Grey Wagtail.
SPRING: Passage waders include Whimbrel, Curlew, Common and Green Sandpipers, Dunlin and Ruff. Garganey, Hobby, Osprey, terns including Black and Little Gulls, Yellow Wagtail, Wheatear and Whinchat.
SUMMER: Gadwall, Pochard, Tufted Duck and Shoveler breed; Reed and Sedge Warblers, Hobby.
AUTUMN: Black-necked Grebe, Osprey, Black Tern, Little Gull; passage waders may include Curlew Sandpiper, Spotted Redshank and Little Stint. There is a chance of a rarity or storm-blown seabird such as Sabine's Gull.
WINTER: All commoner dabbling and diving ducks, plus Goldeneye and Goosander. Smew, Long-tailed Duck and Red-breasted Merganser are regular. Gull roost may include Mediterranean Gull, plus Glaucous or Iceland Gulls. Firecrest, Chiffchaff and Bearded Tit are often recorded.

ACCESS
OS MAP: 172/182 REF: ST 570 600
The best point for roadside viewing is Herriot's Bridge at the southern end on the A368 and at Heron's Green on the eastern side on the B3114. Trails on the north-eastern side of the lake go from the car park off Denney Road.

FACILITIES
Hides accessed by permit only.

29 EXMOOR NATIONAL PARK

NATIONAL PARK
68,635 ha (169,601 acres)
Heather moorland, tumbling streams, wooded valleys and fields, plus a stretch of coastline; such a diverse array of habitats gives this small National Park a good range of species.

Due to the loss of large areas of moorland to agriculture, the typical upland species associated with this habitat are fairly thin on the ground. Black Grouse has been lost and Red Grouse are hard to track down.

Away from the moorland, sessile oak woods hold most interest, with the typical western specialities of Pied Flycatcher, Redstart and Wood Warbler all present. Porlock Marsh on the coast attracts a few wildfowl and waders. It is worth a look in spring and autumn for passage waders.

KEY BIRDS

ALL YEAR: Buzzard, Kingfisher, Lesser Spotted Woodpecker, Merlin, Red Grouse, Woodcock, Dipper, Grey Wagtail, Stonechat, Raven.
SPRING AND SUMMER: Curlew, Lapwing, Snipe, Nightjar, Cuckoo, Tree Pipit, Redstart, Whinchat, Wheatear, Ring Ouzel (scarce), Wood Warbler, Pied Flycatcher.
AUTUMN: Chance of passage waders at Porlock.
WINTER: Fairly quiet on moorland; resident woodland birds; wildfowl and waders at Porlock.

ACCESS

OS MAP: 180/181 REF: ST 050 350
Anywhere with suitable habitat is worth exploring. Porlock Marsh is easily reached from Porlock village; a public footpath leads to the shingle bank.

30 CHAPEL WOOD

RSPB RESERVE
6 ha (15 acres)
This small reserve encompasses a wooded valley 16 km (10 miles) from Barnstaple.

KEY BIRDS

ALL YEAR: Sparrowhawk, Buzzard, Green, Great Spotted and Lesser Spotted Woodpeckers, Dipper, Grey Wagtail, Raven.
SPRING AND SUMMER: Warblers, Redstart, Pied Flycatcher.

ACCESS

OS MAP: 180 REF: SS 483 413
Take the A361 from Barnstaple to Ilfracombe, turn left towards Spreacombe, 3 km (2 miles) north of Braunton.

31 LUNDY ISLAND

THE NATIONAL TRUST
959 ha (2,368 acres)
Lundy, derived from the Norse *Lun-dey* and meaning Puffin Island, sits out in the Bristol Channel, 16 km (10 miles) off the Devon coast. Spectacular sea cliffs, boggy moorland and a wooded valley are the key habitats.

Spring and autumn are the most popular seasons to visit for migrants and rarities. However, the summer months provide breeding seabirds and the opportunity of seeing European Storm Petrels and Manx Shearwaters on the boat crossing.

Millcombe Valley with its trees and bushes, situated in the south east of the island provides a perfect haven for tired migrants. A blackboard at the Marisco Tavern lists recent sightings.

KEY BIRDS

ALL YEAR: Shag, Peregrine, Rock Pipit, Raven.
SPRING: Manx Shearwaters start to appear off the island in March. Merlin, Whimbrel, Firecrest, warblers, hirundines, Yellow Wagtail, Ring Ouzel, Pied and Spotted Flycatcher, Whinchat, Redstart, Black Redstart, Wheatear, and the potential for scarce migrants such as Golden Oriole, Dotterel and Hoopoe.
SUMMER: Manx Shearwater and European Storm Petrel are most easily seen from the boat. A few Puffin, Guillemot and Razorbill breed, along with Kittiwake, Fulmar, Great Black-backed and Lesser Black-backed Gulls, and Curlew.
AUTUMN: As for spring, plus finches and thrushes in late autumn, and a good chance of rarities.

ACCESS

OS MAP: 180 REF: SS 130 450
Day crossings to Lundy run throughout the year, normally departing from Bideford. For sailing times, bookings and accommodation details, contact the Lundy Sales Office, The Quay, Bideford, North Devon EX39 2LY.

SOUTH-EAST ENGLAND

If you stand on the white cliffs above Dover on a clear day, the French coast is clearly visible. The 34 km (21 miles) separating us is no great distance. No wonder then that the south-east acts as the arrival-and-departure lounge for thousands of migrant birds. New colonists have made this journey, too. The first Cetti's Warbler arrived in Britain in 1961, and was breeding in Kent by 1973. More recently, the Little Egret, which not long ago was a much sought-after rarity, now breeds and is a common sight.

The south-east enjoys a mild and, compared to much of Britain, a dry climate, which suits many species of birds on the northern edge of their range. Many of these reside in our heaths, where species such as Dartford Warbler, Woodlark and Nightjar thrive. The New Forest and Surrey heaths such as Thursley are excellent sites in which to see them. These same sites play host to many other members of our fauna and flora at the northern limit of their European ranges.

From the Thames Estuary in the north of the region round to Langstone Harbour in the west, the coastline is dotted with birding hotspots. Jutting out into the Channel, both Beachy Head in Sussex and Dungeness in Kent offer outstanding birding in spring and autumn when migrants are on the move. The south coast encompasses salt marsh, estuaries and marshland that swarm in winter with wildfowl and waders escaping their frozen northern breeding grounds.

KEY

1) New Forest
2) Titchfield Haven
3) Yar Estuary
4) St Catherine's Point
5) Langstone Harbour and Farlington Marshes
6) Chichester Harbour, Thorney Island and Pilsey Island
7) Pagham Harbour
8) Arundel
9) Pulborough Brooks
10) Thursley Common
11) London Wetland Centre
12) Staines Reservoir
13) Beachy Head
14) Fore Wood
15) Rye Harbour
16) Tudeley Woods
17) Bough Beech Reservoir
18) Dungeness
19) New Hythe and Burham Marshes
20) Sandwich Bay
21) Pegwell Bay
22) Blean Woods
23) Oare Marshes
24) Shellness and Swale
25) Stodmarsh
26) Elmley
27) Nor Marsh and Motney Hill
28) Northward Hill
29) Cliffe Pools
30) Lee Valley Country Park
31) Rye Meads

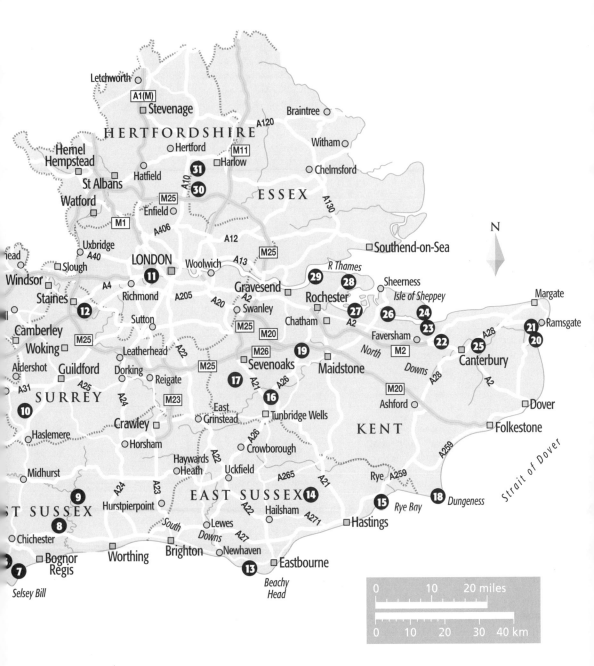

Letchworth ○

A1(M)

■ Stevenage

HERTFORDSHIRE

Hemel
Hempstead
St Albans
Watford ■

○ Hertford

Hatfield ○

A120

Braintree ○

M11

■ Harlow

Witham ○

Chelmsford ○

M25

Enfield ○

A10

31

30

ESSEX

A130

E S S E X

M1

A406

A12

Uxbridge ○
□ Slough
A40
ead ○

Windsor
○
Staines
12

A4

LONDON

11

Woolwich ○

A13

M25

Southend-on-Sea

Richmond ○

A205

A20

R Thames

Gravesend

A2

29

28

Sheerness

Isle of Sheppey

Margate ■

Camberley
Woking ○

M25

Sutton ○

Swanley ○

Rochester

27

26

Faversham ○

24

23

Ramsgate ○

21

20

Chatham ■

A2

Leatherhead ○

A22

M25

M20

North

M2

22

25

Canterbury

Aldershot ○
A31
Guildford
○

A25

A24

Dorking ○

Reigate ○

M26

Sevenoaks

19

Maidstone

Downs

A28

A2

S U R R E Y

M23

17

A21

A26

16

East
Grinstead ○

Tunbridge Wells

M20

Ashford ○

Dover ■

10

Crawley

○ Haslemere

○ Horsham

A26

Crowborough ○

K E N T

Folkestone ■

Midhurst ○

Haywards
○Heath

A22

Uckfield ○

A265

Rye

A259

A259

18

Dungeness

Strait of Dover

A24

A23

EAST SUSSEX

14

A21

15

Rye Bay

9

Hurstpierpoint ○

Hailsham ○

A271

ST SUSSEX

A22

South

Lewes ○

A27

Hastings ■

8

○ Chichester

□ Bognor
Regis

Worthing

Downs

Brighton

○Newhaven

Eastbourne

7

Selsey Bill

13

Beachy
Head

0   10   20 miles

0   10   20   30   40 km

N

25

1   NEW FOREST

VARIOUS, INCLUDING FORESTRY ENTERPRISE
37,600 ha (92,912 acres)
Ancient and new woodlands interspersed with
vast areas of heath and bogs make the New
Forest a rich hunting ground for the birder as
well as those keen on rare plants and insects.

Dartford Warblers are best located in spring
when their scratchy song can be heard.
Woodlarks like the heavily-grazed grassy areas,
known locally as lawns. The best time to locate
them is during early-morning visits in spring from
mid-March to late April, when they sing and
display from the tops of tall trees.

Some locations are particularly productive for
birds. For example, Beaulieu Heath has a good
population of Dartford Warblers and Woodlarks.
Acres Down has a ridge overlooking heath and
forest, and is one of the best spots to search for
raptors such as Honey Buzzard and Goshawk.
Here, a morning visit is usually more productive
than an afternoon visit.

Autumn and winter can be disappointing.
However, a few species such as Hawfinch are
easier to see. Try Pitts Wood enclosure between
Hampton Ridge and Cockley Plain. The heath
here also attracts Hen Harrier in winter and
Dartford Warbler in summer. Another site for
Hawfinch is the Bolderwood Grounds. It is also a
good site for Firecrest.

KEY BIRDS
ALL YEAR: Goshawk, Mandarin, Woodcock,
Lesser Spotted Woodpecker, Stonechat,
Crossbill, Hawfinch; Dartford Warbler and
Woodlark are best in spring and summer as they
can be elusive in winter.
SPRING AND SUMMER: Honey Buzzard, Hobby,
Curlew, Nightjar, Tree Pipit, Nightingale,
Redstart, Whinchat, Wheatear, Grasshopper and
Wood Warblers, Firecrest.
WINTER: Hen Harrier, occasional Great Grey
Shrike, Brambling.

ACCESS
OS MAP: 184/195 REF: SU 300 100
Beaulieu Heath: leave Lyndhurst on the B3056
to Beaulieu Road Station. Just before the bridge
there is a car park on the right.

Bolderwood Grounds: leave Lyndhurst on the
Stoney Cross Road. Turn left in Emery Down for

Bolderwood. After 4 km (2.5 miles) there is a car
park in the fork of two roads.

Acres Down: take the minor road running
between Emery Down and the A31. If travelling
north from Emery Down, take a turning on the
left after 3 km (2 miles) marked 'no through
road', opposite the turning for Newtown. Carry
on to the car park. Walk up to the ridge.

Pitts Wood enclosure is along the B3078 east
of Fordingbridge. Continue for about 5 km
(3 miles) to the Ashley Walk car park, then
follow the main path across the valley to Pitts
Wood.

2   TITCHFIELD HAVEN

NNR
87 ha (215 acres)
Behind the shore of the Solent, south-east of
Southampton, this small reserve is a patchwork of
reed beds, freshwater scrapes and wet meadows.
Migrant waders and passerines appear on passage.
A winter visit may produce a Bittern.

KEY BIRDS
ALL YEAR: Water Rail, Cetti's Warbler and
Bearded Tit.
SPRING AND SUMMER: Common Tern, warblers.
SUMMER: Breeding birds include Sedge Warbler.
A few waders occur on the Humber.
AUTUMN: Passage waders.
WINTER: Bittern, large population of Black-tailed
Godwits, wintering wildfowl and waders.

ACCESS
OS MAP: 196 REF: SU 535 025
Open from 9.30am to 5pm (4pm in winter),
Wednesday to Sunday, plus Bank Holidays.
Accessed from the A27 west of Fareham.

FACILITIES
Information desk, hides, tearoom and a shop.

3   YAR ESTUARY

NNR
Close to Yarmouth Harbour, this estuary with its
various habitats, is the most accessible site on the
Isle of Wight if visiting without a vehicle.

Reed beds and damp woodland add interest to
a site that is good for estuarine waders and
wildfowl in winter.

KEY BIRDS

ALL YEAR: Shelduck, Reed Bunting, Cetti's Warbler, resident woodland birds.
SPRING AND AUTUMN: Wintering estuarine waders and wildfowl arriving and departing. Passage waders include Spotted Redshank, Greenshank, Common Sandpiper and Whimbrel.
SUMMER: Common and Little Terns, Sedge and Reed Warblers.
WINTER: Brent Goose, Wigeon, Teal, Goldeneye, estuarine waders including Black-tailed Godwit and Spotted Redshank. Kingfisher, Grey Wagtail and Rock Pipit.

ACCESS

OS MAP: 196 REF: SZ 354 897
From the ferry in Yarmouth Harbour, follow River Road (A3054) south past the car park before turning into Mill Road to Yarmouth Mill, then take the footpath along the seawall.

4 ST CATHERINE'S POINT

THE NATIONAL TRUST
As the most southerly tip of the Isle of Wight, the Point is a good seawatching site, and during spring and autumn receives its fair share of passage migrants. Scrub, small, stone-walled fields, low cliffs and grassland are the main habitats.

For passage migrants an early-morning visit is best, but like all migration sites, birds can and do arrive at any time of day. Seawatching is best in spring from mid-April to mid-May, with onshore south, south-westerly to north-easterly winds. In autumn, gales are needed to witness a good passage of birds.

KEY BIRDS

SPRING AND AUTUMN: Passerine migrants such as Ring Ouzel, Firecrest, Pied Flycatcher, warblers and chats, chance of a Hoopoe or Serin in spring. Seabird passage includes divers, seaduck, Manx Shearwater, Gannet, auks, gulls and terns. Whimbrel, Bar-tailed Godwit, Pomarine Skua in spring. Possible Sabine's Gull and Little Auk during gales in autumn.

ACCESS

OS MAP: 196
Reached from the A3055 in Niton, proceed south. A track leads to the lighthouse, and there are various paths from which to explore the area.

5 LANGSTONE HARBOUR AND FARLINGTON MARSHES

RSPB / HAMPSHIRE WILDLIFE TRUST
700 ha (1,730 acres)
The inter-tidal mud flats, freshwater marsh, reed bed and grazing land of these two adjacent sites attract an abundance of wildfowl and waders throughout the year. The sea wall enclosing the marshes gives a good vantage point.

A visit on a rising tide is good for views of waders as they are pushed off the mud by the rising water, and flocks wheel around, settling to roost on some of the islands and within the sea wall.

Passage migrants that use the Farlington Reserve are the other big attraction. It is a good site for early-arriving Sand Martins and Wheatears in March, and during both spring and autumn scarce species put in an appearance.

KEY BIRDS

ALL YEAR: Water Rail, Little Egret, Mediterranean Gull, Cetti's Warbler.
SPRING AND AUTUMN: Garganey, Hobby, Wood Sandpiper, Curlew Sandpiper, Common Sandpiper, Green Sandpiper, Ruff, Little Stint, Avocet, Greenshank, Spotted Redshank, Whimbrel, Little Ringed Plover, both godwits, Black Tern and Little Gull in the harbour, Wheatear, Whinchat, Cuckoo, Yellow Wagtail, Ring Ouzel, Firecrest, Pied Flycatcher (autumn), various warblers. Autumn may produce a rare wader, while Black Redstart, Spotted Crake and Wryneck are all possibilities.
WINTER: Occasional divers, a regular flock of Black-necked Grebes, often Slavonian Grebe, Brent Goose, Wigeon, Teal, Pintail, Shoveler, Goldeneye, Red-breasted Merganser, sometimes Long-tailed Duck. Waders include all the typical estuarine species, plus Green Sandpiper and a few Greenshank. Peregrine, often Merlin and Short-eared Owl, Hen Harrier, and in some winters Long-eared Owls roost. Often Water Pipit, Bearded Tit, Twite and sometimes Snow and Lapland Buntings.

ACCESS

OS MAP: 196/197 REF: SU 685 045
From the A27 east of Portsmouth, turn off on to the roundabout that leads to the A2030. There is an entrance to the car park from the roundabout.

6 CHICHESTER HARBOUR, THORNEY ISLAND AND PILSEY ISLAND

RSPB RESERVE

1,200 ha (2,965 acres)

Wintering wildfowl and waders are the main draw to these sites. Pilsey Island is a small island off the tip of Thorney Island, which hosts the largest wader roost in Chichester Harbour.

Thorney Island can be explored by taking the coastal footpath. It is an 8 km (5 mile) walk, with good views of Pilsey Island obtainable midway around.

KEY BIRDS

ALL YEAR: Little Grebe, Water Rail, Little Egret, Barn Owl, Cetti's Warbler, Redshank, Mediterranean Gull.

SPRING AND AUTUMN: Estuarine wildfowl and waders. Whimbrel, terns, gulls such as Mediterranean and a few passerine migrants.

SUMMER: Terns in the harbour.

WINTER: Estuarine waders with large roost at Pilsey, also Avocet, Golden Plover and Spotted Redshank. Wildfowl include Brent Goose, Pintail, Wigeon, Scaup, Eider, Red-breasted Merganser, Teal. Chance of Hen Harrier, Merlin, Peregrine, Short-eared and Barn Owls. Kingfisher, Rock Pipit, Snow Bunting and Stonechat.

ACCESS

OS MAP: 197 REF: SU 770 006

Leave the A27 at Emsworth. Either take the footpath from Emsworth Marina, or park along the access road to Thorney Island.

7 PAGHAM HARBOUR

NNR

440 ha (1,087 acres)

A good path runs around the whole harbour. The harbour mouth is bordered by shingle spits, the beach on the south side protecting some wet grassland and reed-fringed pools known as the Severals. Just inland from the Severals is Church Norton, with wooded areas and a graveyard attractive to migrants. The Ferry Pool, which is opposite the visitor centre, can be outstanding for passage waders in autumn. The harbour is at its best in winter when thousands of wildfowl and waders can be seen.

KEY BIRDS

ALL YEAR: Little Egret, Shelduck, Oystercatcher, Redshank, Barn Owl, Little Owl, Lesser Spotted Woodpecker.

SPRING: Passage waders, terns, and offshore, divers, scoters, grebes, a few auks and skuas. Passerine migrants, with occasional Osprey and Garganey.

SUMMER: Returning waders by July, terns.

AUTUMN: Passage waders, Black Tern, Little Gull, passerine migrants include Redstart.

WINTER: Brent Goose, Wigeon, Pintail, Teal, Goldeneye, Eider, Red-breasted Merganser. Hen Harrier, Merlin, Short-eared Owl, Water Rail; all estuarine waders plus Avocet. Occasional wintering Twite, Chiffchaff, Firecrest; offshore, Slavonian Grebe.

ACCESS

OS MAP: 197 REF: SZ 857 966

From the A27 Chichester bypass, take the B2145 to Selsey. The reserve car park is 0.8 km (½ mile) south of Sidlesham village on the left. A car park at Church Norton can be reached by carrying on and turning left where signposted.

FACILITIES

A visitor centre is open at weekends. There are hides and limited wheelchair access.

8 ARUNDEL

WWT

24 ha (60 acres)

Primarily a captive collection, there are, however, wader scrapes, a reed bed and open water which all attract a good range of wild birds.

KEY BIRDS

ALL YEAR: Water Rail, Cetti's Warbler.

SUMMER: Breeding Redshank, Oystercatcher, Common Tern, Sedge and Reed Warblers.

WINTER: Bewick's Swan roost, Wigeon, Teal, Snipe, Green Sandpiper, Kingfisher.

ACCESS

OS MAP: 197 REF: TQ 020 081

Open daily from 9.30am, except Christmas Day. Reached by taking the road alongside the Castle.

FACILITIES

Reserve centre, shop and café, plus hides and an extensive captive waterfowl. Disabled access.

9 PULBOROUGH BROOKS

RSPB RESERVE

170 ha (420 acres)

After intensive agricultural use diminished the value of the flood meadows for birds, the Brooks have now been restored to their former glory, making them one of the south-east's most impressive wetlands.

Winter is the best time for a visit, with wildfowl being of most interest. A circular route around the reserve takes three hours to complete.

KEY BIRDS

ALL YEAR: Lapwing, Redshank, Snipe, Teal, Mandarin, Woodcock, Little Owl, Barn Owl, Sparrowhawk, Lesser Spotted Woodpecker.
SUMMER: Breeding waders and wildfowl sometimes includes Garganey. Hobby, Yellow Wagtail, Nightingale, woodland breeding birds.
WINTER: Bewick's Swan, Wigeon, Gadwall, Teal, Pintail, Shoveler, sometimes White-fronted Goose; Ruff, Jack Snipe, Peregrine and Merlin possible; often good numbers of thrushes.

ACCESS

OS MAP: 197 REF: **TQ 054 170**

Open daily from 9am to sunset, closed on Christmas Day. The reserve is signposted from the A29. Pulborough is 3 km (2 miles) away.

FACILITIES

Visitor centre, hides, wheelchair access.

10 THURSLEY COMMON

NNR

250 ha (618 acres)

A lowland heath with bogs and scattered pine and birch woodland, Thursley should be visited in spring and summer for the heath specialities of Dartford Warbler, Woodlark and Nightjar. In winter there is little bird interest, with the more interesting residents being hard to find.

Paths cross the heath, with boardwalks over the boggy areas, favoured by Curlews and Redshank in summer.

KEY BIRDS

ALL YEAR: Dartford Warbler, Woodlark, Stonechat, in some years Crossbill.
SPRING AND SUMMER: Hobby, Curlew, Snipe, Redshank, Woodcock, Nightjar, Tree Pipit, Nightingale, Redstart.
WINTER: Hen Harrier, and occasionally Great Grey Shrike.

ACCESS

OS MAP: 186 REF: **SU 900 417**

From the A3 take the B3001 to Elstead. At the village green turn left (just past pub). The Moat car park is 1.6 km (1 mile) further along on the left. The turning is easily missed.

11 LONDON WETLAND CENTRE

WWT

35 ha (86 acres)

Five years in the making, this new reserve at Barn Elms on the banks of the River Thames was once a reservoir complex. Now a wetland, its lagoons, reed beds and grazing marsh are attracting ever-increasing numbers of birds. Therefore, the following is just a rough guide and is likely to change over the next couple of years as the site settles down and habitats develop.

KEY BIRDS

ALL YEAR: Great Crested and Little Grebes, Mute Swan, Pochard, Lapwing, Redshank, Reed Bunting.
SPRING AND SUMMER: Chance of Garganey, Hobby and Little Egret, various passage waders including Common and Green Sandpipers, Snipe, Yellow Wagtail, Whinchat, Wheatear.
SUMMER: Little Ringed Plover, Reed and Sedge Warblers.
WINTER: Gadwall, Shoveler, Wigeon, Teal, Tufted Duck and Pochard, chance of other diving duck; Peregrine regular.

ACCESS

OS MAP: 176 REF: **TQ 228 771**

Open from 9.30am to 4pm in winter, and 5pm in summer, daily except Christmas Day. It is located on the A306 just south of Hammersmith Bridge. Nearest tube is Hammersmith, and the 283 is a special 'duck bus' which runs directly to the centre.

FACILITIES

These are excellent with hides, including the three-storey Peacock Tower complete with lift, an observatory, café and restaurant, art gallery, exhibitions and more. There is wheelchair access.

12 STAINES RESERVOIR

THAMES WATER

170 ha (420 acres)

Below the flight path of Heathrow this large, concrete-banked reservoir is primarily of interest for passage migrants and wintering wildfowl. The Black-necked Grebes that occur in small numbers in autumn are a speciality.

A causeway separates the two basins, providing the ideal vantage point from which to view.

⚐ KEY BIRDS

SPRING AND AUTUMN: Black Tern, Little Gull; passage waders, especially Common Sandpiper, Dunlin, Greenshank, Ringed and Little-ringed Plovers. Black-necked Grebes often linger into winter.

WINTER: Grebes, Pochard, Tufted Duck, Goldeneye, often sawbills and a few dabbling duck; sometimes Black Redstart.

⚐ ACCESS

OS MAP: **176** REF: **TQ 053 733**

Take the A3044 north of Staines, between King George V1 and Staines Reservoirs. If travelling north, park on the verge by the access path on the right.

13 BEACHY HEAD

EASTBOURNE COUNCIL

Extends for 6.5 km (4 miles)

The spectacular starting point of the South Downs, Beachy Head's white cliffs rise to some 150 m (500 feet) above the sea. Migrant passerines and seawatching mean this is primarily a site for spring or autumn. A number of sites both east and west of the head should be visited, with Birling Gap, Whitbread Hollow and Belle Tout Wood being those most visited by birders.

From April to mid-May seawatching can be excellent from Birling Gap – southerly or south-easterly gales are best. For passerine migrants the opposite is true – during spring birds rarely linger, but in autumn numbers build, and there is more chance of a rarity.

⚐ KEY BIRDS

SPRING: Offshore passage includes Red- and Black-throated Divers, grebes, Fulmar, Gannet, Brent Goose, scoters, Red-breasted Merganser,

Eider, Garganey, Bar-tailed Godwit, Whimbrel, skuas including Pomarine in late April / May, terns and gulls. Passerine migrants include Grasshopper Warbler, Redstart, Pied Flycatcher, Wheatear, Whinchat, Ring Ouzel and (annually) Hoopoe and Serin.

AUTUMN: Offshore, skuas and occasional shearwaters. Passerines as for spring, especially large numbers of Sylvia warblers; good chance of Wryneck; rarities are annual. Arrival in late autumn of winter thrushes, finches and buntings.

⚐ ACCESS

OS MAP: **199** REF: **TV 586 956**

The B2103 runs just inland of the cliffs. Birling Gap has a car park and is west of the head just before a bend at the bottom of a hill. Belle Tout is just east of Birling Gap, and Whitebread Hollow is just east of the head.

14 FORE WOOD

RSPB RESERVE

55 ha (136 acres)

Supporting a range of woodland species, Fore Wood is deciduous with coppiced areas. It is best visited in spring or early summer. After heavy rain, take good footwear as it can get muddy.

⚐ KEY BIRDS

ALL YEAR: Green, Great Spotted and Lesser Spotted Woodpeckers, Nuthatch, Treecreeper, Marsh Tit.

SPRING AND SUMMER: Nightingale, plus common warblers, Spotted Flycatcher.

⚐ ACCESS

OS MAP: **199** REF: **TQ 758 123**

Reached off the A2100 Battle to Hastings Road, on the outskirts of Crowhurst. Park at Crowhurst village hall. Walk up the road for 0.8 km (½ mile) to the entrance on the left at the top of the hill.

15 RYE HARBOUR

LNR

360 ha (890 acres)

At one time the sea bed, Rye Harbour is a vast area of shingle dotted with gravel pits and backed by farmland. Birding is good throughout the year. Cover is sparse so passage migrant interest usually centres on waders, terns and gulls.

To cover the entire area, a full day is needed, otherwise a visit to the hides overlooking the more productive sites can be achieved in two to three hours. Good paths make walking easy.

KEY BIRDS

ALL YEAR: Teal, Gadwall, Shoveler, Pochard, Tufted Duck, Ruddy Duck, Grey Partridge, Oystercatcher, Ringed Plover, Mediterranean Gull, Corn Bunting.
SPRING AND AUTUMN: Hobby, Garganey, passage waders, Little Gull, Black Tern, often Roseate Tern, chats and wagtails, chance of a rarity.
SUMMER: Little, Common and Sandwich Terns, Yellow Wagtail, Wheatear.
WINTER: Offshore, Red-throated Diver, Brent Goose, Eider, Common Scoter, Guillemot; on the pits a chance of a rarer grebe, sawbill or Long-tailed Duck; Wigeon, Scaup and Goldeneye. Hunting over the shingle and farmland, Merlin, Peregrine, Short-eared Owl and Hen Harrier. Waders roost on islands in the pits and include Knot and Grey Plover. Bittern and Water Rail on the pits with reed beds.

ACCESS
OS MAP: **189/199** REF: **TQ 941 188**
From Rye, go west on the A259. Turn left to Rye Harbour on the town's outskirts. Follow this road to the end and around to the right to a car park. A path leads to the reserve along the river.

FACILITIES
An information point in the car park, and hides and a good tarmac path allowing disabled access.

16   TUDELEY WOODS

RSPB RESERVE
120 ha (296 acres)
The ancient coppiced oak woodland and restored heathland of Tudeley are at their best in spring and summer. An early-morning visit in May will find the wood alive with birds, while the heath comes to life at dusk with the churring of Nightjars.

KEY BIRDS
ALL YEAR: Sparrowhawk, Woodcock, Tawny Owl, Green, Great Spotted and Lesser Spotted Woodpeckers, Nuthatch, Treecreeper, Marsh Tit, Hawfinch.
SPRING AND SUMMER: Nightingale plus other warblers, Tree Pipit, Nightjar on heath.
WINTER: Thrushes, Redpoll, Siskin, Brambling, sometimes Crossbill.

ACCESS
OS MAP: **188** REF: **TQ 618 434**
Leave Tonbridge on the A21. After 1.6 km (1 mile) take the minor road on the left just before a garage, signposted for Capel. The reserve is a short way along here.

17   BOUGH BEECH RESERVOIR

KENT WILDLIFE TRUST
125 ha (308 acres)
Mixed broad-leaf woodland, hedgerows and fields surround this reservoir in west Kent. Muddy margins from mid-summer into late autumn attract a few passage waders.

Viewing is from the causeway that separates the North Lake from the reservoir. A feeding station in the orchard close to the visitor centre attracts a range of woodland birds, notably Bramblings.

KEY BIRDS
ALL YEAR: Great Crested Grebe, Grey Heron (small heronry), Mandarin, Little Owl, Lesser Spotted, Great Spotted and Green Woodpeckers, Kingfisher, Grey Wagtail.
SPRING AND AUTUMN: A few passerine migrants such as Wheatear and Yellow Wagtail. Terns include a few Black Tern annually. Passage waders include Whimbrel (spring), Curlew, Redshank, Common and Green Sandpipers and Greenshank. Snipe in late autumn; Osprey and recently Little Egrets have become annual.
SUMMER: Little Ringed Plover, Common Tern, Lesser Whitethroat, Reed Warbler.
WINTER: Gadwall, Wigeon, Shoveler, Teal, Pochard, Tufted Duck, feral geese, Snipe, Green Sandpiper, Water Rail, Brambling.

ACCESS
OS MAP: **188** REF: **TQ 496 489**
From Sevenoaks (junction 5 off M25) take the B2042 to Ide Hill from where the reservoir can be seen. Follow the road down the hill, taking the left-hand turning signposted to the reservoir.

FACILITIES
Visitor centre open between April and October on Wed, Sat and Sun, and Bank Holidays.

DUNGENESS
RSPB RESERVE (486 ha/1,200 acres)

Sticking out into the English Channel, Dungeness is a huge shingle spit, with gravel pits, scrub and reed beds providing welcome habitat for a good range of birds. Due to its geographic location close to the continent it is important for studying migration, and is Kent's premier seawatching site, hence the bird observatory established in 1952.

The shingle extraction industry has created a number of gravel pits, suitable for a good range of wintering wildfowl, while the islands provide a safe refuge for breeding gulls and terns. Dominating the skyline, the nuclear power stations at Dungeness have benefited

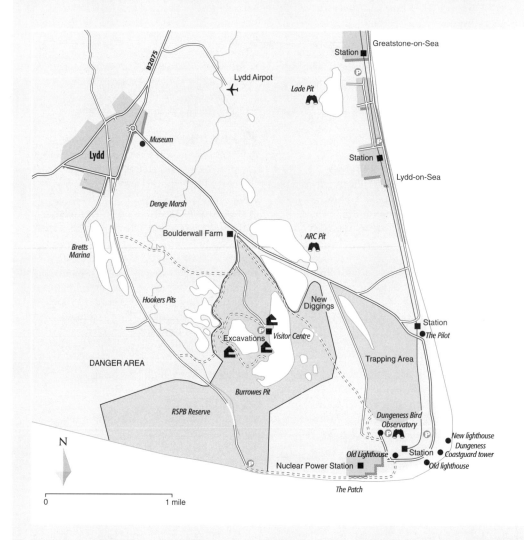

some birds, with Black Redstart nesting on the structure, and the warm water outflow known as 'The Patch' attracting gulls and terns.

The RSPB has had a long relationship with Dungeness, and today manages an ever-increasing area, with exciting plans for the future. From the RSPB Reserve centre, there is a circular trail with hides overlooking gravel pits, a favoured haunt of wintering Smew. They are often joined by other sawbills and the rarer grebes. Away from the pits, the dry bramble-filled moat surrounding the bird observatory and the large area of scrub close by known as the 'Trapping Area' are where most passerine migrants lurk.

Seawatching is best from the Coastguard Tower, or the hide on the beach. Like most south-coast sites it is best in spring for the variety and numbers of species passing, including the flocks of Pomarine Skuas that annually pass offshore between mid-April and mid-May.

KEY BIRDS

ALL YEAR: Common dabbling and diving duck, Mediterranean Gull, Bearded Tit, Black Redstart.

SPRING: Offshore passage of Manx Shearwater, divers, grebes, scoters, Garganey, Eider, Red-breasted Merganser, waders, especially Whimbrel and Bar-tailed Godwit, terns, gulls, auks and skuas, especially Pomarine. Migrants in the Trapping Area may include Golden Oriole and Serin.

SUMMER: Breeding gulls and terns, Wheatear, Yellow Wagtail, possible Roseate Tern and Little Gull.

AUTUMN: Offshore during gales there is a possibility of petrels, Manx Shearwater and Sooty Shearwater. Black Tern and Little Gull on The Patch. Migrants include Redstart, Whinchat, Pied Flycatcher, Ring Ouzel, crests and various warblers, plus a chance of Wryneck, Melodious Warbler and Red-backed Shrike. Finches and thrushes in late autumn, and passage waders.

WINTER: Offshore, divers and grebes. On the pits, Black-necked, Red-necked and Slavonian Grebes, Smew, Goosander, Goldeneye, Bewick's Swan, Merlin, Peregrine, Golden Plover, Ruff, Stonechat. Often wintering Glaucous Gull on the beach.

ACCESS

OS MAP: 189 REF: TR 063 196
South-east of Lydd, take the Dungeness Road. The RSPB reserve is on the right 2.4 km (1½ miles) from the Lydd roundabout. It opens daily from 9am.

OS MAP: 189 REF: TR 085 173
The bird observatory and beach are reached by continuing past the gravel pits and taking the next right turn after the power station entrance.

FACILITIES

The RSPB reserve has a visitor centre and hides with disabled access. The bird observatory offers accommodation and is open throughout the year. Contact DBO, 11 RNSSS, Dungeness, Kent TN29 9NA.

Smew
Mergellus albellus

The male Smew is easily identified. Its black and white plumage makes it one of our most striking ducks, and the female, with its compact shape, grey body and red head, is also distinctive.

Large numbers of Smew winter across the Channel on the continent, with just a few making it to Britain each year to traditional wintering sites such as Dungeness. Here, usually from mid-winter, there is a regular flock, which favours the reserve's gravel pits.

Numbers vary annually depending on the severity of the weather in Europe. If a big freeze occurs then hundreds of Smew may arrive in Britain, and may then turn up on any suitable lake or gravel pit.

19 NEW HYTHE AND BURHAM MARSHES

KENT WILDLIFE TRUST

202 ha (500 acres)

These two sites are separated by the River Medway. Burham Marshes consists of a little grazing marsh and a reed bed. New Hythe is a mosaic of lakes, willow scrub and hedgerows.

New Hythe is one of the more reliable sites in Kent for Smew. Rare grebes and the odd diver occasionally turn up. New Hythe will take half a day to explore fully, along a network of paths around the lakes. Burham has a footpath along the river bank from which to view.

KEY BIRDS

ALL YEAR: Great Crested and Little Grebes, Water Rail, Kingfisher, Cetti's Warbler (New Hythe), Bearded Tit (Burham).

SPRING AND AUTUMN: Occasional terns; passage waders may include Whimbrel overhead in spring. Wheatear, Yellow Wagtail and Whinchat.

WINTER: Occasional visits by rarer grebes and a chance of Smew. Gadwall, Teal, Wigeon, Pintail, Tufted Duck, Pochard. Bitterns winter annually.

ACCESS

OS MAP: 188 REF: TQ 714 615

New Hythe is best accessed by coming off the M20 at junction 4. Take the A228 north over two roundabouts. Soon after the end of a dual carriageway, take the turning on the left opposite a Royal Mail depot, then immediately right, over the A228, then right as if going back on to the A228, but turn off left to the car park. Proceed under a low bridge to the lakes. Burham can be reached by taking a minor road north out of Aylesford to Burham. Park by the church and proceed out to the marshes.

20 SANDWICH BAY

SANDWICH BAY BIRD OBSERVATORY TRUST

400 ha (988 acres)

Primarily of interest for migrants, Sandwich Bay has a mix of habitats ranging from mature gardens and scrub, to a wader scrape, meadows and sand dunes. The areas of cover within the Sandwich Bay Estate, in which the bird observatory is situated, are best for migrants. Information can be obtained at the observatory.

A number of paths dissect the area. However, you should respect the privacy of the residents.

KEY BIRDS

SPRING: Migrants include Ring Ouzel, Wheatear, Whinchat, Redstart, Black Redstart, various warblers, with annual Golden Oriole and rarities.

AUTUMN: As for spring plus Pied Flycatcher and generally more birds. Rarities such as Wryneck and Icterine Warbler and, in late autumn, chance of Pallas's Warbler. Finches and thrushes arrive.

WINTER: Raptors, Golden Plover, Twite, Snow Bunting, possible Shorelark.

ACCESS

OS MAP: 179 REF: TR 355 575

Travel east out of Sandwich towards Royal St George's golf course, go through the toll gate. The observatory is a short way down on the right.

FACILITIES

The bird observatory offers accommodation. There is a visitor centre, a field study centre, and disabled access. Contact SBBO, Guildford Road, Sandwich Bay, Sandwich, Kent CT3 9PF.

21 PEGWELL BAY

KENT WILDLIFE TRUST

121 ha (300 acres)

Close to Sandwich Bay, Pegwell Bay is of main interest for waders and wildfowl. Mud flats, salt marsh and a limited area of coastal scrub are easily covered in quite a short space of time.

KEY BIRDS

ALL YEAR: Oystercatcher, Redshank, Ringed Plover.

SPRING AND AUTUMN: Passage waders, with Kentish Plover just about annual in spring.

SUMMER: Sandwich and Little Terns, Yellow Wagtail, possible Mediterranean Gull.

WINTER: Estuarine waders and wildfowl including Brent Goose. Stonechat, possible Snow Bunting.

ACCESS

OS MAP: 179 REF: TR 342 635

The car park is on the A256 Sandwich to Ramsgate road at Pegwell Bay.

FACILITIES

Hide overlooking the mud flats.

22 BLEAN WOODS

RSPB RESERVE
309 ha (765 acres)
Close to Canterbury, this impressive wood is mainly oak and sweet chestnut coppice. A network of trails allows exploration. Spring is the best season for a visit.

KEY BIRDS
ALL YEAR: Sparrowhawk, Tawny Owl, Woodcock, Lesser Spotted, Great Spotted and Green Woodpeckers, Hawfinch (scarce).
SPRING AND SUMMER: Hobby, Nightjar, Tree Pipit, Turtle Dove, Nightingale, Redstart and warblers.

ACCESS
OS MAP: 179 REF: TR 126 592
If coming off the A2 from the west, take the first turning to Canterbury, and then the second turning on the left to Rough Common. The reserve is along here on the left.

FACILITIES
Limited disabled access on good paths.

23 OARE MARSHES

KENT WILDLIFE TRUST
67 ha (165 acres)
Situated on the south side of the Swale, Oare's grazing marsh and floods are overlooked by two hides. Waders and wildfowl are of prime interest.

This is also a good site for viewing the Swale. With its extensive mud flats, estuarine waders are much in evidence and roost on the reserve.

KEY BIRDS
ALL YEAR: Shelduck, Eider (non-breeding birds on Swale), Redshank, Lapwing, Oystercatcher.
SPRING AND AUTUMN: Passage waders, occasional Temminck's Stint, Little Egret, Garganey, Whinchat, Yellow Wagtail.
SUMMER: Garganey, Avocet, Black-tailed Godwit, Common and Little Terns.
WINTER: Estuarine waders and wildfowl, plus seaduck, divers and grebes on the Swale.

ACCESS
OS MAP: 178 REF: TR 013 648
Three kilometres (2 miles) north of Faversham, follow signs to Oare and Harty Ferry.

FACILITIES
Hides and an information centre open at weekends and on Bank Holidays.

24 SHELLNESS AND SWALE

NNR
Shellness is a spit composed of shells and sand washed up from Whitstable's cockle beds. The main attractions of the point are the Snow Buntings and often Shorelarks that winter, and a wader roost. In autumn during northerly gales, it is also a good vantage point for the mouth of the Swale, where seawatching can be excellent. During winter there is often a range of seaduck, divers and grebes to view.

The main part of the reserve comprises a large flood surrounded by hides and a path, which attracts similar species to the flood at Elmley (*see* page 38). The Swale side of the reserve is bordered by salt marsh favoured in some years by wintering Twite.

KEY BIRDS
ALL YEAR: Shelduck, Teal, Gadwall, Shoveler, Eider (non-breeding birds), Marsh Harrier, Snipe, Redshank, Corn Bunting.
SPRING AND AUTUMN: Garganey, passage waders as for Elmley (*see* page 38). In autumn, in north or ideally north-westerly winds, Great and Arctic Skuas, chance of Long-tailed and Pomarine Skuas, Manx Shearwater, European and Leach's Storm Petrels, Little Gull. Chance of Sabine's Gull and, from late October, Little Auk.
SUMMER: Garganey, Avocet, Black-tailed Godwit, returning passage waders.
WINTER: As for Elmley plus, annually, Snow Bunting on Shellness, in some years Shorelark, Twite on salt marsh. Wader roost including Knot and Oystercatcher on Shellness. Seaduck, divers and grebes in the mouth of the Swale.

ACCESS
OS MAP: 178 REF: TR 052 682
Located at the eastern end of Sheppey, drive through Leysdown-on-Sea, past the caravan park and Muswell Manor, along a track to the car park. A path leads out to Shellness, another path leads to the flood along a raised embankment.

FACILITIES
Hides overlooking the flood.

STODMARSH
NNR (170 ha/420 acres)

Bordering the River Great Stour north-east of Canterbury, Stodmarsh is an outstanding site for wetland birds. Formerly known as Stud-marsh because Augustinian monks once bred horses here, the marshes today encompass wet meadows, damp woodland and vast reed beds. There are lagoons and wader scrapes, too.

The reserve is well served with a network of paths that allows access to all the main habitats. There is much to see throughout the year. Overhead in summer, Hobbies gather

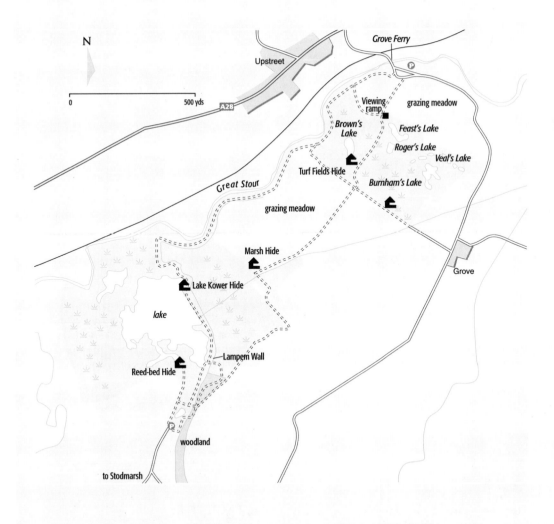

to feast on the abundant insect life; it is not unusual to witness 20 or more in the air at once. The reed beds often resound to the pinging calls of Bearded Tits, and singing Reed and Sedge Warblers. Cetti's Warblers emit their explosive song from suitable scrubby habitat. Stodmarsh was the English stronghold for this species when it first started colonizing the area in the early 1970s, since when they have spread across southern England.

The main route through the reserve is a raised path, called the Lampen Wall, which runs through the reed bed at the Stodmarsh end and follows the River Stour as it nears Grove Ferry. During winter the Lampen Wall provides a good vantage point for watching birds such as Hen Harrier coming into roost, and if you are lucky you may spot a flying Bittern. The wet meadows towards Grove Ferry occasionally attract the odd family party of Whooper or Bewick's Swans, and are annually the haunt of Water Pipits best found from mid-December through to mid-April.

KEY BIRDS
ALL YEAR: Little Egret, Gadwall, Teal, Shoveler, Pochard, Tufted Duck, Water Rail, Marsh Harrier, Snipe, Redshank, Kingfisher, Lesser Spotted Woodpecker, Bearded Tit, Cetti's Warbler.
SPRING AND AUTUMN: Garganey, Hobby, often Osprey, Black Tern, Black-tailed Godwit, Spotted Redshank, Greenshank, Whimbrel, possible Grasshopper Warbler. Spotted Crakes are becoming annual in autumn at Grove Ferry.
SUMMER: Common Tern, Hobby, Reed and Sedge Warblers, Garganey.
WINTER: Wintering wildfowl, including Wigeon, often Bewick's Swan and occasional Whooper Swan; White-fronted Goose is regular. Hen Harrier roosts, plus Short-eared Owl, Bittern, Water Pipit, Green Sandpiper and roosting Corn Bunting.

ACCESS
OS MAP: 179 REF: TR 222 618
Access points at Stodmarsh village or Grove Ferry, see map opposite.

FACILITIES
Hides suitable for wheelchair access.

Hobby
Falco subbuteo

This dashing falcon, with pointed slim wings, a slim body and long tail resembles a giant Swift in flight. A summer visitor from its African winter quarters, the Hobby arrives in Britain during April.

Hobbies often congregate at good feeding sites such as Stodmarsh, where on occasion you can see a number in the air at once. Summer evenings are best, as they hawk over the reed beds and pools for one of their favourite foods – dragonflies – eating their prey in midair.

The Hobby is a secretive breeder, nesting high up in trees in wooded areas, and it can be remarkably elusive around its nest site.

26   ELMLEY

RSPB RESERVE
1,400 ha (3,459 acres)
Bordering the Swale Estuary on the Isle of
Sheppey, Elmley provides interest throughout the
year and is one of the best sites in Britain for
birds of prey. Visit in winter for often spectacular
numbers of wildfowl and waders, while in spring
and autumn, passage waders often reveal a rarity.

KEY BIRDS
ALL YEAR: Shelduck, Little Egret, Wigeon,
Gadwall, Teal, Shoveler, Marsh Harrier, Ringed
Plover, Snipe, Redshank, Barn Owl, Corn Bunting.
SPRING: Garganey, passage waders include
Temminck's Stint (near annual), Black-tailed
Godwit and Whimbrel. Chance of Montagu's
Harrier.
SUMMER: Garganey, Black-tailed Godwit, Avocet,
Common and Little Terns, Yellow Wagtail.
AUTUMN: Returning waders include Spotted
Redshank, Greenshank, Little Stint, Curlew
Sandpiper.
WINTER: Estuarine waders roost. Brent and
White-fronted Geese, seaduck are regular on the
Swale. Raptors include Peregrine, Merlin, Hen
Harrier and Short-eared Owl. In irruption years
chance of a Rough-legged Buzzard; sometimes
Snow Bunting and Lapland Bunting (scarce).

ACCESS
OS MAP: 178 REF: **TQ 938 680**
After crossing the Kingsferry Bridge on to the
Isle, the reserve entrance is along a straight bit of
road on the right. The main flood and hides are
a 2.5 km (1½ mile) walk from the car park.

FACILITIES
Wheelchair access to one hide. For those unable
to walk far, and the disabled, permission can be
sought to drive to the hides.

27   NOR MARSH AND MOTNEY HILL

RSPB RESERVE
These two adjacent sites comprise salt marsh and
mud flats, attracting the typical estuarine
wildfowl and waders. Nor Marsh is an
inaccessible island, best viewed from the
Riverside Country Park, which in itself can be
good for passerine migrants. Motney Hill can be
viewed from the sea wall. A telescope is useful.

KEY BIRDS
ALL YEAR: Shelduck, Oystercatcher, Redshank.
SPRING AND AUTUMN: Passage waders include
Whimbrel and Black-tailed Godwit. A few
passerine migrants in country park.
SUMMER: Common Tern breeds.
WINTER: Brent Goose, Wigeon, Pintail, Teal,
chance of seaduck and rarer grebes, Grey Plover,
Dunlin, Black-tailed Godwit and Avocet.

ACCESS
OS MAP: 178 REF: **TQ 810 700**
Nor Marsh is best viewed from Horrid Hill,
reached from the Riverside Country Park off the
B2004 east of Gillingham. Motney Hill is
reached from the car park along Motney Hill
Road just east of the country park on the same
road. View from the sea wall.

28   NORTHWARD HILL

RSPB RESERVE
202 ha (500 acres)
Home to the largest heronry in Britain,
Northward Hill overlooks a vast area of grazing
land bordering the Thames. Little Egrets have
recently started to breed, and there is now an
impressive evening roost in autumn.
    Paths cut through the woodland. The heronry
is out of bounds in the breeding season.

KEY BIRDS
ALL YEAR: Lapwing, Redshank, Grey Heron,
Little Egret, Marsh Harrier, Long-eared, Tawny,
Little and Barn Owls, Great Spotted, Lesser
Spotted and Green Woodpeckers.
SPRING: A few passage waders on the marsh,
including Whimbrel and Ruff.
SUMMER: Avocet, Black-tailed Godwit,
Grasshopper Warbler, Nightingale.
AUTUMN: Passage waders on marsh.
WINTER: White-fronted Goose, Wigeon, Teal,
Hen Harrier, Merlin and Peregrine.

ACCESS
OS MAP: 178 REF: **TQ 780 765**
From the A228 Rochester to Grain road, take a
minor road to High Halstow. The reserve is
signposted and on the north side of the village.

29 CLIFFE POOLS

RSPB RESERVE
700 ha (1,730 acres)
An outstanding site in spring and autumn for passage waders. Breeding birds include Avocet and Garganey. In winter the lagoons support large numbers of wildfowl and waders, with a number of estuarine species roosting.

KEY BIRDS
ALL YEAR: Little Egret, Shelduck, Gadwall, Teal, Shoveler, Pochard, Tufted Duck, Water Rail, Avocet, Oystercatcher, Ringed Plover, Dunlin, Snipe, Little and Barn Owls, Corn Bunting.
SPRING: Garganey, passage waders as for autumn, Whinchat, Wheatear.
SUMMER: Garganey, Common Tern, Yellow Wagtail, passage waders from early July.
AUTUMN: Passage waders include Curlew, Green and Wood Sandpipers, Temminck's and Little Stints, Spotted Redshank, Greenshank, Black-tailed Godwit, chance of a rarity; Little Gull.
WINTER: Red-throated Diver; occasional rarer grebes including Black-necked and Slavonian. Wigeon, Pintail, Goldeneye, estuarine waders plus Golden Plover. Merlin, Hen Harrier, Peregrine, Short-eared Owl, occasionally Long-eared Owl.

ACCESS
OS MAP: **178** REF: **TQ 730 767**
Take the B2000 to Cliffe village, when you get to a sharp right-hand bend, go straight on down the track, past the farm to the pools.

30 LEE VALLEY COUNTRY PARK

RIVER LEE COUNTRY PARK
4,050 ha (10,000 acres)
The Lea Valley has a varied birdlife. Reservoirs such as Walthamstow and King George V attract large numbers of wintering wildfowl. The Fishers Green area within the Lee Valley Country Park is one of the most popular sites. A small reed bed adjacent to the Fishers Green car park has become the best site in Britain to view Bitterns.

KEY BIRDS
ALL YEAR: Great Crested and Little Grebes, Grey Heron, Gadwall, Shoveler, Tufted Duck, Pochard, Ruddy Duck, Sparrowhawk, Snipe, Lesser Spotted Woodpecker, Redshank, Kingfisher, Reed Bunting.
SPRING AND AUTUMN: A few passage waders plus terns, including Black.
SUMMER: Shelduck, Little-ringed Plover.
WINTER: All common dabbling and diving ducks, Goosander, Smew, Bittern, Long-eared Owl, Water Pipit and Jack Snipe.

ACCESS
OS MAP: **166** REF: **TL 378 027**
Permits are required to visit both Walthamstow and King George V Reservoirs. For Fishers Green and the Bittern hide, take the B194 from Waltham Abbey north, turn off left on a sharp bend, to Fishers Green car park (after Fishers Green Lane). Walk over the bridge opposite and the Bittern hide is on the right. Normally this is locked until around 8.30am.

FACILITIES
Numerous hides and paths in River Lee Country Park. Fishers Green is a good starting point.

31 RYE MEADS

RSPB / THE WILDLIFE TRUSTS
25 ha (62 acres)
These two reserves have a mosaic of habitats that includes scrapes, scrub, reeds and a lake. Both reserves have a good range of breeding birds, including raft-nesting Common Terns. In winter, Bittern and Jack Snipe are rarer possibilities.

KEY BIRDS
ALL YEAR: Great Crested and Little Grebes, Gadwall, woodpeckers, Kingfisher.
SPRING AND SUMMER: Common Tern, various species of warbler and breeding wildfowl.
WINTER: Bittern, Water Rail, Teal, Shoveler, Snipe, Jack Snipe, Redpoll, Siskin, chance of Water Pipit on the meadows.

ACCESS
OS MAP: **166** REF: **TL 387 099**
In Hoddesdon follow Rye Road to Rye House Railway Station. Pass the station and proceed over bridge. Car park is adjacent to Rye House Gatehouse. The Wildlife Trusts reserve is open from 9am to 5pm, and the RSPB reserve from 10am to 5pm. Closed Christmas and Boxing Days.

FACILITIES
Hides with wheelchair access.

EAST ANGLIA

Home to legendary bird reserves such as Cley and Minsmere, East Anglia, encompassing the counties of Essex, Suffolk, Norfolk and Cambridgeshire, is visited by more birdwatchers than any other region in the British Isles. Rare breeding species such as the dazzling Golden Oriole, Breckland's Stone Curlews, and Bitterns booming from reed beds stretching from southern Suffolk to North Norfolk are part of the popularity. Other big attractions are the migrant hotspots dotted along the North Norfolk coast. Sites such as Blakeney Point can be excellent in spring and autumn. Indeed, with a string of outstanding reserves and many resident birdwatchers in the villages and towns, the North Norfolk coast has become the birding capital of Britain.

Winter attractions include spectacular numbers of waders in the Wash, while, further south, thousands of birds use the many coastal reserves. Inland, the Ouse Washes, flooded in winter, are famed for their huge concentrations of wildfowl, most notably Bewick's and Whooper Swans.

Summer is a season of plenty, too. Busy-looking tern colonies, wader scrapes patrolled by Avocets, reed beds quartered by Marsh Harriers, heaths resonating to the Nightjars' song – the list of attractions is as long as it is varied.

With the land rarely rising above 91 m (300 ft), East Anglia is very flat, yet the landscape has a distinctive beauty. The Norfolk Broads is popular for boating holidays, and the wild feel and open spaces of the Suffolk and Norfolk coasts draw many visitors to the region. Combine this with the outstanding birding on offer, and little wonder why birders flock here in their thousands.

KEY

1) Hanningfield Reservoir	14) Dingle Marshes	26) Titchwell
2) Abberton Reservoir	15) Breydon Water and Berney Marshes	27) Holme Bird Observatory
3) Colne Point	16) Walberswick	28) Snettisham
4) Fingringhoe Wick	17) Carlton Marshes	29) Welney
5) Old Hall Marshes	18) Strumpshaw Fen	30) Ouse Washes
6) Stour Estuary	19) Surlingham Church Marsh	31) Nene Washes
7) Landguard Point	20) Buckenham Marshes	32) Mayday Farm Forest Trail
8) Trimley Marshes	21) Hickling Broad	33) Lackford Lake
9) Bradfield Woods	22) Cley	34) The Brecks at Weeting Heath
10) Wolves Wood	23) Blakeney Point	35) Fowlmere
11) Havergate Island	24) Holkham	36) Wicken Fen
12) North Warren	25) Scolt Head Island	
13) Minsmere		

The Wash

○ Hunstanton

㉗ ㉖ ㉕ ㉔

Wells-○
next-the-Sea

㉓ ㉒

Sheringham ○

○ Cromer

A148

㉘

A148

○ North Walsham

○ Aylsham

A149

King's Lynn

East
Dereham

A140

A1067

A149

㉑

○ Caister-on-Sea

□ Wisbech

A47

A10

Swaffham

A47

Norwich

The
Broads

A47

□ Great Yarmouth

□ March

Downham
Market

NORFOLK

㉖ ㉘ ㉙

㉗ ㉙ ㉕

㉕

A146

⑮

A141

Attleborough ○

A11

A140

㉗ Lowestoft

㉙

Chatteris ○

㉚

Brandon ○

㉞

A143

Bungay ○

⑰

Thetford

A11

A143

SUFFOLK

A12

Southwold ○

⑯

-SHIRE

□ Ely

A1165

㉜

Mildenhall

㉝

A11

⑬ ⑭

A14

Newmarket

A14

A14

Bury
St Edmunds

A134

Saxmundham ○

⑫

○ Aldeburgh

Cambridge

M11

A11

Haverhill

⑨

Stowmarket

A14

Orford
Orford Ness

㊱

A10

A505

㉟

Sudbury

A134

Hadleigh

⑩

Woodbridge ○

Ipswich

⑪

㉟

ESSEX

Braintree

A120

⑧

Felixstowe

⑥ ⑦

Harwich

A12

The Naze

Witham

A12

②

Colchester

④

M11

Harlow

M11

Chelmsford

⑤

Maldon

③

□ Clacton-on-Sea

①

A130

Chigwell ○

Brentwood

Foulness
Island

M25

Southend-on-Sea

R Thames

Gravesend

N

0		10		20 miles
0	10	20	30	40 km

41

1   HANNINGFIELD RESERVOIR

ESSEX WILDLIFE TRUST
392 ha (970 acres) including 40 ha (100 acres) of woodland

This reservoir south of Chelmsford has the bonus of a mixed woodland in its south-eastern corner. These ancient coppiced areas are rich in fauna and flora, including an array of woodland birds.

The reservoir attracts large wintering flocks of wildfowl and, in summer, large numbers of Swifts and hirundines.

KEY BIRDS
ALL YEAR: Gadwall, Tufted Duck, Pochard, Coot, Grey Heron, Cormorant, Kingfisher and resident woodland birds.
SPRING AND AUTUMN: A few passage waders such as Common and Green Sandpipers, Osprey, terns.
SUMMER: Common Tern, Hobby, sometimes large numbers of Swifts, martins, woodland warblers.
WINTER: Wintering dabbling and diving ducks, a chance of the rarer grebes and sawbills.

ACCESS
OS MAP: 167 REF: **TQ 725 972**
Turn off the A130 at Rettenden on to South Hanningfield Road. After 3 km (2 miles) turn right at the T-junction with Hawkswood Road. The visitor centre is 1.6 km (1 mile) further on.

FACILITIES
View from the causeway and from hides, the visitor centre is just past the causeway. There is wheelchair access to a hide. The visitor centre opens from 9am daily except Mondays, but is open on Bank Holidays.

2   ABBERTON RESERVOIR

ESSEX WILDLIFE TRUST
500 ha (1,235 acres)

Situated 6 km (4 miles) from the coast, Abberton ranks as one of the country's top inland sites. Its location means many coastal birds visit. Thousands of wildfowl congregate in autumn and remain through the winter months in nationally important numbers.

A good range of waders and terns can be expected during passage periods. The numbers of waders are dependent on water levels. Summer months are enlivened by a large colony of tree-nesting Cormorants.

Two causeways crossing the south-western end provide good vantage points. The Essex Wildlife Trust has a small reserve with a lagoon just south of the village of Layer-de-la-Haye with nature trails allowing limited access.

KEY BIRDS
ALL YEAR: Great Crested Grebe, Grey Heron, Cormorant, Tufted Duck, Gadwall, Shoveler, Shelduck, Ruddy Duck, Ringed Plover.
SPRING AND AUTUMN: Passage migrants include Garganey, Osprey, Little Gull and terns including Black, various waders include Whimbrel, Curlew, Spotted Redshank, Common Sandpiper; also Yellow Wagtail and a few passerine migrants. In autumn Red-crested Pochard is regular.
SUMMER: Cormorant colony, Common Tern, wildfowl and passage waders from mid-July.
WINTER: Divers and rarer grebes occur annually, with Black-necked Grebe most likely. Bewick's Swan and White-fronted Goose visit; Wigeon, Teal, Pintail, Pochard, Goldeneye, Smew, Goosander; occasional raptors such as Merlin.

ACCESS
OS MAP: 168 REF: **TL 963 185**
From Colchester take the B1026 south. Drive through Layer-de-la-Haye, and the visitor centre is about 1.6 km (1 mile) further on. Continue another 0.8 km (½ mile) to one of two causeways. The second causeway, near Layer Breton, is reached by turning right after 1.6 km (1 mile).

FACILITIES
A visitor centre and hides with wheelchair access. The centre is open from 9am until 5pm daily except Mondays.

3   COLNE POINT

ESSEX WILDLIFE TRUST
276 ha (683 acres)

Colne Point is the best-developed shingle spit on the Essex coast. Sand and shingle ridges harbour nesting birds as well as nationally rare plants. The salt marsh, inter-tidal pools and mud flats are the feeding ground for passage and wintering wildfowl and waders.

Colne Point is a good migration watch point too, when the weather conditions are favourable, passerine migration can then be impressive.

Before a visit check the tides as the car park can become flooded and parts of the reserve may not be accessible. It is often muddy and it may be necessary to wade at any time of year.

KEY BIRDS

ALL YEAR: Oystercatcher, Ringed Plover, Redshank.
SPRING AND AUTUMN: Whinchat, Wheatear, plus in the right conditions large movements of pipits, wagtails, Skylark, finches and hirundines. Migrant raptors are recorded regularly. Estuarine waders and wildfowl on mud flats.
SUMMER: Little Tern, Skylark, Reed Bunting.
WINTER: Offshore, often divers, grebes and seaduck. Typical estuarine waders and wildfowl including Brent Goose. Chance of Snow Bunting and Shorelark.

ACCESS
OS MAP: 168 REF: TM 108 125
From Clacton take the B1027 to St Osyth, then Lee Wick Farm Lane, to a car parking space on the seaward side of the sea wall – note this can flood. During the breeding season, walk below the high-tide mark as birds are nesting on the spit.

4   FINGRINGHOE WICK

ESSEX WILDLIFE TRUST
50 ha (124 acres)
Comprised of disused gravel pits and scrub bordering the River Colne, this reserve attracts wildfowl, waders and passage migrants. Waders and wildfowl are at their best in autumn and winter. A rising tide ensures good views from the river banks.

Various species of warbler breed in the scrub, including a healthy population of Nightingales.

KEY BIRDS

ALL YEAR: Little Grebe, Kingfisher, various woodland species.
SPRING AND AUTUMN: Little Egret, passage waders, Whinchat and Wheatear.
SUMMER: Nightingale, Sedge Warbler, Lesser Whitethroat, Whitethroat, Blackcap.
WINTER: Brent Goose, Shelduck, Teal, Wigeon, Gadwall, Pochard, Tufted Duck, Red-breasted Merganser, Goldeneye, Avocet, estuarine waders, chance of raptors, Twite.

ACCESS
OS MAP: 168 REF: TM 046 197
Take the B1025 from Colchester to Abberton, then a minor road towards Fingringhoe. Take a right turn to South Green – the reserve is signposted from here.

FACILITIES
Open daily except Mondays, Christmas and Boxing Days. The reserve centre opens 9am to 5pm. There are hides and nature trails with limited disabled access.

5   OLD HALL MARSHES

RSPB RESERVE
500 ha (1,236 acres)
Old Hall Marshes comprise an extensive area of coastal grazing marsh, salt marsh, small reed beds, tidal creeks and two small islands in the estuary.

Although cold and bleak in winter, this is the best season for a visit. A public footpath running along the sea wall gives a good vantage point to enjoy the thousands of wildfowl and waders.

During passage periods, a good range of waders uses the reserve, and a number of rarities have been found in recent years. The grazing marshes support breeding populations of waders and wildfowl in summer.

KEY BIRDS

ALL YEAR: Lapwing, Redshank, Snipe, Marsh Harrier, Barn Owl, Corn Bunting.
SPRING AND AUTUMN: Passage waders may include stints, sandpipers, godwits, Whimbrel. Passerine migrants include Wheatear and Whinchat; chance of a rarity.
SUMMER: Shelduck, Shoveler, Pochard, Common Tern, Bearded Tit, Yellow Wagtail, Avocet.
WINTER: Grebes including Slavonian. Red-throated Diver, Bewick's Swan, White-fronted Goose, Brent Goose, Wigeon, Teal, Goldeneye, Eider, Red-breasted Merganser, occasional Long-tailed Duck, Hen Harrier, Merlin, Peregrine, Short-eared Owl, estuarine waders, Twite.

ACCESS
OS MAP: 168 REF: TL 975 125
Located south-east of Tiptree, accessible from a minor road to Salcott from Tollesbury. After 0.8 km (½ mile) a track on the right leads to the footpath following the sea wall.

6 STOUR ESTUARY

RSPB RESERVE

101 ha (250 acres)

Straddling the Essex / Suffolk border, this reserve includes Stour Wood, best visited in spring, and the estuary, which is best in winter for wildfowl and waders.

The woodland is predominantly oak and sweet chestnut coppice, supporting all three species of woodpecker and summer visitors, including Nightingale. The estuary is shallow so diving ducks are discouraged, but it proves highly attractive to species such as Wigeon and a good range of waders. Noteworthy is the large number of Black-tailed Godwits that use the estuary.

KEY BIRDS

ALL YEAR: Green, Great Spotted and Lesser Spotted Woodpeckers.
SPRING AND AUTUMN: Passage and arriving and departing estuarine waders in the estuary.
SUMMER: The wood has a good range of breeding summer visitors, including Nightingale.
WINTER: Most interest on the estuary, with Brent Goose, Shelduck, Wigeon, Teal, Pintail, Goldeneye, Black-tailed Godwit and typical estuarine waders.

ACCESS

OS MAP: 169 REF: TM 191 310
The reserve lies 8 km (5 miles) west of Harwich. Take the B1352 from Ramsey to Wrabness, and the reserve is 0.8 km (½ mile) east of Wrabness.

FACILITIES

There are trails and hides. It can be wet underfoot.

7 LANDGUARD POINT

SUFFOLK WILDLIFE TRUST

16 ha (40 acres)

Primarily a site for migrants, Landguard is an area of short-cropped turf, shingle banks and tamarisk scrub bordering Felixstowe Docks.

A bird observatory has existed on the site since 1983. Migrants can be plentiful, and Landguard has a long list of rarities to its name. A few interesting species breed, but, spring and autumn are the key times for a visit.

KEY BIRDS

SPRING AND AUTUMN: Passerine migrants include commoner chats, warblers, finches and thrushes. More regularly occuring scarce species include Wryneck, Bluethroat, Barred and Icterine Warblers, Firecrest and Ortolan Bunting, and annually an outstanding rarity may be found.
AUTUMN: Although not known for seawatching, autumn often produces a few skuas and occasional shearwaters.
SUMMER: Little Tern, Ringed Plover, Wheatear, Black Redstart.

ACCESS

OS MAP: 169 REF: TM 283 317
Take the A14 almost to the docks south of Felixstowe town. When almost at the docks, turn down Manor Terrace to the car park at the end.

8 TRIMLEY MARSHES

SUFFOLK WILDLIFE TRUST

84 ha (208 acres)

Living proof of what can be created for birds, Trimley was once farmland, before its transformation into the wetland it is today. Situated on the banks of the River Orwell, it attracts a good range of waders throughout the year, most notably in autumn.

KEY BIRDS

ALL YEAR: Gadwall, Shoveler, Redshank.
SPRING AND AUTUMN: Garganey; good variety and number of passage waders that include Ruff, Little and Temminck's Stints, Curlew Sandpiper, Common, Green and Wood Sandpipers, Greenshank, Whimbrel, Spotted Redshank (autumn).
SUMMER: Garganey, Avocet, Marsh Harrier, Common and Little Terns.
WINTER: Estuarine waders and wildfowl, plus Peregrine and Merlin.

ACCESS

OS MAP: 169 REF: TM 260 352
From the A14 north of Felixstowe, turn off to Trimley St Mary. The car park is at the top of Cordy's Lane.

FACILITIES

A visitor centre is open at weekends; hides.

9 BRADFIELD WOODS

NNR / SUFFOLK WILDLIFE TRUST
65 ha (161 acres)
As an ancient coppiced woodland, Bradfield Woods has been described as one of the most outstanding ancient woods left in Britain. Best visited in spring and summer, the reserve offers a wide range of breeding woodland species, including star songsters such as Nightingale.

The ancient status of the wood (coppiced since at least the thirteenth century) means that it is particularly rich in woodland flora.

KEY BIRDS
ALL YEAR: Sparrowhawk, Woodcock, Tawny Owl, Great Spotted Woodpecker, Treecreeper, Nuthatch, tits.
SPRING AND SUMMER: Nightingale, Blackcap, Chiffchaff and Willow Warbler, plus numerous other woodland species.
WINTER: Redpoll, Brambling, thrushes.

ACCESS
OS MAP: 155 REF: TL 935 581
The reserve is to the south-east of Bury St Edmunds off the A14. Take minor roads to the village of Bradfield St George and the wood is on the road between here and Felsham.

FACILITIES
A visitor centre, a hide and three trails of 0.8 km (½ mile), 1.6 km (1 mile) and 3 km (2 miles).

10 WOLVES WOOD

RSPB RESERVE
37 ha (91 acres)
Wolves Wood is an ancient woodland consisting of oak, ash, hornbeam, hazel and birch. Coppiced in the traditional way, the wood is rich in woodland birds, as well as plants and mammals, plus 20 or so recorded species of butterfly.

An early morning visit from May to early June is likely to be most productive.

KEY BIRDS
ALL YEAR: Woodcock, Tawny Owl, Great Spotted and Lesser Spotted Woodpeckers, Goldcrest, Marsh and Willow Tits, Nuthatch, Treecreeper, Hawfinch (scarce).

SPRING AND AUTUMN: Nightingale, Lesser Whitethroat, Whitethroat, Blackcap, Garden Warbler.
WINTER: Fieldfare and Redwing.

ACCESS
OS MAP: 155 REF: TM 054 436
Located 3 km (2 miles) east of Hadleigh on the A1071.

11 HAVERGATE ISLAND

RSPB RESERVE
108 ha (267 acres)
Havergate is a low embanked island in the River Ore. Within the embankment are shallow brackish lagoons dotted with islands: the perfect breeding sites for Avocets and terns.

Outside the breeding season, autumn is a good time for a visit because passage and wintering wildfowl, and waders use the lagoon.

KEY BIRDS
ALL YEAR: Avocet, Ringed Plover, Oystercatcher, Redshank.
SPRING AND AUTUMN: Passage waders, and arriving and departing winter and summer visitors.
SUMMER: Common and Sandwich Terns, Little Tern visits, Shelduck, Black-headed Gull.
WINTER: Occasionally Bewick's Swan and White-fronted Goose, Wigeon, Teal, Shoveler, Pintail, occasionally Hen Harrier, estuarine waders.

ACCESS
OS MAP: 169 REF: TM 425 496
Park in Orford. Access is by boat, which needs to be pre-booked with the warden. Trips run between April and August on the first and third Sundays of the month and each Thursday; and from September to March on the first Saturday every month. Apply by post to Reserve Manager, 30 Mundays Lane, Orford, Woodbridge, Suffolk IP12 2LX.

12 NORTH WARREN

RSPB RESERVE

204 ha (506 acres)

Close to Minsmere, this reserve shares similar habitats, including lowland heath, reed beds, woodland and grazing marsh. As a result, a similar range of species can be found.

Apart from the interesting breeding species, a good range of passage waders uses the reserve, and seawatching can be productive. Nature trails allow exploration.

KEY BIRDS

ALL YEAR: Teal, Snipe, Woodlark, Dartford Warbler, Stonechat, Barn Owl.
SPRING AND AUTUMN: Garganey, Yellow Wagtail. Passage waders include Spotted Redshank, Ruff, Greenshank and Wood Sandpiper. Offshore, chance of skuas, terns, occasional shearwaters.
SUMMER: Bittern, Marsh Harrier, Hobby, Nightjar, Nightingale.
WINTER: Bewick's Swan, White-fronted Goose, sometimes Tundra Bean Goose, Wigeon, Shoveler, Teal, Gadwall, Pintail. Offshore, scoters, Red-throated Diver, grebes.

ACCESS

OS MAP: 156 REF: TM 472 595

Directly north of Aldeburgh, take the coast road towards Thorpeness – the reserve is easily found along here.

13 MINSMERE

RSPB RESERVE

816 ha (1,972 acres)

Unlike Walberswick, this neighbouring reserve attracts crowds of people. As one of the RSPB's flagship reserves, the facilities match the excellent birdwatching that is available throughout the year.

Extensive reed beds, woodland, heath and the 'scrape' – a flood with plentiful mud – help attract a wide range of birds. Like Walberswick, it is possible to notch up 100 species in a day here in May. Marsh Harriers display over the reed bed and Bitterns boom from within, in spring. During autumn the scrape can be buzzing with passage waders. Passerine migrants favour the scrub along the beach, while offshore from autumn to spring

there is a good chance of locating divers, grebes and seaduck.

Minsmere is justly famous for its Avocets, symbol of the RSPB. They breed on the scrape along with other waders, wildfowl, terns and gulls. The reserve probably has a longer list of breeding birds than any other in Britain.

KEY BIRDS

ALL YEAR: Bittern, various wildfowl, Marsh Harrier, Water Rail, various waders, Barn Owl, Kingfisher, Lesser Spotted Woodpecker, Cetti's Warbler, Bearded Tit, Stonechat, Willow Tit, Dartford Warbler.
SPRING: Passage waders along the river and on pools include Whimbrel, Common Sandpiper, Wood Sandpiper, Green Sandpiper, Spotted Redshank, Greenshank and godwits. Avocet, Little Gull, Black Tern, Wheatear, Whinchat, Redstart, Black Redstart. Chance of rarities such as Spoonbill.
SUMMER: Avocet, Little Tern, Nightjar, Woodlark, Nightingale, Grasshopper Warbler, Reed Warbler and Sedge Warbler. Tree Pipit, Yellow Wagtail, Redstart. Occasional Savi's Warbler.
AUTUMN: As for spring, plus the chance of a drift migrant. Arctic Skua offshore.
WINTER: Offshore, a few Eider, scoters, divers and grebes. Pintail, Wigeon, Bewick's Swan. Hen Harrier and Short-eared Owl roost in the reed bed, Merlin, Peregrine, estuarine waders plus a few Ruff, Spotted Redshank. A chance of Water Pipit on the meadows, Shorelark, Snow Bunting and Twite along the beach. Scarcer gulls might include Mediterranean, and Caspian Gull has been recorded.

ACCESS
OS MAP: 156 REF: TM 452 680

From the A12 take a minor road to Westleton. There are signs from the centre of the village to the reserve. Alternatively, the beach and a public hide can be reached from the National Trust car park at Dunwich Cliff. The reserve is open daily from 9am except Tuesdays, Christmas Day and Boxing Day.

FACILITIES

Facilities are excellent, with a large visitor centre, a café and most hides allowing wheelchair access.

14 DINGLE MARSHES

RSPB RESERVE / SUFFOLK WILDLIFE TRUST
263 ha (650 acres)

An extension of the Walberswick reserve, Dingle Marshes stretches to Dunwich.

A path from the beach car park at Dunwich runs along the coastal side of the reserve. Continue and you will end up at Walberswick, a 4 km (2½ mile) walk. There is a circular trail and a hide overlooking the reed bed from a vantage point on the edge of Dunwich Forest.

KEY BIRDS

ALL YEAR: Bittern, various wildfowl, Marsh Harrier, Water Rail, various waders, Barn Owl, Kingfisher, Lesser Spotted Woodpecker, Cetti's Warbler, Bearded Tit, Willow Tit.
SPRING: Passage waders along the river and on pools include Whimbrel, Common, Wood and Green Sandpipers, Spotted Redshank, Greenshank and godwits. Avocet, Little Gull, Black Tern, Wheatear, Whinchat, Redstart, Black Redstart. Chance of rarities such as Spoonbill.
SUMMER: Avocet, Little Tern, Nightingale, Grasshopper Warbler, Reed and Sedge Warblers, Tree Pipit, Yellow Wagtail, Redstart. Occasional Savi's Warbler.
AUTUMN: As for spring, plus the chance of a drift migrant. Arctic Skua offshore.
WINTER: Offshore, a few Eider, scoters, divers and grebes. Pintail, Wigeon, Bewick's Swan. Hen Harrier and Short-eared Owl roost in the reed bed, Merlin, Peregrine, estuarine waders plus a few Ruff, Spotted Redshank. A chance of Water Pipit on the meadows. Shorelark, Snow Bunting and Twite along the beach.

ACCESS
OS MAP: 156 REF: TM 480 720
From the A12 take a minor road to Westleton, and from here a minor road to Dunwich. Park in the beach car park. Walk north. Alternatively, a hide overlooking the reed bed can be reached from the Forest Enterprise car park off Blythburgh Road.

15 BREYDON WATER AND BERNEY MARSHES

RSPB RESERVE
150 ha (370 acres)

Breydon Water is an estuary fed by the Rivers Yare, Bure and Waveney, and meets the sea south of Great Yarmouth. The area is productive for breeding and wintering wildfowl and waders.

The reserve regularly attracts rarities. During passage periods a good range of passage waders can be expected, along with gulls and terns. Both the north and south shores of the estuary are served by footpaths, with hides at the eastern end. The north-eastern corner of the estuary tends to be particularly productive for waders, and is best visited on a rising tide.

KEY BIRDS

ALL YEAR: Shelduck, Shoveler, Oystercatcher, Snipe, Redshank, Bearded Tit.
SPRING AND AUTUMN: Passage species include Brent Goose, Spoonbill (occasional), Little Egret, Garganey, Marsh Harrier, Osprey, Hobby, Avocet, Little Stint, Curlew Sandpiper, Spotted Redshank, Greenshank, Whimbrel, Green, Common and Wood Sandpipers, Ruff, and terns including Black.
SUMMER: Common Tern, returning passage and winter waders.
AUTUMN: As for spring, plus the chance of a drift migrant. Arctic Skua offshore.
WINTER: Occasional divers, grebes, Bewick's Swan, White-fronted Goose, Brent Goose, various dabbling and diving ducks, typical estuarine waders, raptors including Peregrine, Merlin, Hen Harrier and Short-eared Owl.

ACCESS
OS MAP: 134 REF: TG 465 055
The eastern end of the estuary is crossed by the A47. Park in the ASDA car park on the east side of the road. Footpaths run along both banks. Berney Marshes is a 12 km (8 mile) trip from here. Boat trips run from the marina at Burgh Castle (north of Belton). Details from the RSPB (*see* page 171).

WALBERSWICK
NNR (700 ha/1,729 acres)

Few reserves possess such a varied range of habitats as Walberswick, which boasts a huge reed bed, woodland, scrub, muddy scrapes, seashore, heath and river. Such variety means it is possible to see more than 100 species in a single day in May.

Walberswick's impressive reed bed extends inland for more than 3 km (2 miles). Along its ditches lurk Bitterns, while Bearded Tits and Marsh Harriers are much more easily seen. A network of paths criss-crosses the reed bed and leads you to the other habitats the reserve has to offer.

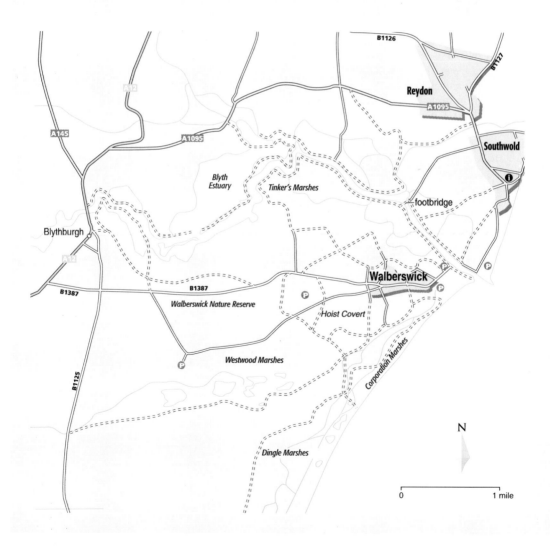

The heaths are part of the Suffolk Sandlings, once an extensive area that has been eroded to the remnants that are left today. They attract all the typical lowland heath specialities. Visit at dusk to locate Nightjars that give their presence away by a distinctive churring call. During the day in spring the heath resonates with the scratchy songs of Dartford Warblers and the liquid, fluty notes of Woodlarks.

Scrub and woodlands are home to a variety of resident woodland species, joined in summer by summer migrants that include Nightingale and Redstart. The River Blyth marks the northern boundary of the reserve, and fans out into the Blyth Estuary a little way upstream from its mouth – a favoured haunt of waders at low tide. The adjoining grazing marshes are grazed by wildfowl such as Wigeon, and occasionally graced by small parties of Bewick's Swans.

Due to the size of this reserve, a whole week could be employed to explore. However, if limited by a day or even half a day, then a walk out through Hoist Covert and through both Corporation Marshes and Westwood Marshes is as good a route as any to unearth some of Walberswick's birds. The beauty of the extensive system of paths is that circular routes of varying lengths can be planned, based on the time available.

KEY BIRDS

ALL YEAR: Bittern, various wildfowl, Marsh Harrier, Water Rail, various waders, Barn Owl, Kingfisher, Lesser Spotted Woodpecker, Cetti's Warbler, Bearded Tit, Stonechat, Willow Tit, Dartford Warbler.
SPRING: Passage waders along the river and on pools include Whimbrel, Common Sandpiper, Wood and Green Sandpipers, Spotted Redshank, Greenshank and godwits. Avocet, Little Gull, Black Tern, Wheatear, Whinchat, Redstart, Black Redstart. Chance of rarities such as Spoonbill.
SUMMER: Avocet, Little Tern, Nightjar, Woodlark, Nightingale, Grasshopper Warbler, occasional Savi's Warbler, Reed and Sedge Warblers, Tree Pipit, Yellow Wagtail, Redstart.
AUTUMN: As for spring, plus the chance of a drift migrant. Arctic Skua offshore.
WINTER: Offshore, a few Eider, scoters, divers and grebes. Pintail, Wigeon, Bewick's Swan. Hen Harrier and Short-eared Owl roost in the reed bed. Merlin, Peregrine, estuarine waders plus a few Ruff, and Spotted Redshank. A chance of Water Pipit on the meadows, Shorelark, Snow Bunting and Twite along the beach. Scarcer gulls might include Mediterranean Gull, and Caspian Gull has been recorded.

ACCESS

OS MAP: 156 REF: TM 460 733
There are numerous access points to the reserve from Walberswick and the B1387. See map.

Bittern
Botaurus stellaris

Stealth, camouflage and a secretive nature mean the Bittern is one of the most difficult of Britain's breeding birds to see. At Walberswick the Bittern is most likely to be seen in flight, with fast wing beats, neck retracted and flying low over the reeds – even then it does not make things easy. The best chance of seeing a bird in flight is to visit in early morning when Bitterns fly to and from fishing sites. In June and July when they are feeding the young, a patient wait should be rewarded.

In spring, the Bittern emits a distinctive low-pitched booming call that can be heard from a considerable distance, and can sound like a muffled foghorn.

17 CARLTON MARSHES

SUFFOLK WILDLIFE TRUST

40 ha (100 acres)

Situated at the western end of Oulton Broad, within the Waveney Valley, this reserve's grazing marsh, fen and peat pools support a typical range of Broadland birds.

During the summer the dykes abound with marsh plants, including the localized Water Soldier, and insects such as the rare Norfolk Hawker Dragonfly.

KEY BIRDS

ALL YEAR: Redshank, Marsh Harrier, Barn Owl, Bearded Tit, Cetti's Warbler.

SPRING AND SUMMER: Sedge and Reed Warblers, Yellow Wagtail, Cuckoo.

WINTER: Short-eared Owl and Hen Harrier are possible. A few waders present including Snipe, also Kingfisher.

ACCESS

OS MAP: 134 REF: TM 508 920

The reserve is on the south-western side of Oulton Broad. If travelling south along the A146 in Lowestoft, take Burnt Hill Lane on the right soon after the petrol station, and follow this road to a car park at the end.

FACILITIES

There is a visitor centre.

18 STRUMPSHAW FEN

RSPB RESERVE

243 ha (600 acres)

Strumpshaw Fen is primarily a reed bed with some open water, bordered by scrub. The reserve has year-round appeal for the species that winter on the pools, and those that breed in the reed bed, including reed-bed specialities of Bittern, Marsh Harrier and Bearded Tit. An added attraction in summer is the Swallowtail Butterfly, on the wing in June and sometimes in August.

KEY BIRDS

ALL YEAR: Little and Great Crested Grebes, Water Rail, Gadwall, Shoveler, Pochard, Tufted Duck, Snipe, Lapwing, Redshank,

Kingfisher, Green, Great Spotted and Lesser Spotted Woodpeckers, Cetti's Warbler, Bearded Tit.

SPRING AND SUMMER: Bittern, Marsh Harrier, Garganey, Grasshopper Warbler, Yellow Wagtail.

WINTER: Pintail, Teal, Goldeneye, Merlin, Hen Harrier.

ACCESS

OS MAP: 134 REF: TG 330 006

Take the A47 from Norwich to Great Yarmouth, turn off to Brundall, pass through Brundall, under the railway bridge, and then take the minor road (Low Road) to the right. The car park is 0.8 km (½ mile) further on.

FACILITIES

Information point and hides.

19 SURLINGHAM CHURCH MARSH

RSPB RESERVE

93 ha (230 acres)

Just across the River Yare from the RSPB's Strumpshaw Fen reserve, this marsh is typical of the Broads – a mix of reed and sedge fen, open water, ditches, alder and willow carr. Typical Broadland birds reside.

KEY BIRDS

ALL YEAR: Wildfowl plus Water Rail, Marsh Harrier, Bearded Tit, Cetti's Warbler, Kingfisher.

SPRING AND AUTUMN: A few passage waders, including Green Sandpiper; possible Wood Sandpiper.

SUMMER: Little-ringed Plover, Cuckoo, Grasshopper, Reed and Sedge Warblers.

WINTER: Various dabbling ducks, sometimes geese, Hen Harrier, Snipe, Jack Snipe, chance of Water Pipit.

ACCESS

OS MAP: 134 REF: TG 304 066

On the A146 from Norwich to Lowestoft, take the minor roads to Surlingham. Park at the Church and access the reserve from here.

FACILITIES

There are two hides.

20 BUCKENHAM MARSHES

RSPB RESERVE
116 ha (287 acres)

This area of grazing marsh is best known for the flock of Taiga Bean Geese that traditionally winters here. The geese tend to arrive in November, but, to be sure of seeing them, a visit from December through to January is best. They are often joined by White-fronted Geese. In recent years the geese have favoured nearby Cantley Marshes.

KEY BIRDS
WINTER: Taiga Bean Goose, White-fronted Goose, Wigeon, Teal, Pintail, Golden Plover, Snipe, Redshank, Hen Harrier, Merlin and Water Pipit.

ACCESS
OS MAP: 134 REF: TG 352 056
On the A47 from Norwich to Great Yarmouth, turn off to Brundall, pass through Brundall, proceed to Buckenham and park at Buckenham Station. Walk across the railway, following the track out to the hide.

Cantley Marshes are reached by continuing east from Buckenham and taking Burnt House Road, which leads straight ahead from a sharp left-hand bend.

21 HICKLING BROAD

NNR / NORFOLK WILDLIFE TRUST
542 ha (1,355 acres)

This is the largest of the Norfolk Broads, and is the most productive for birds. Situated just 5 km (3 miles) from the coast, its varied habitats, ranging from open water and extensive reed beds to wader scrapes, grazing marsh and scrub, attract a good range of migrant birds. In addition, the site supports the classic reed-bed specialities such as the Bittern.

The reserve has a number of paths, leading to hides and taking you through various Broadland habitats. The best sites for waders are the Rush Hills and Coot Swim scrapes, overlooked by hides, which have to be reached by boat.

On the opposite side of the Broad is the Weaver's Way, a path skirting the reed bed, which allows views of the open water. Marsh Harriers are usually easy to see from here, along with other reed-bed birds. This is also a good site for Swallowtail Butterflies in June and August.

KEY BIRDS
ALL YEAR: Bittern, various wildfowl, Marsh Harrier, Water Rail, Barn Owl, Bearded Tit, Lesser Spotted Woodpecker, Cetti's Warbler.
SPRING AND AUTUMN: Garganey, Osprey, Spoonbill (almost annual), passage waders include Temminck's Stint in May, Black Tern, Little Gull, Whinchat.
SUMMER: Garganey, Grasshopper Warbler, Reed and Sedge Warblers, Redshank, Yellow Wagtail.
WINTER: Whooper Swan, Wigeon, Teal, Pintail, Scaup, Goldeneye, Hen Harrier, Merlin, Snipe, Golden Plover.

ACCESS
OS MAP: 134 REF: TG 428 222
The reserve is reached by turning off the A149 to Hickling. Once in Hickling Green, take Stubbs Road by the Greyhound pub – the reserve is signposted. To take the boat trip that includes a visit to the scrapes, advance booking is necessary. Contact the Hickling Broad Visitors' Centre, Stubb's Road, Hickling NR12 OBN.

The Weaver's Way path is found by turning off the A149 at Potter Heigham. Park by the church and take the footpath out to the broads. A circular route can be taken.

FACILITIES
The visitor centre opens from 10am to 5pm daily between April and September. There is wheelchair access to the visitor centre and some of the hides.

CLEY

NORFOLK WILDLIFE TRUST (180 ha/445 acres)

This quaint North Norfolk village complete with windmill has long been an outstanding birding site, although in recent years the reserve has seen a decline.

The reserve, which is a series of scrapes, blocks of reed bed and wet grazing marsh, attracts migrants and breeding birds. Winter brings flocks of wildfowl and waders to the fields and scrapes, which are in turn hunted over by harriers, Peregrine and Merlin. As dusk falls, resident Barn Owls appear, silently quartering the meadows and reeds in search of prey. Winter often brings a rarity or two, perhaps a Red-breasted Goose or Black Brant in amongst the Brent Geese.

Spring wader passage, although not on a par with autumn, is still productive. Temminck's Stints are annual in May. The reed beds, during spring and summer, resound with the songs of Reed and Sedge Warblers and with the deep booming call of the Bittern. By July, the scrapes are swarming with waders as northern breeders such as Curlew Sandpiper,

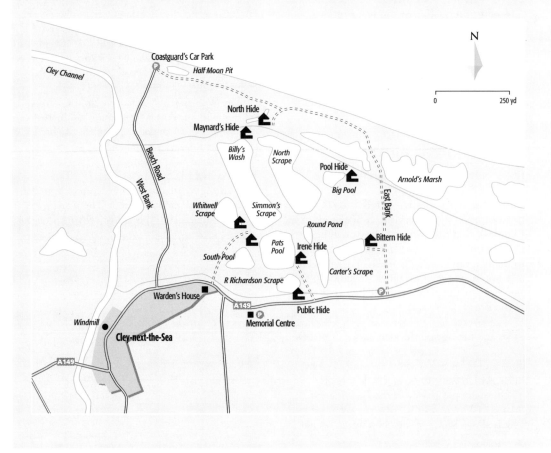

Ruff and Spotted Redshank stop off to refuel on their journey south. Spoonbills often appear either alone or in small parties from mid-July, by which time wader passage is in full swing. By August, there is always the chance of a rarity being discovered.

Whenever an easterly wind blows, it brings a promise of drift migrants, perhaps a Bluethroat in spring or Icterine Warbler in autumn. During such conditions, any cover is worth checking. Walsey Hills is one of the more productive areas to search. Seawatching in autumn can be good, with birders normally gathering on the beach behind the beach car park. By late autumn, Little Auks appear in favourable conditions, and there are often grebes and divers passing or sitting offshore.

KEY BIRDS
ALL YEAR: Bittern, Egyptian Goose, Barn Owl, Bearded Tit.
SPRING: Spoonbill, Garganey, Marsh Harrier, Kentish Plover, Little-ringed Plover, Little Stint, Temminck's Stint, Curlew Sandpiper, Dunlin, Ruff, Black-tailed Godwit, Whimbrel, Curlew, Spotted Redshank, Greenshank, Redshank, Green and Common Sandpiper, Sandwich, Common, Arctic, Little and Black Terns, Yellow Wagtail, Bluethroat, Redstart, Whinchat, Stonechat, Wheatear, Grasshopper Warbler, occasional Savi's Warbler, Sedge and Reed Warblers.
SUMMER: Breeding Avocet, Marsh Harrier, often lingering Little Gull.
AUTUMN: As for spring, with waders, especially, being more numerous. Additional species after easterly winds may include rare drift migrants such as Yellow-browed Warbler, Wryneck, Icterine and Barred Warblers. Offshore, auks, divers, grebes, skuas, terns and gulls can be seen.
WINTER: Offshore, grebes and divers along with seaduck. On reserve, Brent Goose, Shelduck, Wigeon, Teal, Gadwall, Pintail, Hen Harrier, Merlin, Peregrine, Grey Plover, Dunlin, Black-tailed Godwit, Curlew, Redshank, sometimes Snow Bunting, occasional Shorelark.

ACCESS
OS MAP: 133 REF: TG 054 441
Open all year. Closed on Mondays except Bank Holidays. The Memorial Centre (visitor centre) is open from 10am to 5pm between April and October, and from 10am to 4pm between November and mid-December. Admission is free for children under 16 and NWT members. There is a charge for non-members. The reserve centre is 0.8 km (½ mile) east of Cley village along the A149 coast road.

FACILITIES
There are hides, and the visitor centre has toilets and a shop.

Avocet
Recurvirostra avosetta

Boisterous when breeding, and unmistakable to identify, Avocet just cannot be missed at Cley from spring through to autumn. The symbol of the RSPB, the Avocet became extinct in Britain in the 19th century, before recolonizing in the 1940s in neighbouring Suffolk.

Avocets nest in the open on islands and areas of mud, normally from mid-April. They are fiercely protective of their young. Easily spotted at Cley, their black-and-white plumage and upturned bill can be confused with no other wader. The bill is used to sweep through shallow water from side to side, with the curved part slightly open. Their prey, which includes worms, insects and crustaceans, is located mainly by touch.

During winter, Avocets form large flocks at various locations in southern England.

23 BLAKENEY POINT

NNR / THE NATIONAL TRUST
526 ha (1,300 acres)

Blakeney Point is the end of a long shingle spit that runs east to Weybourne. During summer the point hosts a breeding colony of gulls and terns. However, it is the migrants and regular appearance of rarities that attract most birders.

An easterly wind can bring drift migrants such as Bluethroats and Wrynecks, with always the chance of something rarer. In autumn, in the right conditions, large numbers of migrants use the scant cover, both on the point and along the shingle ridge leading back to Cley.

The point is a hard slog on shingle from the Coastguard's car park at Cley, but to cover all the likely migrant traps on the point, a necessity. Also, boats run from Morston Quay and Blakeney.

Blakeney Harbour, with its extensive mud flats, salt marsh and grazing marsh, should not be ignored. From autumn into winter, large flocks of Brent Geese and estuarine waders can be seen.

⚑ KEY BIRDS

SPRING AND AUTUMN: Passage waders and wildfowl in harbour, and moving offshore, skuas, gulls, terns, seaduck, divers and grebes plus a chance of shearwaters, petrels, Little Auk and Sabine's Gull. Migrants on the point may include all common passerine summer migrants plus Ring Ouzel, Firecrest, Pied Flycatcher, Redstart, Black Redstart, Wryneck, Red-backed Shrike, Icterine Warbler, Bluethroat and also in autumn Barred Warbler, Yellow-browed Warbler and Red-breasted Flycatcher. Dotterel is almost annual in August and September. Thrushes and Goldcrest in late autumn.
SUMMER: Sandwich, Common, Little and Arctic Terns, and breeding gulls.
WINTER: Wildfowl and waders in Blakeney Harbour.

⚓ ACCESS
OS MAP: 132/133 REF: TG 000 465
Walk along the shingle from the Cley Coastguard's car park, reached, in turn, by taking a left turn on the eastern side of the village of Cley. Boats leave from Morston Quay, west of Blakeney.

🏠 FACILITIES
Hides overlook the tern colony.

24 HOLKHAM

NNR
3,953 ha (9,768 acres)

Consisting of grazing marsh, salt marsh, dunes and pine woods, this site is good for migrants and annual rarities in autumn, and in winter for wildfowl, notably geese.

The pines and dunes are best explored for migrants, and although not to be ignored in spring, autumn brings a far wider range of species. Winds with an easterly influence are needed to produce scarce drift migrants such as Wryneck, Yellow-browed Warbler and Red-breasted Flycatcher. But even without such conditions migrants and rarities still occur.

The geese, mainly Pink-footed with some White-fronted, are best viewed from Lady Anne's Drive. These large flocks regularly attract rarer species such as Taiga Bean Geese. If visiting in winter, take a look at the sea, as offshore there are often divers, grebes and seaduck.

⚑ KEY BIRDS
ALL YEAR: Feral Greylag Goose, Canada and Egyptian Geese, Redshank, Stonechat.
SPRING AND AUTUMN: Migrant chats, flycatchers and warblers; in the right conditions in autumn, drift migrants such as Wryneck, Barred, Icterine and Yellow-browed Warblers, Red-breasted Flycatcher, Bluethroat; in late autumn, chance of a vagrant such as Pallas's Warbler.
WINTER: Pink-footed, White-fronted and Brent Geese, occasional Taiga Bean Goose, Wigeon, raptors, and offshore seaduck, divers and grebes. On salt marsh and tide line, Snow Bunting, chance of Shorelark and Twite.

🌲 ACCESS
OS MAP: 132 REF: TF 890 450
Reached from the A149 coast road at Holkham, turn down Lady Anne's Drive opposite Holkham Park or, alternatively, from Wells, take the road north along the western edge of the harbour and park at the end.

25 SCOLT HEAD ISLAND

NNR
425 ha (1,050 acres)
This 6 km (3¼ mile) long island of sand dunes has salt marsh on its landward side and is considered

to be the best example of this habitat in Britain. Important for a breeding colony of gulls and terns, Scolt Head also attracts migrants, and in winter, the surrounding mud and salt marsh is well populated by wildfowl and waders.

KEY BIRDS

SPRING AND AUTUMN: Passage migrants, typical of those appearing on the North Norfolk coast (*see* under Holkham).
SUMMER: Breeding terns and gulls.
WINTER: Estuarine waders and wildfowl.

ACCESS
OS MAP: **132** REF: **TF 810 465**
The island can be reached by foot across the saltings. However, this can be precarious and there is a danger of being caught out by the tide. Regular boat trips run from Burnham Norton between April and September. The tern colony at the western end is out of bounds between April and August.

26 TITCHWELL

RSPB RESERVE
162 ha (400 acres)
This is one of Britain's most popular bird reserves. A reed bed is home to Marsh Harriers and Bearded Tits, which are often easier to see than elsewhere due to the raised path that gives a good view across the reeds. Avocets breed on the brackish lagoons that are favoured by passage waders.

During winter, Snow Buntings and often Shore Larks feed along the tide line or on the edge of the salt marsh. Walk west along the beach and you reach Thornham Point, a favourite spot for Shorelarks, and in autumn a few passerine migrants often lurk in the bushes.

Well placed hides ensure good views can be enjoyed of many of the birds. Rarities, which have included long-staying Black-winged Stilt, are discovered here each year.

KEY BIRDS

ALL YEAR: Bittern, Little Egret, Marsh Harrier, Water Rail, Bearded Tit.
SPRING: Passage waders, a few migrant passerines, plus Spoonbill, Black Tern and Garganey.
SUMMER: Little Tern, Avocet, Reed and Sedge Warblers, returning passage waders by mid-July.
AUTUMN: Passage waders include Spotted

Redshank, Greenshank, Curlew, Green and Wood Sandpipers, Little and sometimes Temminck's Stints, Knot. Chance of Redstart, crests and other migrant passerines.
WINTER: Estuarine waders and wildfowl, plus offshore divers (regularly) and rarer grebes, scoters, Long-tailed Duck, Red-breasted Merganser, Eider, Brent Goose. Hen Harriers roost, plus Snow Bunting and Shorelark.

ACCESS
OS MAP: **132** REF: **TF 749 436**
Off the A149 coast road between Titchwell and Thornham.

FACILITIES
A visitor centre and tea bar. Hides are accessible to wheelchairs.

27 HOLME BIRD OBSERVATORY

NORFOLK WILDLIFE TRUST
160 ha (400 acres)
This reserve is primarily of interest for migrants. Outside spring and autumn, offshore divers, grebes and seaduck congregate. However, it is the annual harvest of scarce migrants and rarities that attracts most birders. An easterly or northerly wind in inclement weather is most productive.

KEY BIRDS

ALL YEAR: Sheldnck, Redshank, Barn Owl.
SPRING: Warblers, chats and flycatchers; annually Bluethroat, Red-backed Shrike and Icterine Warbler.
SUMMER: Avocet, Yellow Wagtail.
AUTUMN: As for spring, plus Pied Flycatcher, Redstart, Wryneck, chance of Red-breasted Flycatcher, Barred, Icterine and Yellow-browed Warblers, plus rarities. Late autumn sees arrival of Goldcrest, finches, thrushes and Skylark.
WINTER: Offshore seaduck include Long-tailed Duck; divers and rarer grebes. Twite possible.

ACCESS
OS MAP: **132** REF: **TF 717 450**
Accessed from the A149 coast road – turn off into Holme at the Hunstanton end of the village. Take a right turn along a gravel track signposted to the reserve. A permit is needed to enter the Norfolk Ornithologist's Association reserve – obtainable daily from 9am to 5pm.

28 SNETTISHAM

RSPB RESERVE
1,600 ha (3,000 acres)
The 40 km (25 mile) wide Wash is Britain's most important estuary for migratory and wintering waders and wildfowl, which number tens of thousands. Bordering the southern shore, Snettisham is one of the best points from which to view the impressive numbers of birds using the mud flats. Pits on the reserve provide a safe haven for roosting waders, and, in the past, spectacular flocks of Knot have roosted. More recently this spectacle has become less reliable.

However, a visit on an incoming tide in autumn or winter will provide sightings of wader flocks wheeling over the mud, appearing like plumes of drifting smoke as their patterns continually change. The Wash is a safe roosting site for Pink-footed Geese, and they can be seen in the skies overhead at dawn and dusk after their daily feeding forays into the nearby arable fields.

KEY BIRDS
ALL YEAR: Redshank, Ringed Plover, Oystercatcher.
SPRING AND SUMMER: A few migrants, including passage waders. Avocet, Common Tern, Marsh Harrier.
AUTUMN AND WINTER: Spectacular numbers of waders, particularly Knot, also Oystercatcher, Redshank and Dunlin in big numbers. Additional species include Bar- and Black-tailed Godwits, Grey Plover, Curlew, Golden Plover, Sanderling, Turnstone and Spotted Redshank (a few). Pink-footed Goose roost, Brent Goose, Wigeon, Teal, Gadwall, Tufted Duck, Pochard, Goldeneye. On pits, occasional rarer grebes, divers and wind-blown Little Auk possible. Along the beach, Snow Bunting and occasionally Twite. Hen Harrier, Merlin and Peregrine.

ACCESS
OS MAP: 132 REF: TF 630 310
From the A149 at Snettisham take the beach road to the caravan and car park. Proceed past the holiday chalets to the reserve.

FACILITIES
There are hides overlooking the pits. Disabled visitors can drive to the first hide.

29 WELNEY

WWT
324 ha (800 acres)
Famed for its wild swans, Welney is at its best in winter when the Ouse Washes flood, acting as a haven for thousands of wildfowl escaping the icy grip of their northern breeding grounds.

At their peak, Bewick's Swans can number close to 5,000 birds, with Whooper Swans regularly exceeding 1,000. During daylight you are guaranteed to see hundreds of Whoopers, but, the Bewick's are largely absent, feeding out in the fields. They arrive at or soon after dusk, and can then be seen under floodlights with a mass of other wildfowl, as welcome food is put out.

This ritual is one of the attractions of Welney, as birders can sit in comfortable chairs viewing from a heated observatory, and continue enjoying the birds until after dark. The thousands of other wildfowl include both dabbling and diving ducks, along with geese. Waders vary in number depending on water levels.

During the summer months the meadows are exposed once more from the seasonal flooding of winter, and provide nesting sites for various wildfowl, and waders such as the Avocet, which has recently colonized the area.

KEY BIRDS
ALL YEAR: Gadwall, Shoveler, Tufted Duck, Pochard, Water Rail, Oystercatcher, Lapwing, Redshank, Snipe, Barn Owl, Kingfisher.
SPRING AND SUMMER: On passage, Little Gull, Black Tern and various waders. Arrival of summer visitors. Garganey, Marsh Harrier, Ruff, Black-tailed Godwit, Avocet, warblers, Yellow Wagtail and Hobby. Spotted Crakes may be heard calling at night.
AUTUMN: From July, passage waders include Little Stint, Knot, Dunlin, Whimbrel, Curlew, Spotted Redshank and Green, Wood and Common Sandpipers. Terns include Black, Common and occasionally Sandwich.
WINTER: Whooper, Bewick's and Mute Swans, White-fronted and occasionally the odd Taiga Bean or Pink-footed Geese, Shelduck, Wigeon, Teal, Pintail, Ruddy Duck, Hen Harrier, Merlin, Peregrine, Short-eared Owl, Golden Plover; chance of Scaup, Goldeneye, Smew and Goosander in cold weather.

⛴ ACCESS
OS MAP: **143** REF: **TL 546 944**

Open daily from 10am to 5pm except Christmas Day. From the A10 near Littleport, turn off at the roundabout to the A1101, towards Wisbech. This road eventually follows the New Bedford River, and where it crosses it, travel straight on. The reserve is a little further on.

🏠 FACILITIES
Visitor centre, tearoom, hides and heated observatory. Swans are fed twice daily. There is wheelchair access.

30 OUSE WASHES

RSPB RESERVE
2,500 ha (6,178 acres)

On the Cambridgeshire bank of the Ouse Washes, this reserve shares the same habitat and species to that of Welney. However, wildfowl are not fed here, so are usually far more distant and generally not concentrated, as at Welney.

In spring, Ruff may be encountered lekking, and Spotted Crakes heard rather than seen. Over 70 species breed. Hides are dotted along the embankment for over 5 km (3 miles), allowing long walks to be enjoyed. Barn Owls can be encountered hunting, normally towards dusk, at any season. Like at Welney, a variety of other raptors also occurs. Mass panic amongst the wildfowl often gives their presence away in winter.

🦅 KEY BIRDS
ALL YEAR: Gadwall, Shoveler, Tufted Duck, Pochard, Water Rail, Oystercatcher, Lapwing, Redshank, Snipe, Barn Owl, Kingfisher.
SPRING AND SUMMER: On passage, Little Gull, Black Tern and various waders. Arrival of summer visitors. Garganey, Marsh Harrier, Ruff, Black-tailed Godwit, Avocet, warblers, Yellow Wagtail and Hobby; Spotted Crakes may be heard late at night.
AUTUMN: From July, passage waders; terns.
WINTER: Whooper, Bewick's and Mute Swans, White-fronted and occasionally the odd Taiga Bean or Pink-footed Geese, Shelduck, Wigeon, Teal, Pintail, Ruddy Duck, Hen Harrier, Merlin, Peregrine, Short-eared Owl, Golden Plover; chance of Scaup, Goldeneye, Smew and Goosander in cold weather.

⛴ ACCESS
OS MAP: **143** REF: **TL 471 861**

Located east of Manea – follow signs from the B1093 in Manea.

🏠 FACILITIES
There is a visitor centre and hides, with limited wheelchair access.

31 NENE WASHES

RSPB RESERVE
283 ha (700 acres)

Important for its breeding waders and waterfowl, the reserve's wet grassland and ditches are flooded in winter, attracting a good range of wildfowl, waders and hunting raptors.

Mid- to late winter is normally the most productive time for a visit. Barn Owls are frequently seen hunting towards dusk, as are Hen Harriers that often create panic amongst the flocks of Golden Plover, Lapwing and dabbling ducks out on the washes. Spring brings various waders, some of which remain to breed along with secretive Garganey, and there is a chance of passage migrants such as Black Terns.

🦅 KEY BIRDS
ALL YEAR: Barn Owl, Redshank, Snipe, Lapwing, Kingfisher.
SPRING AND SUMMER: Passage migrants such as Black Tern, Ruff and various other waders. Garganey, Marsh Harrier, Hobby, Black-tailed Godwit, Yellow Wagtail.
AUTUMN: Can be quiet; passage waders may include Greenshank, Wood and Green Sandpipers.
WINTER: Bewick's Swan, Shelduck, Wigeon, Pintail, Teal, Shoveler, Golden Plover, Ruff, Dunlin, Black-tailed Godwit, Hen Harrier, Peregrine, often Merlin and Short-eared Owl, Stonechat, chance of Water Pipit.

⛴ ACCESS
OS MAP: **142** REF: **TL 318 992**

This site is susceptible to disturbance. In order to limit this, the best point to view from is the South Barrier Bank, accessed via Eldernell Lane off the A605 which is just east of Coates. Park in the car park at the end of the lane.

32 MAYDAY FARM FOREST TRAIL

FOREST ENTERPRISE

Traditionally, this site has been one of the most reliable for Goshawks. They display and soar over the plantations in early spring. Otherwise, the forest trails pass through felled areas and clearings favoured by Woodlarks, Nightjars and Tree Pipits.

There are a number of other trails in the area that should be equally productive for birds, including a chance of Golden Pheasant.

KEY BIRDS

ALL YEAR: Goshawk, Golden Pheasant, Woodcock, Crossbill, Hawfinch, Woodlark.
SUMMER: Nightjar, Tree Pipit, various warblers.
WINTER: Although scarcer in winter in recent years, there is always a chance of a Great Grey Shrike here.

ACCESS

OS MAP: 144 REF: TL 783 864
If travelling south from Brandon on the B1106, the entrance is 1.6 km (1 mile) past the Brandon Country Park, on the right.

33 LACKFORD LAKE

SUFFOLK WILDLIFE TRUST
16 ha (39 acres)
These gravel pits on the edge of Breckland are of most interest for their wintering wildfowl. A few passage waders, terns and the occasional Osprey occur, and there is a good range of breeding birds, including both waterfowl and woodland species.

KEY BIRDS

ALL YEAR: Great Crested Grebe, Water Rail, Sparrowhawk, occasional Goshawk, Kingfisher, Crossbill (regular), plus common woodland birds.
SPRING AND AUTUMN: Passage waders, terns, occasional Osprey.
SUMMER: Shelduck, Little-ringed Plover and Ringed Plover, Redshank, Hobby, Reed and Sedge Warblers.
WINTER: Cormorant, Shoveler, Gadwall, Pochard, Tufted Duck, Goldeneye, Goosander and occasional rarer grebes. Large gull roost.

ACCESS

OS MAP: 144 REF: TL 800 708
From the A11 take the A1101 towards Bury St Edmunds. The reserve entrance is a track on the left-hand side of the road between Lackford and Flempton.

FACILITIES

Hides and a visitors' hut. One hide is accessible to wheelchairs.

34 THE BRECKS AT WEETING HEATH

NNR / NORFOLK WILDLIFE TRUST
137 ha (339 acres)
This is the easiest site in Britain to see Stone Curlew. They return in mid-March and breed on the stony heath, and are easily viewed from hides. Woodlarks, too, regularly show well in front of the hides, and for botanists the reserve is a treasure trove, with rarities such as Spiked Speedwell.

KEY BIRDS

SPRING AND SUMMER: Curlew, Stone Curlew, Wheatear, Woodlark, Crossbill.

ACCESS

OS MAP: 144/143 REF: TL 756 881
Open from April to August. Leave Brandon north on the A1065, turning left to Weeting on the B1106. Turn left at the village green towards Hockwold. The reserve is 1.6 km (1 mile) further on along on the left.

FACILITIES

Hides and a visitor centre.

35 FOWLMERE

RSPB RESERVE
101 ha (250 acres)
A fenland oasis in a desert of arable farmland, Fowlmere's reed beds and scrubby woodland are a refuge for marsh and woodland birds. Local industries once thrived on the site as the natural springs were used to cultivate watercress commercially and the reed beds were harvested by villagers for thatch.

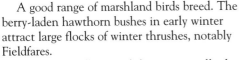

A good range of marshland birds breed. The berry-laden hawthorn bushes in early winter attract large flocks of winter thrushes, notably Fieldfares.

A circular walk around the reserve will take around half a day.

KEY BIRDS

ALL YEAR: Little Grebe, Water Rail, Sparrowhawk, Kingfisher, Reed Bunting.
SPRING AND SUMMER: Warblers include Reed, Sedge, Grasshopper, Garden and Willow Warblers, Chiffchaff, Blackcap, Lesser Whitethroat and Whitethroat. Spotted Flycatcher, Hobby.
AUTUMN AND WINTER: A few dabbling ducks, Green Sandpiper, Snipe, occasional Hen and Marsh Harriers and Merlin, Redwing, Fieldfare, Siskin, Redpoll, roost of Corn Bunting.

ACCESS

OS MAP: 154 REF: TL 407 461
From junction 10 of the M11, proceed west along the A505, turning off for Fowlmere village. If approaching from the east, take the left-hand fork out of the village and the reserve entrance track is next to a cemetery.

36 WICKEN FEN

THE NATIONAL TRUST
295 ha (730 acres)
Tucked away on the flat Cambridgeshire Fens, this is one of Britain's oldest and best-documented reserves. Its mosaic of habitats that include open water, reed beds, sedge beds, grazing marsh, scrub and woodland gives the site a long and varied list of birds.

Due to its location away from the coast, the fen is of most interest for its breeding birds and winter visitors, which include regular Bitterns and Hen Harriers. Breeding birds of interest include Nightingale, Cetti's Warbler and Grasshopper Warbler and often Garganey. Barn Owls are regularly seen on or close to the reserve.

Two main trails take you through the main habitats and include a boardwalk. A half-day visit is sufficient to explore most of the reserve.

KEY BIRDS

ALL YEAR: Little and Great Crested Grebes, Snipe, Shoveler, Pochard, Tufted Duck, Water Rail, Woodcock, Redshank, Barn Owl, Great Spotted and Lesser Spotted Woodpeckers, Bearded Tit.
SPRING AND AUTUMN: Garganey, Marsh Harrier, a few passage waders including Green Sandpiper and Greenshank, Common Tern.
SUMMER: Garganey (scarce), Hobby, Spotted Crake possible, Cuckoo, Yellow Wagtail, Nightingale, Cetti's Warbler, Grasshopper Warbler, Reed Warbler, Sedge Warbler, Garden Warbler, Lesser Whitethroat, Whitethroat, Blackcap.
WINTER: Occasional Bittern, Wigeon, Gadwall, Teal, Pintail, Sparrowhawk, Hen Harrier, Short-eared Owl, Kingfisher, Brambling, Corn Bunting.

ACCESS

OS MAP: 154 REF: TL 563 705
From the A10 north of Cambridge, take the A1123 east to Wicken – the reserve is signposted off to the right in the village.

FACILITIES

There is an information centre, and hides including a tower hide. Also a boardwalk and limited wheelchair access.

THE MIDLANDS

I t is true that a lack of coastline can limit the numbers of species on offer and the chance of a good range of rarities. Yet the Midlands makes up for this with some quite outstanding birding sites, one of which – Rutland Water – is a match for any coastal site. Rutland Water is home to the British Birdwatching Fair held annually in August.

The region is a transitional zone from the southern lowlands to the northern uplands, and separates east from west. Reservoirs dominate the birding scene, with the already mentioned Rutland Water being the jewel in the crown. On the edge of the Peak District, woodlands support oak wood specialities of Redstart, Pied Flycatcher and Wood Warbler, while in the south and west of the region, lowland woods and scrub are filled with the song of the Nightingale.

With so many water-based sites, wintering wildfowl are a major feature, so where better to go for a winter visit than The Wildfowl & Wetlands Trust grounds at Slimbridge? This reserve and its collection – the vision of the great conservationist Sir Peter Scott – is today perhaps the most visited site in the region and has no rival for viewing wildfowl in winter.

Migrants are a big feature at many sites. Passage waders use the many lake and reservoir margins and specially-created wader scrapes on some reserves. Other obvious migrants include flocks of terns, Little Gulls and the Osprey – a favourite migrant for the reservoir watcher. This latter species has been successfully re-introduced as a breeding summer visitor to Rutland, and so it may not be long before this majestic raptor is a frequent sight during summer across the region.

KEY

1) Slimbridge
2) Cotswold Water Park
3) Highnam Woods
4) Nagshead
5) Symond's Yat Rock
6) Otmoor
7) Church Wood
8) The Lodge
9) Tring Reservoirs
10) Paxton Pits
11) Grafham Water
12) Eyebrook Reservoir
13) Pitsford Reservoir
14) Rutland Water
15) Attenborough Gravel Pits
16) Summer Leys
17) Wyre Forest
18) Draycote Water
19) Upton Warren
20) Sandwell Valley
21) Chasewater
22) Belvide Reservoir
23) Coombes Valley
24) Blithfield Reservoir

Glossop

NOTTINGHAM-
SHIRE

A6

Dronfield

A61

A1

Buxton

A619 Chesterfield

DERBYSHIRE

Matlock

M1

Mansfield

Newark-
on-Trent

A617

A53

Leek

23

A6

Ripley

Castle-
-Lyme

STOKE-ON-
TRENT

Ashbourne

A52

DERBY

NOTTINGHAM

15

A52

STAFFORDSHIRE

Stone

Uttoxeter

A50

A453

Melton
Mowbray

Stafford

24

Burton upon Trent

A46

A38

A42

A6

A518

M6

LEICESTERSHIRE

RUTLAND

22

Cannock

Lichfield

M42

Telford

M54

21

Walsall

A606 Stamford

Wisbech

LEICESTER

CAMBRIDGESHIRE

A47

Peterborough

March

AMPTON

WEST
MIDLANDS

M69

Uppingham

12

A43

A141

Dudley

20

A5

M1

Corby

Oundle

A1(M)

Chatteris

urbridge

BIRMINGHAM

Market
Harborough

Kettering

Ely

A10

Huntingdon

minster

COVENTRY

M6

Rugby

A14

A1

Newmarket

M42

13

A449

19

Leamington Spa

18

NORTHAMPTON-
SHIRE

11

10

A14

A428

RCESTERSHIRE

Redditch

Warwick

Daventry

16

St Neots

Cambridge

Stratford
upon Avon

Northampton

A11

RE

M5

A442

Evesham

A46

WARWICKSHIRE

A5

Towcester

Bedford

8

A10

M11

A505

rcester

A44

Banbury

Milton
Keynes

BEDFORDSHIRE

A46

Moreton-in-Marsh

A422

M1

A6

Tewkesbury

Stow-on-the-Wold

Chipping
Norton

A421

Leighton
Buzzard

Dunstable

3

Cheltenham

M40

A5

Luton

cester

A436 A40

A44

Witney

Bicester

9

Aylesbury

1

Stroud

Kidlington

6

A41

BUCKINGHAM-
SHIRE

Cirencester

Oxford

Thame

A413

Malmesbury

Abingdon

Amersham

2

OXFORDSHIRE

High Wycombe

Swindon

Marlow

M40

N

M4

7

Chippenham

A346

Maidenhead

A4

Marlborough

Melksham

Devizes

WILTSHIRE

Salisbury
Plain

arminster

Amesbury

A36

A338

A303

Salisbury

A36

0   10   20   30 miles

0 10 20 30 40   60 km

61

SLIMBRIDGE
WWT (800 ha/1,977 acres)

Situated on the banks of the River Severn, Slimbridge is the headquarters of The Wildfowl & Wetlands Trust (WWT). It is an outstanding site for birding in winter, when hundreds of Bewick's Swans can be enjoyed at very close quarters. The Bewick's arrive at Slimbridge from their Arctic breeding grounds 4,025 km (2,500 miles) away in Arctic Russia. While a few hang around on Swan Lake during the day, the majority fly in to feed here and on Rushy Pen during the late afternoon. At dusk this spectacle can be enjoyed from a comfortable observatory.

Out on the grazing marsh bordering the Severn, White-fronted Geese feed along with a variety of other wildfowl (Slimbridge is the most important wintering site in Britain for White-fronts). In some years, a Lesser White-fronted Goose is discovered among the flocks, while annually Taiga Bean and Pink-footed Geese appear.

Slimbridge contains the largest collection of captive wildfowl in the world and wild ducks, notably Pintail, Gadwall, Pochard and Tufted Duck, mingle in the grounds with their captive cousins. In winter, Peregrine and Merlin hunt over the marshes.

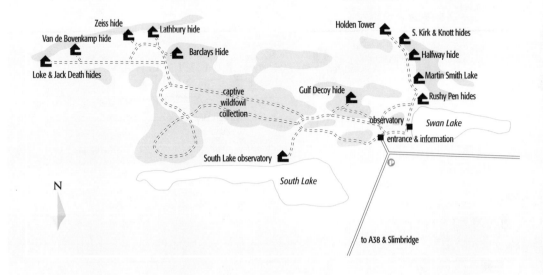

A small feeding station attracts a few woodland birds, and, it is also favoured by Water Rails; in winter there are few better sites to see this often secretive species. Very comfortable hides and observatories are spread around the grounds, and a visit to all the attractions can easily take a whole day.

If visiting in winter it is worth staying on after dark, both for the evening swan feeds under floodlight, and for the spectacular display of tens of thousands of Starlings arriving to roost. They swirl around in huge flocks before coming to rest.

Outside the winter months there are always birds to see, and during passage periods a few migrants occur, mainly waders. Terns, a few Little Gulls and passerine migrants such as Wheatear, Whinchat and Yellow Wagtail are likely. Early spring can see the arrival of Garganey. Summer is quiet for wild birds; nevertheless, many of the captive ducks will have ducklings, making it a popular day out for younger visitors.

KEY BIRDS

ALL YEAR: Little and Great Crested Grebes, Gadwall, Tufted Duck, Sparrowhawk, Lapwing, Redshank, Little Owl, Kingfisher, Reed Bunting, Great Spotted Woodpecker.
SPRING: Passage waders along the river and on pools include Whimbrel, Common Sandpiper, Wood and Green Sandpipers, Spotted Redshank, Greenshank, Avocet, godwits, Little Gull, Black Tern, Wheatear, Whinchat, Redstart, Black Redstart. Chance of rarities such as Spoonbill.
AUTUMN: Swans and geese arrive towards the end of October. Passage waders include Ringed Plover, Knot, godwits, Dunlin, Grey Plover, Spotted Redshank, Greenshank, Ruff, Green, Common and Wood Sandpipers and Curlew Sandpiper. Chance of Mediterranean Gull.
WINTER: Bewick's Swan, White-fronted Goose, plus regularly Brent, Pink-footed, Barnacle and Taiga Bean Geese; chance of a vagrant Lesser White-fronted Goose; Wigeon, Teal, Pintail, Pochard, Peregrine, Merlin, Water Rail, Dunlin, Redshank, Curlew, Golden Plover, Snipe and Ruff.

ACCESS

OS MAP: 162 REF: SO 723 048
Easily accessed off the M5. Drive through the village of Slimbridge, and keep going to the end of this road. The reserve and centre is open from 9am daily except Christmas Day.

FACILITIES

Good disabled facilities, the Discovery Centre has a shop, café and exhibitions. There are hides and comfortable observatories.

Bewick's Swan
Cygnus columbianus

Superficially similar to Whooper Swans, Bewick's differ by having a rounder looking head, stockier body and shorter neck, and the yellow patch on the bill does not extend beyond the nostril as it does in Whooper Swans.

Bewick's Swans are a winter visitor to Western Europe, migrating from their breeding grounds in Arctic Russia. Their arrival at Slimbridge is gradual, starting in mid-October; it may be January before the last birds arrive, gradually being pushed across Europe to Britain with the onset of cold weather. They then leave in mild winters in February, with the bulk of the birds gone by early March.

2   COTSWOLD WATER PARK

GLOUCESTERSHIRE WILDLIFE TRUST
5,666 ha (14,001 acres)
Located in the Thames Valley, this site consists of over 100 pits created from the gravel extraction industry. Hedgerows, woodlands and marshy areas add variety of habitat. The park is divided into a western and eastern end, with around 70 lakes on the Gloucestershire / Wiltshire border, and around 30 to the east in Wiltshire. Birding is good throughout, but the best areas are at the western end.

During passage periods, birds use the Thames Valley as a migration flyway, resulting in a good number appearing in the park.

KEY BIRDS
ALL YEAR: Grebes, feral Greylag and Canada Geese, Tufted Duck, Red-crested Pochard, Sparrowhawk, Redshank, Lapwing, Ringed Plover, Kingfisher, woodpeckers, Grey Wagtail.
SPRING AND AUTUMN: Garganey, Common and Black Terns, Little Gull, passage waders, Wheatear, Whinchat, Yellow Wagtail, hirundines, warblers, Hobby, Osprey.
SUMMER: Hobby, Ringed and Little-ringed Plovers, Common Tern, Cuckoo, Nightingale, warblers, Spotted Flycatcher, Yellow Wagtail.
WINTER: Chance of a diver, rarer grebe or sawbill such as Smew; Peregrine, Teal, Gadwall, Wigeon, Pintail, Shoveler, Pochard, Ruddy Duck, Goldeneye, Goosander, Water Rail, Golden Plover, Green Sandpiper, Siskin, Redpoll, gulls.

ACCESS
OS MAP: **163** REF: **SU 026 957**
The lakes are numbered. At the western end Lake 34 has a hide and logbook, and is a nature reserve. It and the surrounding lakes offer a good range of species. Access is from the A419 Swindon to Cirencester road, turning off at Cerney Wick. The lakes are south of Somerford Keynes. In the eastern section the reserve at Whelford Pools is worth visiting. Take minor roads off the A417 east of Cirencester to Whelford.

3   HIGHNAM WOODS

RSPB RESERVE
122 ha (300 acres)
Five kilometres (3 miles) west of Gloucester,

Highnam Woods is an ancient woodland. Its main feature is a good population of Nightingales. The site also supports a good woodland bird community, and interesting fauna.

KEY BIRDS
ALL YEAR: Sparrowhawk, Buzzard, Green, Great Spotted and Lesser Spotted Woodpeckers.
SPRING AND SUMMER: Nightingale plus good variety of other summer visitors.

ACCESS
OS MAP: **162** REF: **SO 778 190**
Leave Gloucester on the A40 westbound. The reserve is near the village of Highnam and signposted from the A40.

FACILITIES
A hide overlooks a winter feeding station.

4   NAGSHEAD

RSPB RESERVE
300 ha (740 acres)
Within the Forest of Dean, Nagshead contains a mix of trees. This provides the ideal habitat for a good variety of woodland birds, which include Hawfinch that come to feed on the beech mast and hornbeam fruit in winter.

During the summer months Nagshead is well known for its Pied Flycatchers.

KEY BIRDS
ALL YEAR: Buzzard, Woodcock, Tawny Owl, Lesser Spotted, Great Spotted and Green Woodpeckers, Grey Wagtail, Treecreeper, tits, Goldcrest, Redpoll, Siskin, Crossbill, Hawfinch.
SPRING AND SUMMER: Hobby, Turtle Dove, Tree Pipit, Redstart, Wood Warbler and various other warblers, Spotted and Pied Flycatchers.
AUTUMN AND WINTER: Fieldfare and Redwing, mixed tit flocks.

ACCESS
OS MAP: **162** REF: **SO 607 085**
The reserve is signposted from the road running west from Parkend to Coleford.

FACILITIES
An information centre is open at weekends from mid-April to the end of August. There are two nature trails and hides.

Cley in Norfolk has long been a mecca to birders.

Above: Marsh Harriers have spread from their East Anglian stronghold to colonize reed beds across Britain.

Above: Titchwell in north Norfolk is one of the RSPB's most popular reserves.

Above: Weeting Heath in the Brecks is the place to see Stone Curlews.

Above: Slimbridge offers a wildfowl extravaganza in winter.

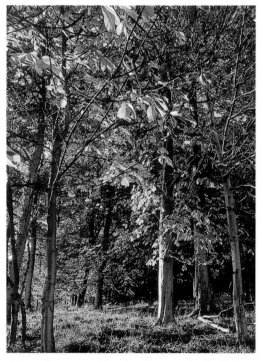

Above: Autumn at Nagshead reserve in the Forest of Dean.

Above: Nuthatches are one of many woodland species resident at Nagshead.

Above: Grafham Water has nearly 10 miles of shoreline.

Above: Goosanders prefer to breed on fast-flowing rivers, such as those found on the Welsh reserve of Dinas.

Above: Rutland Water is one of the largest man-made reservoirs in Europe.

Above: After a successful re-introduction programme at Rutland Water, Ospreys are once more breeding in England.

Above: A Cormorant on its cliff-top nest.

Above: Turnstones, such as this juvenile, are a common sight from autumn through to spring along Britain's rocky coasts.

Above: Red Kites can be enjoyed at close quarters at Gigrin Farm.

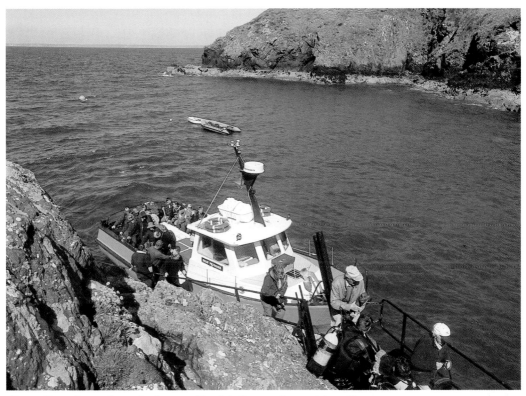

Above: Day trippers leave the boat at Martin's Haven after a visit to Skomer.

Above: A river running through the beautiful Dinas reserve in mid-Wales.

Above: A view across the Dovey Estuary at Ynys-Hir.

5 SYMOND'S YAT ROCK

RSPB / FOREST ENTERPRISE

Symond's Yat Rock overlooks a spectacular gorge through which the River Wye snakes. This rock is the perfect viewpoint from which to watch raptors. Pride of place go to a pair of Peregrine Falcons that nest annually within sight of the rock, and can be watched through telescopes set up by the RSPB.

Buzzard, Goshawk and Hobby are regularly seen, too, and migrant raptors such as Osprey and Honey Buzzard are possible. It is best to avoid early morning visits as the gorge can be misty and raptors tend not to soar too early in the day.

KEY BIRDS

SPRING AND SUMMER: Peregrine, Goshawk, Sparrowhawk, Kestrel, Hobby, Buzzard, chance of Red Kite and passage raptors such as Osprey and Honey Buzzard.

ACCESS

OS MAP: 162 REF: SO 563 160
North-east of Monmouth, the viewpoint is reached off the B4432 just south of the A40.

FACILITIES

Forest Enterprise and the RSPB run the viewpoint between April and August.

6 OTMOOR

RSPB RESERVE
106 ha (262 acres)

Once extensive marshlands, Otmoor suffered major habitat degradation due to drainage. However, the site is currently being returned to a wetland that will, when finished, be a site of national importance for birds.

There are around 90 species of bird breeding on the site, while winter brings large numbers of wildfowl, and wintering raptors such as Peregrine and Short-eared Owl. During spring and autumn passage waders are a feature.

KEY BIRDS

ALL YEAR: Little Grebe, Shoveler, Pochard, Tufted Duck, Sparrowhawk, Water Rail, Lapwing, Snipe, Little Owl, Marsh and Willow Tits, Reed Bunting.

SPRING AND AUTUMN: Marsh Harrier, Little-ringed and Ringed Plovers, Ruff, Black-tailed Godwit, Whimbrel, Greenshank, Green Sandpiper, Whinchat, Wheatear.
SUMMER: Hobby, Quail, Curlew, Redshank, Yellow Wagtail, Grasshopper Warbler, common warblers, Corn Bunting.
WINTER: Shelduck, Wigeon, Gadwall, Teal, Pintail, Hen Harrier, Merlin, Peregrine, Golden Plover, Jack Snipe, Short-eared Owl, Stonechat.

ACCESS

OS MAP: 164 REF: SP 570 126
Situated north of Oxford, from the A40 turn on to the B4027 near Wheatley, turn off to Beckley. Once in Beckley follow the road past the Abingdon Arms, keeping left into Otmoor Lane. Park at the end in the RSPB car park.

FACILITIES

The visitors' trail is partly a public bridleway, which can become very wet. Rubber boots may be essential in winter. Better access and facilities are currently under development.

7 CHURCH WOOD

RSPB RESERVE
14 ha (35 acres)

This small wood in the Chilterns offers a good range of woodland birds. Oak, ash and beech predominate, with hazel coppice. All three woodpeckers can be found and Hobby is regularly seen. Interesting butterflies include the Grizzled Skipper, and there are Common Dormice.

KEY BIRDS

ALL YEAR: Sparrowhawk, Woodcock, Little and Tawny Owls, Green, Great Spotted and Lesser Spotted Woodpeckers, Goldcrest, Marsh and Willow Tits.
SPRING AND SUMMER: Hobby, warblers, Spotted Flycatcher.
WINTER: Fieldfare, Redwing.

ACCESS

OS MAP: 175 REF: SU 972 872
Come off the M40 at junction 2 and take the A355 south, turning left for Hedgerley. The track to the reserve is by the pond just past the White Horse pub.

8 THE LODGE

RSPB HEADQUARTERS

45 ha (111 acres)

The reserve is a mix of woodland, heath and a lake with a good range of woodland birds. A visit at any time is likely to be productive.

KEY BIRDS

ALL YEAR: Grey Heron, Sparrowhawk, Woodcock, Tawny Owl, Kingfisher, Green, Great Spotted and Lesser Spotted Woodpeckers, Stonechat.
SPRING AND SUMMER: Turtle Dove, Cuckoo, Nightjar, Tree Pipit, Redstart, various warblers.
AUTUMN AND WINTER: Fieldfare, Redwing, Brambling, Redpoll, Siskin, possible Crossbill.

ACCESS

OS MAP: 153 REF: TL 188 478

Take the B1042 from Sandy towards Potton. The Lodge is 1.6 km (1 mile) from Sandy on the right. The reserve is open daily from 9am.

FACILITIES

Hides with wheelchair access, an information centre and shop.

9 TRING RESERVOIRS

HERTFORDSHIRE AND MIDDLESEX WILDLIFE TRUSTS

19 ha (47 acres)

Tring Reservoirs were created in the early nineteenth century to provide water for the Grand Union Canal. They are best visited in autumn for passage migrants and in winter for wildfowl.

Wilstone Reservoir is the largest, with three smaller reservoirs in a cluster nearby. There are paths allowing access, with a circular walk possible around Wilstone.

KEY BIRDS

SPRING: Fly-over passage waders, plus occasional Black Tern and Osprey; a few migrant passerines.
AUTUMN: Passage waders, dependent on water level, include Common and Green Sandpipers, Greenshank, plovers, Dunlin; chance of scarce species. Terns, Hobby, possible Osprey.
WINTER: Wigeon, Shoveler, Goldeneye, Teal, Pochard, Tufted Duck; chance in reed bed of Bittern, Bearded Tit and Water Rail. Grey Wagtail, bunting roost and gull roost.

ACCESS

OS MAP: 165 REF: SP 905 134

Located east of Aylesbury and just north of the A41, they are reached on the B489.

FACILITIES

Information boards and hides; the hide overlooking Startops reservoir is accessible to wheelchairs.

10 PAXTON PITS

HUNTINGDONSHIRE DISTRICT COUNCIL

58 ha (142 acres)

These mature gravel pits, with scrub, woods and meadow, provide year-round interest to the birder. A highlight in spring and early summer are Nightingales. They are at their most vocal from their arrival in mid-April to at least the end of May, and a dawn visit when most are singing can be magical. Other highlights include a breeding colony of Cormorants, along with a large winter roost, and in winter a good range of wintering wildfowl. With three guided trails, and a number of other paths, the site is easily explored. However, it can be very muddy on some trails.

KEY BIRDS

ALL YEAR: Cormorant, grebes, various wildfowl, Sparrowhawk, Kingfisher, woodland birds.
SPRING AND AUTUMN: Passage waders and terns plus a few passerine migrants and arrival of summer breeders.
SUMMER: Hobby, Common Tern, Nightingale, Grasshopper Warbler (scarce), Lesser Whitethroat, Whitethroat, Reed and Sedge Warblers.
WINTER: Gadwall, Wigeon, Tufted Duck, Pochard, Shoveler, Goldeneye, Teal, Goosander, in some years Smew, chance of odd geese such as White-fronts turning up and perhaps one of the rarer grebes.

ACCESS

OS MAP: 153 REF: TL 197 629

Access is from the A1 at Little Paxton. Take the B1041, turn left into the High Street in Little Paxton and follow the signs.

FACILITIES

An information point and visitor centre open at weekends. There are two hides and good trails, one of which is suitable for wheelchairs.

11　GRAFHAM WATER

WILDLIFE TRUST FOR BEDFORDSHIRE, CAMBRIDGESHIRE, NORTHAMPTONSHIRE AND PETERBOROUGH

600 ha (1,483 acres)

This large reservoir attracts a good number of wildfowl in winter. At passage periods waders use some of its 16 km (10 miles) of shore to refuel and rest, while terns hawk over the open water. The area surrounding the reservoir has a good population of woodland and farmland birds.

KEY BIRDS

ALL YEAR: Grebes, Cormorant, Grey Heron, Shelduck, Gadwall, Teal, Shoveler, Water Rail, Lapwing, Snipe, Great Spotted, Lesser Spotted and Green Woodpeckers.
SPRING AND AUTUMN: Occasional Common Scoter, passage waders. Terns include Arctic, Black, Sandwich and Little. Hobby, Osprey, chats and wagtails.
SUMMER: Common Tern, Cuckoo, Turtle Dove, Swift, Yellow Wagtail, Nightingale, Grasshopper Warbler, plus various other common warblers.
WINTER: Occasional divers, rarer grebes and sawbills. Regulars include Wigeon, Pochard, Tufted Duck, Goldeneye, Goosander, Golden Plover, Snipe and Dunlin; occasional Peregrine.

ACCESS
OS MAP: 153 REF: TL 143 671
Just off the A1. Mander Park and the nature trail are easily found along the southern shore.

FACILITIES
Hides, some accessible to wheelchairs. An information point is open at weekends in summer.

12　EYEBROOK RESERVOIR

CORBY AND DISTRICT WATER CO.

162 ha (400 acres)

Close to Rutland Water, Eyebrook attracts similar species albeit in much smaller numbers and less variety. The reservoir can be viewed from roadside laybys, along its western and north-eastern sides.

KEY BIRDS

ALL YEAR: Buzzard, Sparrowhawk, Red Kite, wildfowl and woodland birds.

SPRING AND AUTUMN: Chance of Garganey, Osprey, passage waders. Little Gull and Black Tern possible after easterly winds.
SUMMER: Osprey, Hobby.
WINTER: Common wildfowl, plus Goosander, Goldeneye; chance of other sawbills and grebes.

ACCESS
OS MAP: 141 REF: SP 853 964
Access from the A6003 south of Uppingham, along minor road to Stoke Dry.

13　PITSFORD RESERVOIR

WILDLIFE TRUST FOR BEDFORDSHIRE, CAMBRIDGESHIRE, NORTHAMPTONSHIRE AND PETERBOROUGH

325 ha (803 acre)

Pitsford is sliced in two by a causeway, and the northern half is the more productive side for birds. Passage waders are dependent on the water levels. During winter wildfowl and a large gull roost are the main attractions. Viewing is good from the causeway, and there is public access to most of the southern half.

KEY BIRDS

ALL YEAR: Grebes, Cormorant, Grey Heron, feral Canada and Greylag Geese, Gadwall, Shoveler, Ruddy Duck, woodland birds.
SPRING AND AUTUMN: Occasional Black-necked Grebe, Garganey and Osprey; passage waders, Common Tern, Hobby, hirundines, Yellow Wagtail, Rock Pipit, Whinchat and Wheatear.
SUMMER: A few species of wildfowl breed.
WINTER: Occasional divers (notably Great Northern) and rarer grebes. Smew, Goosander, Teal, Gadwall, Wigeon, Pintail, Shoveler, Tufted Duck, Pochard, Ruddy Duck, Goldeneye, Golden Plover, Kingfisher, Grey Wagtail, Siskin, Redpoll, chance of Peregrine. Gull roost.

ACCESS
OS MAP: 141 REF: SP 787 702
Access is from the A508 north of Northampton. Turn off at Brixworth for Holcot, which leads to the causeway.

FACILITIES
Nature reserve with hides. Permits to this area from The Wildlife Trusts or on site from the fishing lodge by the causeway.

RUTLAND WATER

LEICESTERSHIRE AND RUTLAND WILDLIFE TRUST (1,200 ha/2,965 acres)

A wetland of international importance, Rutland Water has become one of the country's top birding sites, attracting a wide range of migrant and breeding birds. There are 14 km (9 miles) of shore, with lagoons, pasture, scrub, woodland, reed beds and open water. Twenty-two hides overlooking some of the best areas, and there is much to see throughout the year.

Apart from its birds, Rutland Water's other claim to fame is as the home of the British Birdwatching Fair, attracting more than 10,000 birders from all over the world annually. A further attraction in summer are the Ospreys that are part of a re-introduction project.

Rutland is a vast site to cover, so it is best to concentrate efforts within the nature reserve, where most of the birds gather, and where there is a network of trails as well as good viewing points. Within the reserve there are two parts, the Lyndon Reserve and Egleton Reserve; the latter is best and is also home to the fair.

During winter in excess of 20,000 waterfowl can be present. Divers and the rarer grebes are annual, as are seaduck such as Long-tailed Duck, Common Scoter and Red-breasted Merganser, as well as occasional Shags among the Cormorants. One of the best places to look for these rarer visitors is from the dam.

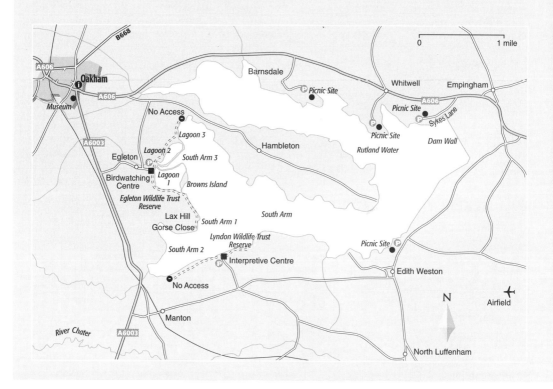

Spring and autumn are seasons of plenty, with good numbers of passage waders: up to 19 species of wader have been recorded on a single day. Terns may be joined by Little Gulls hawking over the open water. Migrant passerines include flocks of Yellow Wagtails, chats, pipits and hirundines.

The Ospreys are a highlight of summer. The re-introduction project has successfully established a population at Rutland. Ospreys here are easy to see, often on show perched at a nest or fishing out over the reservoir. Other summer attractions include breeding waders and wildfowl. There is also the year-round attraction of a thriving Tree Sparrow colony at the Egleton reserve.

🐦 KEY BIRDS

ALL YEAR: Grebes, Cormorant, Grey Heron, Teal, Pochard, Gadwall, Shoveler, Tufted Duck, Ruddy Duck, feral Greylag and Canada Geese, Water Rail, Redshank, Barn Owl, Kingfisher, woodland birds, thriving colony of Tree Sparrows.
SPRING AND AUTUMN: Black-necked Grebe, Garganey, Marsh Harrier, Osprey, Hobby; excellent assortment of passage waders, including occasional estuarine species such as Knot; Black, Common and Arctic Terns with occasional Little and Sandwich Terns; Wheatear, Whinchat, Yellow Wagtail; chance of scarce migrants and rarities.
SUMMER: Black-headed Gull, Common Tern, Shelduck, Osprey, Hobby, Oystercatcher, Little-ringed and Ringed Plovers, Nightingale, Grasshopper, Sedge and Reed Warblers.
WINTER: Divers, rarer grebes, sawbills, possible Shag, Wigeon, Pintail, Scaup, Pochard, Goldeneye, Goosander, Shelduck, occasional Pink-footed, Taiga Bean and White-fronted Geese, wild swans, visiting raptors may include Peregrine, Merlin and Hen Harrier, possible wintering Bittern, Lapwing, Golden Plover, Snipe, Green Sandpiper, Dunlin, Ruff. Gulls may include rarer species.

🚶 ACCESS

OS MAP: 141 REF: SK 866 676
The Egleton reserve is reached off the A6003 south of Oakham, through Egleton village. The Lyndon reserve lies between Manton and Edith Weston along the south shore. The dam can be reached from a car park off Sykes Lane, signposted off the A606 west of Empingham.

🏠 FACILITIES

Egleton: the birdwatching centre on the reserve has an elevated, heated viewing gallery, numerous hides and good paths. The reserve is open from 9am to 5pm daily except Christmas and Boxing Days. Permits to enter the reserve can be obtained from the centre. Some hides are accessible to wheelchairs.
Lyndon: there is an interpretive centre, which is open daily except Mondays.

Osprey
Pandion haliaetus

In 2001, Ospreys bred in England for the first time in generations. Remarkably, not just one pair but two bred, with a pair in the Lake District and another at Rutland Water. The Rutland Water birds were the result of a re-introduction project started in the mid-1990s.

There are few more spectacular sights in birding than watching an Osprey take a fish. Ospreys prey on fish close to the surface of the water, making a shallow dive to grasp their prey. They arrive at Rutland during April, with early individuals in late March, departing for their wintering quarters in Africa in September.

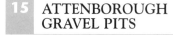

15 ATTENBOROUGH GRAVEL PITS

NOTTINGHAMSHIRE WILDLIFE TRUST
150 ha (370 acres)
Straddling the River Trent, the gravel pits, reed bed, scrub and wood are worthy of exploration at any time of year. Due to the site's location on the Trent, a good variety of migrants pass through.

KEY BIRDS
ALL YEAR: Grebes, Cormorant, Water Rail, feral Canada and Greylag Geese, Gadwall, Teal, Shoveler, Pochard, Tufted Duck, Lapwing, Kingfisher, Green, Great Spotted and Lesser Spotted Woodpeckers, Willow Tit.
SPRING AND AUTUMN: Hobby, Osprey, Marsh Harrier, Garganey, Little-ringed Plover and Ringed Plover, Dunlin, Ruff, Jack Snipe, Whimbrel, Green Sandpiper and Common Sandpiper, Little Gull, Black Tern, Arctic Tern, Yellow Wagtail, Whinchat, Wheatear. Plus scarcer passage waders in autumn and the chance of a rarity.
SUMMER: Little-ringed Plover, Common Tern, Grasshopper Warbler (scarce not annual), common warbler species, Spotted Flycatcher, Yellow Wagtail.
WINTER: Dabbling duck plus Ruddy Duck, Goldeneye, chance of a sawbill, Bittern (just about annual), Snipe, Green Sandpiper.

ACCESS
OS MAP: 129 **REF:** SK 523 343
Just south-west of Nottingham, accessed off the A6005 between Beeston and Long Eaton. The main car park is reached via Barton Lane.

16 SUMMER LEYS

LNR / NORTHAMPTONSHIRE COUNTY COUNCIL
47 ha (116 acres)
One of the top sites in the East Midlands, Summer Leys is a series of mature gravel pits in the Nene Valley. A wader scrape and feeding station in winter help in attracting an impressive array of birds.

Large numbers of Golden Plover roost on the reserve, and another winter attraction are the Tree Sparrows at the feeding station. A circular route takes in the hides, and on good paths the walk takes around two hours.

KEY BIRDS
ALL YEAR: Grebes, Grey Heron, Sparrowhawk, Lapwing, wildfowl, Tree Sparrow.
SPRING AND AUTUMN: Passage migrants include Garganey, Osprey, terns and waders such as Green and Common Sandpipers and (more commonly in autumn) Black-tailed Godwit, Dunlin, Spotted Redshank, Greenshank, Ruff, Little Stint and Curlew Sandpiper. Passerine migrants may include Yellow Wagtail, Whinchat.
SUMMER: Shelduck, Redshank, Oystercatcher, Ringed and Little-ringed Plovers, Common Tern, Black-headed Gull, Hobby.
WINTER: Wigeon, Shoveler, Pochard, Tufted Duck, Gadwall, Pintail, Goldeneye, chance of Smew and Goosander. Woodland birds at feeding station including possible Brambling.

ACCESS
OS MAP: 152 **REF:** SP 886 634
The reserve is east of Northampton, reached by turning off the A45 on to the B573, signposted to Great Doddington. Then turn right, down Hardwater Road signposted to Wollaston. The reserve is on the left.

FACILITIES
There is an information board, hides, a feeding station in winter, and wheelchair access.

17 WYRE FOREST

NNR / WORCESTERSHIRE WILDLIFE TRUST
300 ha (741 acres)
Straddling Worcestershire and Shropshire, Wyre Forest is an outstanding ancient woodland, known for its wildlife, and particularly woodland birds. Dowles Brook runs through the forest, and as is typical of fast-flowing rivers in this region, it supports Dipper and Grey Wagtail. The areas of sessile oak are attractive to Wood Warbler, Pied Flycatcher and Redstart, while the conifers support Long-eared Owl and the less secretive Crossbill.

KEY BIRDS
ALL YEAR: Mandarin, Sparrowhawk, Buzzard, Woodcock, Long-eared Owl, Kingfisher, Green, Great Spotted and Lesser Spotted Woodpeckers, Grey Wagtail, Dipper, common woodland birds plus Hawfinch and Crossbill.
SPRING AND SUMMER: Hobby, Cuckoo, Tree Pipit, Redstart, various common warblers, plus

Wood Warbler, Pied Flycatcher, Nightjar, Firecrest.
WINTER: Thrushes, tit flocks, Siskin, Brambling,
Redpoll.

⚓ ACCESS
OS MAP: 138 REF: **SO 750 760**
The forest lies west of Kidderminster and can be
reached from the B4914 or A456. Dowles Brook:
leave Bewdley town centre on the B4190. Turn
right into Lakes Road after about 0.8 km (½ mile).
Drive through the estate to Dry Mill Lane, go left
and park at the bottom of the hill. Follow the
path along the brook. Callow Hill: the car park is
on the A456 Bewdley to Ludlow road. The best
walk for a good selection of birds is one that
takes you through conifers, mixed woodland and
oak, and along the brook.

🏛 FACILITIES
Forest Enterprise visitor centre and trails at
Callow Hill.

18 DRAYCOTE WATER
SEVERN TRENT WATER
280 ha (691 acres)
Of most interest in winter for its wildfowl and gull
roost. A small feeding station regularly attracts
Willow Tits. Toft Bay is one of the best sites on the
reservoir both for waders and passerine migrants.

⚓ KEY BIRDS
ALL YEAR: Grey Heron, Tufted Duck,
Sparrowhawk, Little Owl, Kingfisher, Green,
Great Spotted and Lesser Spotted Woodpeckers.
SPRING AND AUTUMN: A few passage waders,
including Whimbrel, Common and Green
Sandpipers, Greenshank and Curlew. Terns,
mostly Common but chance of Black; Little
Gull. Passerine migrants include Wheatear,
Yellow Wagtail, Rock and Water Pipits.
SUMMER: Common Tern, Sedge and Reed
Warblers.
WINTER: Annually, rare grebes; occasional diver.
Cormorant, Wigeon, Gadwall, Teal, Shoveler,
Pochard, Goldeneye, Goosander, occasional
Smew. Large Black-headed Gull roost attracts
occasional Glaucous Gulls in late winter.

⚓ ACCESS
OS MAP: 140/151 REF: **SP 460 700**
The reservoir is reached off the A426 Rugby to

Southam road just south of the M45. A permit,
obtainable on site, is needed for much of the
reservoir. Alternatively, there is limited access
through the neighbouring country park.

🏛 FACILITIES
There is a bird information shelter, with
checklist and logbook, on the left of the access
road opposite the lower sailing club car park.

19 UPTON WARREN
WORCESTERSHIRE WILDLIFE TRUST
24 ha (60 acres)
Winter wildfowl and passage migrants are two of
the main interests at Upton Warren. The reserve
is split into two. The Moors Pool is reed fringed
and attractive to wildfowl and warblers. The
Flashes to the south are shallow pools with
islands attractive to waders and wildfowl.

Passage migrants include terns, waders and a
few passerines, while in winter a few waders and
a variety of wildfowl are present.

⚓ KEY BIRDS
ALL YEAR: Grebes, Tufted Duck, Gadwall,
Shoveler, Kingfisher, Cetti's Warbler, Reed
Bunting, Water Rail.
SPRING AND AUTUMN: Passage waders include
Ringed Plover, Common and Green Sandpipers,
Dunlin, Ruff (autumn) and Greenshank; also
terns, wagtails, chats and raptors.
SUMMER: Common Tern, Oystercatcher, Little-
ringed Plover, Redshank, Hobby.
WINTER: Wigeon, Teal, Pochard, Goldeneye,
Curlew; chances of Goosander, Pintail, Rock and
Water Pipits.

⚓ ACCESS
OS MAP: 150 REF: **SO 936 675**
Just off the A38 north-east of Droitwich Spa.
From junction 5 of the M5 take the A38 north.
For the Flashes, turn off the A38 at the Webbs
Garden centre roundabout towards the sailing
club; take immediate left into the birders' car park.
For the Moors Pool, turn east off the A38 by an
AA call box and follow the tarmac track to a car
park. Access is by permit obtained on site.

🏛 FACILITIES
Hides, with West Tower on Moors Pool suitable
for wheelchairs.

20 SANDWELL VALLEY

RSPB RESERVE

10 ha (25 acres)

The Sandwell Valley comprises marsh, pools, a lake, reed bed and woodland, and this array of habitats lies just 6 km (4 miles) from the centre of Birmingham. There is a good range of resident birds within the reserve and neighbouring country park. A feature of the reserve is Forge Mill Lake, which is good for wildfowl in winter, particularly Goosanders. Jack Snipe and Water Rail are regularly seen on the marsh, and during passage periods a few waders pass through.

KEY BIRDS

ALL YEAR: Little and Great Crested Grebes, Grey Heron, Tufted Duck, Little Owl, Kingfisher, Grey Wagtail, Willow Tit and other woodland species.
SPRING AND AUTUMN: A few passage migrants including Hobby, Peregrine, Ringed Plover, Dunlin, Redshank, Greenshank, Common and Green Sandpipers, Yellow Wagtail and Wheatear.
SUMMER: Little-ringed Plover, Common Tern, warblers.
WINTER: Cormorant, Wigeon, Teal, Shoveler, Pochard, Goldeneye, Goosander, Water Rail, possible Jack Snipe, Snipe, thrushes.

ACCESS

OS MAP: 139 REF: SP 035 928

Close to the junction of the M5 and M6, to the north of West Bromwich. Leave the M5 at junction 1 and take the A41 towards Birmingham. After passing the Hawthorns football ground, turn left into Park Lane, which leads into Forge Lane. Turn right at the end on to the A4041, and after 1.6 km (1 mile) turn right into Hampstead Road. Then right into Tannhouse Avenue for the reserve.

FACILITIES

Information centre, hides and wheelchair access.

21 CHASEWATER

BRITISH WATERWAYS BOARD

101 ha (250 acres)

Chasewater is perhaps best known for its winter gull roost, which consistently attracts Iceland and Glaucous Gulls. Late winter is best for the rarer gulls, while during the rest of the winter the site offers winter wildfowl and the chance of a rarer grebe, diver or straying seaduck. During passage periods a few waders appear.

There are footpaths around the reservoir. The gull roost is best watched from the amusement park on the southern shore. The site can experience a great deal of disturbance, so some visits may produce few birds.

KEY BIRDS

ALL YEAR: Grebes, Tufted Duck, Water Rail.
SPRING AND AUTUMN: Occasional Hobby; passage waders include Oystercatcher, Ringed and Little-ringed Plovers, Dunlin, Whimbrel, Common Sandpiper, Curlew and Redshank. Little Gull; terns, including occasional Black, Little and Sandwich; Whinchat and Wheatear.
SUMMER: Warblers breeding around reservoir, otherwise fairly quiet.
WINTER: Wigeon, Teal, Pochard, Goldeneye, Goosander, Ruddy Duck; less regularly Pintail, Gadwall and Scaup. Chance of a diver, rare grebe or seaduck. Kittiwakes appear most often in autumn and March; from mid-November chance of Iceland and Glaucous Gulls in gull roost.

ACCESS

OS MAP: 139 REF: SK 036 074

Reached only from the eastbound carriageway of the A5 north of Brownhills. Turn left from the carriageway into Pool Road, and left again into the amusement park for the gull roost.

22 BELVIDE RESERVOIR

BRITISH WATERWAYS BOARD / WEST MIDLANDS BIRD CLUB

75 ha (285 acres)

A good gull roost occasionally attracting white-winged gulls in late winter and impressive numbers of wintering wildfowl are two of Belvide Reservoir's seasonal attractions. During passage periods it is a good place for migrants, too. Access is restricted to permit holders.

KEY BIRDS

ALL YEAR: Little and Great Crested Grebes, Shoveler, Ruddy Duck, Gadwall, Teal, Tufted Duck, Little and Tawny Owls.
SPRING AND AUTUMN: Possible Garganey, Osprey. Regular passage waders include Little-ringed and Ringed Plovers, Dunlin, Whimbrel, Curlew,

Redshank, and in autumn also Greenshank, possible godwits, Wood Sandpiper, Spotted Redshank, Little Stint and Dunlin; Common, Black and occasional Little Terns; wagtails, chats, warblers and chance of a rarity.

WINTER: Large numbers of wildfowl arrive to moult in autumn. Wigeon, Gadwall, Teal, Pochard, Goldeneye, Goosander, Water Rail, chance of Glaucous and Iceland Gulls in gull roost in late winter.

ACCESS
OS MAP: 127 REF: SJ 870 098
From the A5 Cannock to Telford road, turn off to Horsebrook 3 km (2 miles) west of A449, taking Horsebrook Lane. Then turn right into Shutt Green Lane. The reserve is 0.8 km (½ mile) along here on the right. Annual permits from Miss M. Surman, West Midland Bird Club, 6 Lloyd Square, 12 Niall Close, Edgbaston, Birmingham B15 3LX.

23 COOMBES VALLEY

RSPB RESERVE
104 ha (257 acres)
Tucked away in a steep-sided valley on the edge of the Peak District, Coombes Valley is a delightful reserve. Oak woodland predominates, straddling the Coombes Brook, home to Dipper and Grey Wagtail. The woodland holds the typical oakwood specialities of Redstart, Pied Flycatcher and Wood Warbler, along with a good variety of woodland birds. Steep paths mean good footwear is required.

KEY BIRDS
ALL YEAR: Grey Heron, Sparrowhawk, Woodcock, Tawny, Little and Long-eared Owls, Kingfisher, Great Spotted Woodpecker, Lesser Spotted Woodpecker and Green Woodpecker, Grey Wagtail, Dipper.
SPRING AND SUMMER: Tree Pipit, Pied and Spotted Flycatchers, Wood Warbler, Redstart.
AUTUMN AND WINTER: Thrushes and roving tit flocks, otherwise quite quiet.

ACCESS
OS MAP: 119 REF: SK 005 530
From the A523 Leek to Ashbourne road, turn off to Apesford, and the reserve is on the left after 1.6 km (1 mile).

24 BLITHFIELD RESERVOIR
SOUTH STAFFORDSHIRE WATERWORKS CO.
320 ha (790 acres)
Lying west of Burton Upon Trent, this large reservoir is of most interest in winter, and during passage periods. Cut in two by a causeway, the reservoir's northern end is far more attractive to birds and is a nature reserve. The southern side suffers from disturbance caused by various recreational pursuits. The northern half is accessed by permit only. So, if visits are not planned in advance, viewing is restricted to the causeway.

A variety of wildfowl can be viewed here in winter when there is also a large gull roost. Passage periods can be good, too, with waders and terns passing through.

KEY BIRDS
ALL YEAR: Great Crested Grebe, Cormorant, Shoveler, Tufted Duck, Sparrowhawk, Tawny Owl, Kingfisher, woodpeckers.
SPRING AND AUTUMN: Passage waders include Oystercatcher, Little-ringed Plover, Ringed Plover, Dunlin, Redshank, Common Sandpiper and (particularly in autumn) Spotted Redshank, Wood Sandpiper, Curlew Sandpiper, Little Stint, Ruff and Black-tailed Godwit. Common Tern, Black Tern, Yellow Wagtail, chance of Osprey.
SUMMER: Sedge Warbler, Sand Martin, Spotted Flycatcher, various other breeding birds.
AUTUMN AND WINTER: Occasional visits by rarer grebes, Scaup and Smew, plus the chance of a raptor such as Peregrine. Wildfowl include Wigeon, Gadwall, Teal, Shoveler, Pochard, Goldeneye and Goosander. Gull roost can include Glaucous and Iceland Gulls.

ACCESS
OS MAP: 128 REF: SK 058 237
On the B5013 Rugeley to Abbots Bromley road.

FACILITIES
For access to the nature reserve and hides, apply for a permit from Miss M. Surman, West Midland Bird Club, 6 Lloyd Square, 12 Niall Close, Edgbaston, Birmingham B15 3LX.

WALES

Think of Wales, and the rugged beauty of Snowdonia or the rolling hills of the Brecon Beacons spring to mind. Yet away from these tourist honey pots are less well-known treasures. Take, for instance, the vast expanse of dunes and the endless deserted beaches of Newborough Warren; the tumbling streams and wooded valleys of mid-Wales, realm of the Red Kite, or the long deserted beaches and mudflats bordering the Gower.

Wales is a land of hills, mountains and valleys. Rushing rivers support Dippers, Common Sandpipers and Grey Wagtails and are often bordered by sessile oak woods, home to Pied Flycatcher and a host of woodland birds. The uplands, both moorland and mountain, are home to sought after species such as Ring Ouzel and Black Grouse, the latter a species that has suffered widespread decline.

The Welsh coast is famed for its beauty, and is a popular destination for walkers, as well as offering great birding. Just off the Pembrokeshire coast is a special group of islands, teeming with birds. The islands include Grassholm, which is home to an impressive Gannet colony. If you want to get away from the hubbub of daily life, then try a stay on Skomer or Skokholm, the former can also be explored on a day trip. Nearby, Ramsey Island, an RSPB reserve, attracts visitors keen to see the Choughs, a rarity in Britain. These birds can also be easily seen on Anglesey's Holyhead reserve. Here, impressive cliffs swarm with seabirds in summer, making this one of the most popular birding sites in Wales.

N

KEY

1) Kenfig
2) Cwm Clydach
3) Oxwich
4) Llanelli
5) Grassholm
6) Skomer
7) Skokholm Island
8) Ramsey Island
9) Strumble Head
10) Dinas and Gwenffrwd
11) Dyffryn Woods
12) Gigrin Farm
13) Cors Caron
14) Lake Vyrnwy
15) Ynys-hir
16) Mawddach Valley (Coed Garth Gell)
17) Bardsey Island
18) Newborough Warren
19) Valley Lakes
20) Cemlyn Lagoon
21) Conwy
22) Point of Ayr
23) South Stack

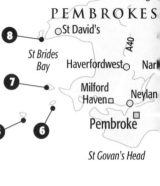

1 KENFIG

NNR
486 ha (1,200 acres)
This reserves consists of a freshwater pool with reed beds, sallows and sand dunes stretching to the coast. It is one of the best sites in Wales for migrants, and seawatching can be rewarding during spring and autumn from Sker Point.

Various species of warbler breed, and interesting flora includes the Fen Orchid. In winter the pool attracts wildfowl and there is a chance of a rare grebe. Bitterns visit, and down on the foreshore a few waders will be present.

KEY BIRDS

ALL YEAR: Great Crested Grebe, Tufted Duck, Sparrowhawk, Oystercatcher, Ringed Plover, Water Rail, Cetti's Warbler, Stonechat.
SPRING: Occasional Garganey, Whimbrel, Common, Sandwich and Black Terns, Grasshopper Warbler, various other passage waders and passerines.
SUMMER: Grasshopper, Reed and Sedge Warblers; offshore, Manx Shearwater.
AUTUMN: Seabirds offshore, particularly in rough weather the chance of shearwaters, petrels and skuas. Passage migrants on reserve, waders along foreshore.
WINTER: Bittern is regular. Shoveler, Gadwall, Pochard, Goldeneye, Ruddy Duck, chance of Smew and seaduck. Among the dunes Short-eared Owl, Merlin, Peregrine, occasional Hen Harrier, Snipe, possible Jack Snipe. On the foreshore a few waders include Purple Sandpiper, offshore the chance of grebes, divers and seaduck. Golden Plover on fields at Sker.

ACCESS

OS MAP: 170 REF: SS 802 811
Leave the M4 at junction 37, taking the A4229 towards Porthcawl. Immediately after the second roundabout (South Cornelly), take the first right down a lane that comes out at a golf club. Turn right. The reserve is a little further on, on the left.

FACILITIES

Two hides overlook the pool. It is worth noting that it can be very wet underfoot, so wellingtons are recommended. The visitor centre is open at weekends and Bank Holidays.

2 CWM CLYDACH

RSPB RESERVE
69 ha (170 acres)
Consisting mainly of oak with a mix of birch, beech, alder and ash, this woodland holds the typical species found in Welsh oak woods, notably Redstart, Wood Warbler and Pied Flycatcher. All three species of woodpecker occur too, and on the higher ground above the wood, Wheatear and Tree Pipit can be found in summer.

The wood lines the banks of the River Clydach, which holds species typical of fast-flowing rivers, including Dipper and Grey Wagtail. There are good trails including a short 1.6 km (1 mile) route and a long 11 km (7 mile) route. During winter, Red Kites are seen regularly.

KEY BIRDS

ALL YEAR: Sparrowhawk, Buzzard, Green, Great Spotted and Lesser Spotted Woodpeckers, Grey Wagtail, Dipper, Marsh and Willow Tits, Raven.
SPRING AND SUMMER: Tree Pipit, Redstart, Whinchat, Wheatear, Wood Warbler, Pied Flycatcher.
AUTUMN AND WINTER: Red Kite, Redwing, Snipe, Woodcock, Fieldfare, Brambling, Redpoll.

ACCESS

OS MAP: 159 REF: SN 584 026
The reserve lies north of Swansea. From junction 45 of the M4, proceed to Clydach. Take the minor road from the centre of the village up the Clydach valley, through Craigcenfnparc. Follow this road until you reach the reserve car park.

FACILITIES

There is a short trail suitable for wheelchairs.

3 OXWICH

NNR
258 ha (638 acres)
Situated on the south-east side of the 32 km (20 mile) long Gower Peninsula. This is an area of salt marsh, freshwater marsh, fen, reed bed, fish ponds and woodland bordering the shallow 4 km (2½ mile) long Oxwich Bay.

This range of habitat and coastal location is ideal for a broad range of birds. There are various paths including a board walk and marsh lookout. Burry Inlet on Gower's northern coast is worth visiting in winter for wildfowl and waders. At the southern end of the impressive Rhossili Bay at the Gower's tip is Worm's Head. Rhosilli Down can be good for migrants and both Chough and Peregrine are resident here. Worm's Head, only accessible at low tide, is worth checking for migrants, too. The cliffs here have a sizeable seabird colony. Offshore, seaduck and both Red-throated and Great Northern Divers can be found in winter.

KEY BIRDS
ALL YEAR: Little Grebe, Shelduck, Teal, Sparrowhawk, Buzzard, Water Rail, Cetti's Warbler, Bearded Tit (scarce), Peregrine, Chough, Reed Bunting.
SPRING: Chance of Garganey in early spring, plus arrival of summer visitors.
SUMMER: Reed and Sedge Warblers, Cuckoo, woodland birds.
AUTUMN: Light passage of waders and terns.
WINTER: Shoveler, Pochard, Gadwall, Kingfisher, chance of Bittern, waders on foreshore, chance of grebes, divers and seaduck offshore.

ACCESS
OS MAP: 159 REF: SS 872 773
From Swansea take the A4118, turn off on to the first road signed to Oxwich which will take you through some of the reserve. There is a car park at the end. It can be busy in summer.

4   LLANELLI
WWT
182 ha (450 acres)
The reserve is located on the northern shore of the Burry Inlet and the main attractions are wildfowl, waders and, a relatively recent addition, a roosting site for Little Egrets.

Habitats range from mud flats and salt marsh to reed beds and freshwater pools, and there is a captive collection of wildfowl. Autumn and winter are two of the most productive seasons for a visit, when a good range of waders can be enjoyed, along with dabbling duck, hunting Peregrine and Short-eared Owl.

KEY BIRDS
ALL YEAR: Cormorant, Grey Heron, Little Egret, Oystercatcher, Redshank.
SPRING: Passage waders, plus departing winter species. Chance of Garganey, Marsh Harrier.

SUMMER: Reed Warbler, Sedge Warbler.
AUTUMN AND WINTER: Migrants include Marsh Harrier, Garganey, passage waders include Greenshank, godwits, Whimbrel, Curlew Sandpiper, Green and Common Sandpipers, Ruff, Spotted Redshank. Estuarine waders in winter include Knot, Curlew, Oystercatcher, Dunlin, Redshank and Grey Plover. Teal, Golden Plover, Wigeon, Pintail, plus seaduck in estuary.

ACCESS
OS MAP: 159 REF: SS 533 984
Leave the M4 at junction 47 and take the A4240 towards Llanelli, which joins the A484. The reserve is signposted off this road. Open daily from 9.30am except Christmas Eve and Christmas Day.

FACILITIES
A visitor centre, hides, and good wheelchair access. Captive collection of wildfowl.

5   GRASSHOLM
NNR / RSPB
9 ha (22 acres)
The least accessible of the Pembrokeshire Islands, Grassholm is famous for its Gannets, containing the world's fourth largest colony with 33,000 pairs. The Gannet colony covers most of the island. However, a few other species of seabird may be seen including auks. The boat trip to the island, which is 11 km (7 miles) offshore, may provide views of Manx Shearwaters.

KEY BIRDS
SPRING AND SUMMER: Gannet, Manx Shearwater, Puffin, Guillemot, Razorbill, Shag, Oystercatcher, Kittiwake, Herring and Great Black-backed Gull.

ACCESS
OS MAP: 157 REF: SS 533 984
Boats run from Martin's Haven throughout the summer. Boat trips circumnavigate the island, allowing excellent views of the colony. For details of sailings contact the RSPB's regional Welsh office, or check details from the RSPB website. Martin's Haven is reached by taking the B4327 from Haverfordwest to Marloes. Go through the village and proceed to The National Trust car park at the end. The boat goes from a quay at the bottom of the hill.

SKOMER

WILDLIFE TRUST OF SOUTH AND WEST WALES (291 ha/720 acres)

Lying a short distance from the Pembrokeshire coast, the Island of Skomer neighbours Skokholm, but is far more accessible to visitors, with day trips possible throughout the spring and summer months. Unlike Skokholm's red sandstone cliffs which have few ledges suitable for cliff nesting, Skomer's cliffs are much more conducive to nesting auks, Kittiwakes and Fulmars. The cliff tops are riddled with burrows inhabited by Puffins, with close views possible.

A big attraction is the island's breeding population of Manx Shearwaters. The island supports the world's largest colony with over 100,000 pairs. An overnight stay is

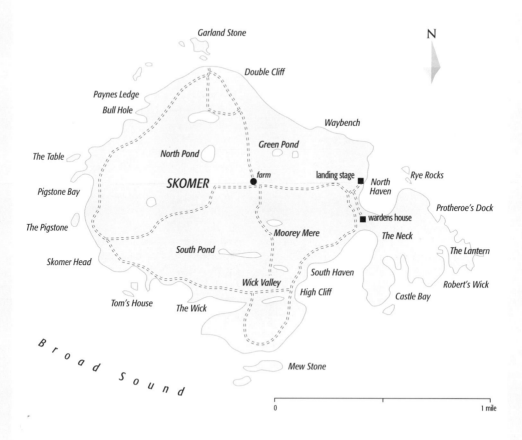

necessary to enjoy the spectacle of thousands of birds returning to their nest sites in old rabbit burrows. Another night-time visitor is the European Storm Petrel, which nests on the boulder beachers and in the stone walls. Occasionally, during the day, you may hear a storm petrel calling from its nest crevice in a wall, but at night they are easily located by listening for their soft purring trill. Both species come ashore in their greatest numbers on moonless nights to try and avoid the predatory Great Black-backed Gulls that patrol the island.

Choughs nest on Skomer, and are relatively easy to see as they soar above the cliffs or feed on the short cliff top turf. Another bird in evidence is the Short-eared Owl, able to live here due to the presence of the Skomer Vole, a larger race of the mainland Bank Vole, on which it preys.

Spring and autumn can be exciting periods on Skomer, with rare birds turning up annually, there is usually a reasonable variety of migrants passing through. Small patches of scrub in the centre of the island, are the best places to look.

A full day is needed to explore the island thoroughly. One of the best spots for viewing seabirds is at The Wick. A circular route can be taken from the landing stage around the island. A visit in May or June is best for the seabirds, while April, May and August are good months for migrants.

KEY BIRDS
SPRING AND SUMMER: Manx Shearwater, Fulmar, European Storm Petrel, Cormorant, Shag, Buzzard, Peregrine, Oystercatcher, Whimbrel, Curlew, Common Sandpiper, Lesser Black-backed Gull, Greater Black-backed Gull and Herring Gull, Kittiwake, Guillemot, Razorbill, Puffin, Short-eared Owl, Rock Pipit, Sedge Warbler, Whitethroat, Chough, Raven; variety of passage migrants, chats, warblers and flycatchers and the chance of a rarity.
AUTUMN: Passage migrants as for spring.

ACCESS
OS MAP: 157 REF: SM 725 095
Boats depart from Martin's Haven on the mainland between April and October, at 10am, 11am and midday daily except Mondays, excluding Bank Holidays.

FACILITIES
There is accommodation available. Contact Wildlife Trust of South and West Wales, 7 Market Street, Haverfordwest,

Pembrokeshire, Wales SA61 1NF; tel: 01437 765462.

Manx Shearwater
Puffinus puffinus

Coos, croons, screams and howls are all words that can be used to describe the sounds of calling Manx Shearwaters. On overcast nights when there is no moon, thousands of shearwaters come ashore during the breeding season to their nesting burrows. The noise of all these birds calling can be quite spine-chilling.

Manx Shearwaters pair for life and are long lived, spending the winter off the coast of South America, before returning to breed during April. On summer evenings, the shearwaters can often be seen gathering off Skomer in rafts on the sea, before coming ashore under the cover of darkness. Once ashore, they shuffle over the ground using their legs and wings to reach their burrow.

7 SKOKHOLM ISLAND

WILDLIFE TRUST OF SOUTH AND WEST WALES

101 ha (250 acres)

Day visits are possible on Mondays only, but the best way to soak up the island's atmosphere is to stay for a week. Large numbers of Puffins nest along the cliff tops, and the island is riddled with thousands of burrows used by nesting Manx Shearwaters.

At night the island comes alive with the eerie sound of shearwaters calling from their burrows. Another night-time visitor is the European Storm Petrel, which nests in the stone walls and boulder beaches.

During spring and autumn migrants can be expected, and although not a regular breeding bird on the island, Choughs from the mainland visit.

KEY BIRDS

SPRING AND SUMMER: Manx Shearwater, European Storm Petrel, Shag, Guillemot, Razorbill, Puffin, Kittiwake, Lesser Black-backed Gull, Great Black-backed Gull, Chough, Peregrine, Raven, Rock Pipit; spring migrants include Wheatear, Whinchat, warblers, Spotted Flycatcher, chance of a rarity.
AUTUMN: Passage migrants as for spring.

ACCESS

OS MAP: 157 **REF:** SM 738 047

Weekly accommodation is available between April and September. Day visits are possible on Mondays from June to August. Details of accommodation and boat sailing times from Wildlife Trust of South and West Wales, 7 Market Street, Haverfordwest, Pembrokeshire SA61 1NF; tel: 01437 765462.

FACILITIES

The boat departs from Martin's Haven. Details on reaching quay listed under Grassholm on page 77.

8 RAMSEY ISLAND

RSPB RESERVE

260 ha (642 acres)

Less than 1.6 km (1 mile) off the coast, Ramsey is the northernmost Pembrokeshire island. It is best known for its Choughs, which favour the island's fields, and nest on the sea cliffs, along with a variety of seabirds.

KEY BIRDS

ALL YEAR: Shag, Buzzard, Peregrine, Oystercatcher, Curlew, Rock Pipit, Chough, Raven, Stonechat.
SPRING AND AUTUMN: Wide variety of passage migrants, arrival of breeding seabirds in spring. During autumn seabirds passing offshore include skuas, and chance of Sooty Shearwater and petrels. Great Northern and Red-throated Divers are often seen.
SUMMER: Fulmar, Manx Shearwater (a few breed), Lapwing, Kittiwake, Guillemot, Razorbill, Puffin, Wheatear.

ACCESS

OS MAP: 157 **REF:** SM 706 237

Open daily except Fridays from Easter until the end of October. Boats leave the lifeboat station at St Justinians at 10am and 1pm. Access details can be checked on the RSPB's website, or by telephone from the Welsh regional office, and in St David's.

Numbers are limited to 40 visitors per day, so book in advance. Contact Thousand Islands Expeditions, Cross Square, St David's; tel: 01437 721686. St Justinians is just west of St David's, situated along a minor road.

9 STRUMBLE HEAD

This west-facing headland is one of the best places in Britain for seawatching. During autumn large numbers of petrels, shearwaters and skuas pass offshore. July to December is best for seabird movements. The ideal conditions are gale force south or south-westerly winds, veering northerly or north-westerly. Early morning and late afternoon are often the most productive periods. Even on a calm day in summer and autumn you can expect to see passing Manx Shearwaters and Gannets.

A wartime bunker set into the cliff has been maintained as a seawatching lookout, and is just a short walk from the car park. Other attractions include the chance of migrants and Choughs.

KEY BIRDS

ALL YEAR: Chough, Peregrine.
LATE SUMMER TO EARLY WINTER: Manx Shearwater, annually Sooty and Balearic Shearwaters, Great and Cory's Shearwaters are almost annual, European Storm and Leach's Petrel, Arctic, Great, Pomarine and Long-tailed Skuas, Sabine's Gull, Kittiwake, auks.

ACCESS
OS MAP: **157** REF: **SM 895 414**
Strumble Head is north-west of Fishguard, along a minor road from Fishguard Harbour.

10   DINAS AND GWENFFRWD

RSPB RESERVE

2,763 ha (6,828 acres)

These two adjoining reserves are examples of the hanging oak woods that cling to many valley sides throughout mid-Wales. They hold the typical species, Pied Flycatcher, Wood Warbler, and Redstart. Above the woodlands there are patches of moorland and bracken-covered slopes. Below, fast-flowing rivers and streams.

Dinas is a compact reserve offering a circular walk and is likely to produce all the specialist birds of the area, including Red Kites. It can, however, be muddy and there are some steep and rugged sections to the path, so good footwear is recommended.

KEY BIRDS
ALL YEAR: Sparrowhawk, Buzzard, Peregrine, Red Kite, Goosander, Woodcock, Green, Great Spotted and Lesser Spotted Woodpeckers, Red Grouse (very few), Grey Wagtail, Dipper, Raven, Willow Tit.
SPRING AND SUMMER: Common Sandpiper, Cuckoo, Tree Pipit, Redstart, Whinchat, Wheatear, Ring Ouzel, Wood Warbler, Spotted and Pied Flycatchers.

ACCESS
OS MAP: **147** REF: **SN 788 472**
Situated north of Llandovery, on minor roads. From the A483, turn off for Rhandirmwyn, and the reserves are on this road beyond the village. Car parking is at the Dinas reserve, and details of the walk available on the Gwenffrwd reserve are available from here.

11   DYFFRYN WOODS

RSPB RESERVE

22 ha (54 acres)

Oak wood and heather moorland holds the typical upland species of mid-Wales. Visit in spring or early summer for the best opportunities for locating the breeding birds. There is a circular walk of about 1.6 km (1 mile).

KEY BIRDS
ALL YEAR: Red Kite, Peregrine, Buzzard, Grey Wagtail, Woodcock, woodpeckers, Dipper, Raven.
SPRING AND SUMMER: Cuckoo, Redstart, Whinchat, Stonechat, Wheatear, Wood Warbler, Pied Flycatcher.

ACCESS
OS MAP: **148** REF: **SN 980 672**
Just south of Rhayader, park in a layby on the A470 Rhayader to Brecon road. Close to Gigrin Farm.

12   GIGRIN FARM

81 ha (200 acres)

Gigrin is the place to see Red Kites as nowhere else offers such close views. Food is placed in front of a row of hides each afternoon. With a captivating display of agility, kites twist and turn, plucking food from the ground with their talons. This spectacle is best viewed in winter, when more than 100 kites have been present. It can be popular, particularly at weekends, so arrive early.

The farm has much to offer throughout the year. Walks winding through the Welsh upland habitats enable many of the typical species of the area to be seen, including Pied Flycatcher and Whinchat. There is the chance of a Goshawk at any time of year, and in winter Bramblings are sometimes attracted to the farm's feeding station.

KEY BIRDS
ALL YEAR: Red Kite, Buzzard, Peregrine, Goshawk, Raven, Sparrowhawk, woodpeckers, Grey Wagtail.
SPRING AND SUMMER: Redstart, Pied Flycatcher, Wood Warbler, Whinchat, Wheatear.
WINTER: Farmland and woodland birds including Brambling and Fieldfare.

ACCESS
OS MAP: **147** REF: **SN 990 678**
The farm is on the outskirts of Rhayader, off the A470. Feeding is at 2pm daily in winter, and at 3pm when the clocks go forward until they change again in October.

FACILITIES
There are hides with wheelchair access, plus a shop and visitor centre.

13 CORS CARON

NNR

101 ha (250 acres)

A raised bog with scrub, a reed bed, wet grassland, woodland and river, not far from Tregaron. A good range of birds breed here including Redstart and Grasshopper Warbler. In winter wildfowl and hunting raptors are attracted to the reserve. Red Kites may be seen all year. There is a good path along the site of an old railway line, which has an observation tower giving good views across the bog.

KEY BIRDS

ALL YEAR: Teal, Red Kite, Goshawk, Sparrowhawk, Buzzard, Peregrine, Water Rail, Snipe, Stonechat, Raven.

SPRING AND SUMMER: Marsh Harrier, Redshank, Tree Pipit, Whinchat, Grasshopper Warbler.

AUTUMN AND WINTER: Whooper Swan, occasional parties of Bewick's Swans, Wigeon, Tufted Duck, Pochard, Goldeneye, Hen Harrier, Golden Plover, Jack Snipe.

ACCESS

OS MAP: **135/146** REF: **SN 697 632**

The reserve is directly north of Tregaron, and accessed off the B4343.

14 LAKE VYRNWY

RSPB RESERVE

7,285 ha (18,000 acres)

At 8 km (5 miles) in length, this is the largest artificial lake in Wales. Although the lake holds plenty of interesting birds, it is the extensive surrounding area with its mix of habitats that range from moorland to deciduous woodland and conifer plantations, which are of most interest.

The uplands support breeding raptors, Ring Ouzel and Red Grouse, whilst in the woodlands a good mix of species include Long-eared Owl, Wood Warbler, Redstart, Crossbill and Pied Flycatcher. Late spring is one of the optimum times to visit for breeding birds. In winter the lake is the centre of attention for its wintering wildfowl.

There are a number of trails, some starting at the southern end at the visitor centre, and of varying length. At the northern end of the lake, the Rhiwargor Island trail takes around an hour and is likely to produce a good range of birds.

KEY BIRDS

ALL YEAR: Great Crested Grebe, Red Grouse, Teal, Goosander, Sparrowhawk, Buzzard, Black Grouse (very few), Peregrine, Goshawk, Siskin, Woodcock, Long-eared Owl, Great Spotted and Green Woodpeckers, Kingfisher, Grey Wagtail, Dipper, Crossbill, Redpoll, Goldcrest, Raven.

SPRING AND SUMMER: Hen Harrier, Merlin and Short-eared Owl, Golden Plover, Curlew, Common Sandpiper, chance of Nightjar, Cuckoo, Redstart, Whinchat, Stonechat, Wheatear, Wood Warbler, various woodland warblers, Pied and Spotted Flycatchers, Ring Ouzel.

AUTUMN AND WINTER: Whooper Swan, Goldeneye, Wigeon, Tufted Duck, Pochard and often Green Sandpiper and Greenshank.

ACCESS

OS MAP: **125** REF: **SJ 020 193**

Situated south of Bala, and west of Welshpool, and reached by minor roads.

FACILITIES

The visitor centre is at the southern end of the lake and is open from 10.30am to 4.30pm daily from April to December, and from December to April at weekends only, at the same times. Various sites are accessible to wheelchairs.

15 YNYS-HIR

RSPB RESERVE

405 ha (1,000 acres)

Varied habitats with an equally varied birdlife can be found in this attractive reserve at the head of the Dyfi estuary.

In winter Greenland White-fronted Geese graze the salt marsh and farmland. Red Kite and Goshawk may be encountered and there is a heronry. The Breakwater and Saltings hides can be good for roosting waders on high tides.

A complete circuit of the reserve is about 8 km (5 miles), so allow at least half a day for this. Alternatively, there are much shorter routes for the less energetic.

KEY BIRDS

ALL YEAR: Grey Heron, Red-breasted Merganser, Sparrowhawk, Buzzard, chance of Red Kite and Goshawk, Snipe, Green, Great Spotted and Lesser Spotted Woodpeckers, Grey Wagtail, Dipper, Kingfisher, Raven.

SPRING AND SUMMER: A few passage waders including Whimbrel; Common Sandpiper, Tree Pipit, Redstart, Whinchat, Wheatear, Grasshopper Warbler, Wood Warbler, Spotted and Pied Flycatcher.
AUTUMN AND WINTER: Various passage waders. Greenland White-fronted Goose, Wigeon, Teal, Pintail, Shoveler, Pochard, Goldeneye, Tufted Duck, Hen Harrier, Merlin, Peregrine, Water Rail, estuarine waders plus Golden Plover, Siskin.

ACCESS
OS MAP: 135 REF: SN 682 963
Reserve is opposite a watermill at Furnace Bridge on the A487 Machynlleth to Aberystwyth road.

FACILITIES
There is a visitor centre, hides, and limited wheelchair access.

16 MAWDDACH VALLEY (COED GARTH GELL)

RSPB RESERVE
46 ha (114 acres)
A spring or early summer visit is best, with one of the biggest attractions to this reserve being its walks. Close by, the estuary adds birding interest, and information on birdwatching in the area can be acquired at the RSPB information centre next to the toll bridge at Penmaenpool.

KEY BIRDS
ALL YEAR: Tawny Owl, Lesser Spotted Woodpecker, Grey Wagtail, Dipper, Buzzard, Raven, Willow Tit.
SPRING AND SUMMER: Tree Pipit, Redstart, Wood Warbler, Pied Flycatcher, and a variety of woodland birds.
AUTUMN AND WINTER: Thrushes, Siskin, Redpoll plus most interest on estuary for wildfowl and waders.

ACCESS
OS MAP: 124 REF: SH 687 191
The wood is reached by parking in the layby on the A496 opposite the Borthwnog Hall Hotel at the head of the estuary. The RSPB information point is by the toll bridge at Penmaenpool.

17 BARDSEY ISLAND

BIRD OBSERVATORY / BARDSEY ISLAND TRUST
17 ha (44 acres)
Home to Bardsey Bird Observatory, this small island off the Lleyn Peninsula is famed not only for birds, but as a burial ground for thousands of saints. The island, with cliffs up to 168 m (550 feet), is predominantly small fields and areas of bracken, scrub and boulder beaches. At its southern end there is a lighthouse linked to the island by a narrow isthmus.

Birding interest is maintained from early spring through to late autumn, with migrants the main attraction. Rarities are found annually.

The summer months offer breeding seabirds and resident Choughs, the island being one of the Welsh strongholds for this species.

KEY BIRDS
ALL YEAR: Cormorant, Shag, Kestrel, Peregrine, Lapwing, Little Owl, Rock Pipit, Chough, Raven.
SPRING: Arrival of seabirds. Passage migrants include a few waders plus Skylark, Tree Pipit, Whinchat, Black Redstart, Redstart, Wheatear, Ring Ouzel, thrushes, various warblers, flycatchers and chance of scarce migrants such as Common Rosefinch or Hoopoe.
SUMMER: Fulmar, Manx Shearwater, European Storm Petrel (scarce), Oystercatcher, Lesser Black-backed and Greater Black-backed Gulls, Kittiwake, Guillemot, Razorbill, Puffin.
AUTUMN: As for spring with a chance of rarities, and offshore seabird passage may involve skuas, terns and shearwaters. Late autumn sees influxes of thrushes, pipits and finches.

ACCESS
OS MAP: 123 REF: SH 11 21
Bardsey is reached by boat from Pwllheli. Most visitors stay on the island, however day trips are organized by the Bardsey Island Trust.

FACILITIES
Accommodation is available at the observatory. The boat leaves Pwllheli Marina on Saturday mornings throughout the season. Bookings to Mrs A. Normand, 46 Maudlin Drive, Teignmouth, Devon TQ14 8SB. Farmhouse accommodation is available from the Bardsey Island Trust, details from Coed Anna, Nanhoron, Pwllheli, Gwynedd LL54 6AB; tel: 01758 730740.

18 NEWBOROUGH WARREN

NNR
648 ha (1,601 acres)
This large reserve on the south-east tip of
Anglesey offers views back towards the
mountains of Snowdonia, and delightful walks
through forest, sand dunes and along the sea and
estuary shore.

A variety of habitats exist within and just
outside the reserve. One of the top spots for birds
is Malltraeth Pool, lying immediately north of
Newborough Forest. The pool lies alongside the
head of the Cefni Estuary. The pool is a good
place for passage waders in spring and autumn,
while the estuary in autumn and winter attracts a
range of wildfowl and waders.

Newborough Forest has one of the largest
winter roosts of Ravens in Europe. On the
southern side, the forest gives way to sand dunes
that are of most interest in summer for a few
breeding species, and for flora.

Towards the estuary on the south-west tip of
the reserve is a peninsula and small rocky isle,
the latter a nesting site for Shags and
Cormorants. The Ynys Llanddwyn peninsula is a
good site from which to scan the sea for seaduck,
divers and grebes in winter, and in summer
various species of tern can be seen.

There is a network of paths throughout the
area, and a full day is needed to explore the area
thoroughly.

KEY BIRDS
ALL YEAR: Little Grebe, Cormorant, Shag, Teal,
Shelduck, Sparrowhawk, Peregrine, Buzzard, Little
Egret, Crossbill, Raven.
SPRING AND SUMMER: Passage waders on pool
may include Whimbrel, Greenshank, godwits,
perhaps Spotted Redshank. Among the dunes
Whinchat, Stonechat, Grasshopper Warbler,
Whitethroat; offshore, Common, Arctic, Roseate
and Sandwich Terns.
AUTUMN AND WINTER: Passage waders as in
spring plus Ruff, Curlew Sandpiper and Little
Stint, a range of estuarine waders. Wildfowl
include Pintail, Shoveler, Tufted Duck,
Goldeneye, Whooper and Bewick's Swans.
Offshore, chance of seaduck, divers and grebes;
hunting raptors in dunes may include Merlin,
Short-eared Owl, Hen Harrier, Kingfisher,
Woodcock, Osprey. Chance of Barn Owl.

ACCESS
OS MAP: 114 REF: SH 414 672
After crossing over the Brittania Bridge on to
Anglesey on the A55, turn on to the A5 then
the A4080 west to Newborough. The dunes and
forest can be accessed from this road. Continue
on to a bridge at the head of the estuary just
before entering Malltraeth. The Cefni Estuary
and Malltraeth Pool can be viewed from the
embankment separating the pool from the
estuary at this point.

19 VALLEY LAKES

RSPB RESERVE
This small reserve on Anglesey has a large
freshwater lake as its centrepiece. There is a
nature trail that extends for around 3 km
(2 miles). Wintering wildfowl are the main
attraction, along with a few breeding species.

KEY BIRDS
ALL YEAR: Grebes, Grey Heron, Gadwall, Teal,
Ruddy Duck, Tufted Duck, Pochard,
Oystercatcher.
SPRING AND SUMMER: Common Tern, Sedge
Warbler, Reed Warbler, a few wildfowl.
AUTUMN AND WINTER: Wildfowl include
Shoveler, Goldeneye. Hen Harrier and Short-
eared Owl are possible.

ACCESS
OS MAP: 114 REF: SH 378 853
The reserve is just west of the A5, reached on
minor roads from Caergeiliog.

20 CEMLYN LAGOON

NORTH WALES WILDLIFE TRUST
25 ha (62 acres)
This brackish lagoon protected from the sea by a
shingle ridge is not to be missed if visiting
Anglesey in summer. The islands on the lagoon
are used as a nesting site for hundreds of pairs of
terns. Sandwich with lesser numbers of Arctic
and Common Terns nest. Roseate Terns used to
breed, but are now a scarce but regular visitor.
The colony can be viewed from the shingle ridge,
but care should be taken not to scare the birds. It
is best to stand below the ridge and look over.

During passage periods migrant waders drop
in, and during winter a few wildfowl use the pool.

🦜 KEY BIRDS

SPRING AND SUMMER: Common, Sandwich, Arctic and chance of Roseate Terns. Black-headed Gull, Shelduck, Red-breasted Merganser.
AUTUMN AND WINTER: Passage waders and in winter a few wildfowl including Shoveler, Goldeneye, Wigeon, Purple Sandpiper on headland.

⛵ ACCESS

OS MAP: 114 REF: SH 337 932
From the A5025 at Tregele, take the minor road signed to the lagoon.

21 CONWY

RSPB RESERVE
37 ha (90 acres)
Created by the RSPB, following the construction of the Conwy tunnel, the reserve is of interest throughout the year. During autumn and winter, large numbers of waders from the nearby Conwy estuary roost here, while passage waders favour the pools.

A good range of migrants can be expected during the spring and autumn, and for such a young reserve this site already has an impressive list of rarities. There are various good nature trails from 0.8 km (½ mile) to 3 km (2 miles).

🦜 KEY BIRDS

ALL YEAR: Lapwing, Redshank, Skylark, Reed Bunting.
SPRING AND AUTUMN: Garganey, Yellow Wagtail, passage waders include Little Stint, Curlew Sandpiper, Spotted Redshank, godwits, Ruff, Green Sandpiper.
SUMMER: Little Ringed Plover, Reed Warbler.
WINTER: Wigeon, Shoveler, Teal, Goldeneye, Red-breasted Merganser, Water Rail, Kingfisher plus roosting estuarine waders, along with visiting raptors.

⛵ ACCESS

OS MAP: 115 REF: SH 799 771
Access from the A55 at exit signed to Conwy and Deganwy. Reserve open from 10am to 5pm daily except Christmas Day.

🏛 FACILITIES

There are good paths and hides accessible to wheelchairs, and a visitor centre.

22 POINT OF AYR

RSPB RESERVE
182 ha (450 acres)
Overlooking the Dee Estuary, this reserve comprises a large shingle spit, and salt marsh, mud flats and sand dunes. The Dee is important for its huge number of estuarine wildfowl and waders that stop off on passage and winter. During winter up to 20,000 waders, mostly Knot, Oystercatcher, Dunlin and Redshank, swarm over the mud flats. At high tide thousands of waders roost at the point, an impressive spectacle viewable from an RSPB hide.

Shelduck, Mallard, Wigeon and Pintail are joined by seaduck, mainly scoters and sawbills, and there is usually a sprinkling of divers, grebes and often auks. Snow Bunting and Twite feed along the shoreline and salt marsh, and are sometimes joined by Shorelark and Lapland Bunting. Seawatching in autumn can, in the right weather, provide Sabine's Gull, Leach's Petrel and Grey Phalarope. Seawatching is best from the lighthouse.

A visit a couple of hours prior to high tide in autumn or winter is recommended.

🦜 KEY BIRDS

ALL YEAR: Cormorant, Shelduck, Oystercatcher, Ringed Plover, Redshank, Kestrel, Stonechat.
SPRING AND AUTUMN: Passage waders and a few passerine migrants such as Whinchat and Wheatear. In autumn seabird passage may include Gannet, Fulmar, Great and Arctic Skuas, Manx Shearwater, plus in stormy weather the chance of a Leach's Petrel, Sabine's Gull, or phalarope.
SUMMER: In late summer pre-migratory roost of Sandwich and Common Terns with chance of Roseate and Black Terns joining them.
WINTER: Divers and grebes, a few auks, gulls, Light-bellied Brent Goose, Wigeon, Teal, Pintail, Shoveler, Scaup, Common Scoter, Goldeneye, Red-breasted Merganser, Hen Harrier, Merlin, Peregrine, Golden Plover, Grey Plover, Knot, Black-tailed Godwit, Sanderling, Dunlin, Curlew, Turnstone, Short-eared Owl, Snow Bunting, Twite, chance of Shorelark and Lapland Bunting.

⛵ ACCESS

OS MAP: 116 REF: SJ 140 840
East of Prestatyn, turn off the A548 at a roundabout to Talacre to enter the reserve.

SOUTH STACK
RSPB (316 ha/781 acres)

Chough, Peregrine and impressive seabird colonies combine to make South Stack a popular reserve during spring and summer. The cliffs here are backed by maritime heath, now a rare habitat in Britain important for its flora. This is a great reserve to watch Choughs at any time of year, but particularly in spring and early summer when they can be seen regularly,

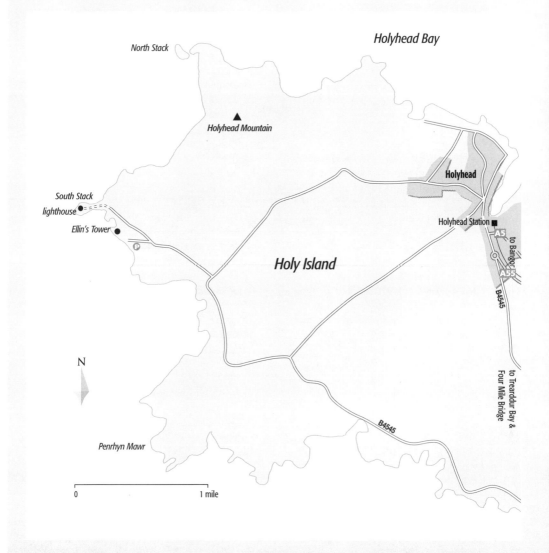

patrolling the cliffs. Early mornings often see them feeding around the café or on the grassy slopes and heath near Ellin's Tower. In winter they can frequently be found feeding in the adjacent fields. Peregrines hunt the cliffs, often terrorizing the massed ranks of auks and Kittiwakes nesting on the cliff ledges.

Guillemots far outnumber other species including Razorbills, Kittiwakes and Shags on the cliffs. Puffins nest in suitable sites and are easily seen albeit at a distance. A colony of Herring Gulls inhabit the perimeter of the lighthouse (built in 1809), which can be reached by a long flight of steps. These steps offer a good vantage point when looking for Chough, and the cliffs here in early summer are covered in a blaze of colour, notably Kidney Vetch, Spring Squill and Thrift. The nationally rare Spotted Rock-rose grows near Ellin's Tower, along with a variety of interesting plants.

The seabirds are best viewed from Ellin's Tower, which also has live pictures of the seabird colony beamed to a television set. A few migrants appear in spring and autumn and a number of rarities have occurred, most notably a Black Lark. During autumn, seawatching can be productive. Manx Shearwater and Gannet are easily seen, and in stormy weather, skuas, shearwaters and large movements of auks are possible.

KEY BIRDS
ALL YEAR: Buzzard, Peregrine, Stonechat, Chough, Raven, Rock Pipit.
SPRING AND SUMMER: Fulmar, Shag, Guillemot, Razorbill, Puffin, Herring Gull, Kittiwake, Whitethroat.
AUTUMN: Seabird passage including Manx Shearwater, Gannet, skuas, chance of Sooty Shearwater and auks. A few passerine migrants.
WINTER: Residents joined by Merlin, and chance of Hen Harrier and Hooded Crow.

ACCESS
OS MAP: 114 REF: SH 205 823
From Holyhead on Anglesey, drive towards Holyhead Mountain, the reserve is well signposted.

FACILITIES
There is an information centre in Ellin's Tower with live television pictures of the seabirds. It is open daily from 11am to 5pm from Easter to September. Nearby, next to the car park, is a café and toilet facilities.

Guillemot
Uria aalge

Guillemots feed mainly on small fish, which they catch by diving from the surface of the sea. They regularly feed in groups. Indeed, this is one of our most sociable seabirds, with nesting pairs on average getting closer to their neighbours than any other bird, some less than 5 cm (2 in) apart in some colonies.

At South Stack, Guillemots are easily seen on the cliff ledges from where they rear their chicks. The young normally fledge on calm evenings when the chicks throw themselves off the cliff ledge and drop down to the sea below. Once re-united with the male parent, they swim out to sea. The males may care for their chick for a further 12 weeks before the chick becomes independent. Females remain on the cliff ledges after fledging for a further three weeks.

NORTHERN ENGLAND

The coast dominates birding in the north, from the classic migrant hot spots of the east coast headlands of Spurn and Flamborough, to the wader-rich estuaries of the west coast. Morecambe Bay, the Dee and, up on the borders, the Solway swarm with waders and wildfowl escaping the Arctic freeze for our milder winter. There are few more spectacular sites in British birding than watching skeins of geese against a winter sky, or great flocks of waders wheeling over vast mud flats.

Visit Leighton Moss in spring and you may be treated to the booming call of a Bittern or a Marsh Harrier quartering the reed bed. The moors and dales resound to the bubbling songs of the Curlew and the plaintive cry of Golden Plover. In the valleys, rushing streams are home to Dipper.

Autumn witnesses the migration of many birds to the east coast. Here, if the east wind blows, the large number of migrants that flood in and out of the country from the continent are joined by much rarer relatives. There is the possibility of sighting a Firecrest or Yellow-browed Warbler flitting about a buckthorn bush on Spurn, or a Red-breasted Flycatcher sallying back and forth from a sycamore on Flamborough Head.

The north is home to England's finest seabird city, the Farne Islands. Each year thousands of visitors flock to these low-lying islands off the Northumberland coast. Here, Arctic Terns, Puffins and a host of other species can be viewed nesting just inches from the paths. Travel north and you reach Coquet Island, an RSPB reserve and home to a thriving colony of Roseate Tern, one of our rarest breeding seabirds. Travel south from the Farnes and you reach another big attraction, the great, east coast seabird city of Bempton Cliffs, which teems with life in summer.

Workington
Whitehaven
21

Isle of Man
○ Andreas
Ballaugh ○ A3 ○ Ramsey
Peel ○ A4
St John's ○ A1 ○ Laxey
Port Erin ○ A5 □ Douglas
Calf of Man **37** ○ Castletown

Barrow-in-Furne
Isle of Wal.

B

KEY

1) Frampton Marsh
2) Freiston Shore
3) Gibraltar Point
4) Tetney Marshes
5) Spurn Head
6) Blacktoft Sands
7) Fairburn Ings
8) Wheldrake Ings –
   Lower Derwent Valley
9) Hornsea Mere
10) Anglers Country Park
   and Wintersett
   Reservoir
11) Flamborough Head
12) Bempton Cliffs

13) Filey Brigg Bird
   Observatory
14) Teesmouth
15) Druridge Bay
16) Coquet Island
17) Lindisfarne
18) Campfield Marsh
19) Farne Islands
20) Geltsdale
21) St Bees Head
22) Haweswater
23) Hodbarrow
24) Walney Island
25) Morecambe Bay
26) Leighton Moss

27) Heysham Nature
   Reserve
28) Martin Mere
29) Hilbre
30) Gayton Sands
31) Marshside
32) Pendle Hill
33) Seaforth
34) Frodsham and the
   Weaver Bend
35) Sandbach Flashes
36) Pennington Flash
37) Calf of Man Bird
   Observatory

MERSEYS

SCOTLAND

Berwick-upon-Tweed

Coldstream

17

19

A1

A697

16
15

Otterburn

Morpeth

Newbiggin-by-the-Sea

A68

NORTHUMBERLAND

The Borders

Ponteland

NEWCASTLE UPON TYNE

TYNE & WEAR

Longtown

18

Brampton

A69

Consett

A692

A1

Washington

Carlisle

20

A96

M6

DURHAM

Durham

Peterlee

A1(M)

A19

Hartlepool

14

CUMBRIA

Penrith

Appleby-in-Westmoreland

Bishop Auckland

Stockton-on-Tees

Middlesbrough

A66

A688

Whitby

A66

Brough

Darlington

A66

A171

22

Ambleside

A685

Scotch Corner

A172

North York Moors

Lake District

Windermere

Hawes

A1

Northallerton

A684

Kendal

A170

Scarborough

Ulverston

A590

26

Kirkby Lonsdale

NORTH YORKSHIRE

Thirsk

A170

13

25

A683

Ripon

A61

Malton

12

11 Flamborough Head

24 Morecambe

Lancaster

A65

A19

A64

Bridlington

27

Skipton

Harrogate

A59

A614

EAST RIDING OF YORKSHIRE

32

A59

A1(M)

A59

York

9

LANCASHIRE

Keighley

Tadcaster

8

Hornsea

Preston

BRADFORD

LEEDS

Market Weighton

Beverley

7

Garforth

A63

M62

A63

HULL

Burnley

WEST YORKSHIRE

Goole

6

Blackburn

Huddersfield

Wakefield

Pontefract

Scunthorpe

5 Spurn Head

A59

Rochdale

M62

M18

10

M1

Thorne

M180

Grimsby

4

Southport

31

M61

Bolton

A62

Barnsley

A159

Doncaster

28

M58

36

A629

MANCHESTER

Rotherham

Gainsborough

Louth

A16

Crosby

33

LIVERPOOL

M62

SHEFFIELD

Lincoln

A46

A158

Birkenhead

Warrington

SOUTH YORKSHIRE

A57

A156

30

M56

Knutsford

A16

River

Runcorn

34

Macclesfield

LINCOLNSHIRE

Skegness

Ellesmere Port

Chester

35

M6

Congleton

3

WALES

CHESHIRE

Sleaford

Boston

A15

A52

Grantham

A17

2

A1

1

A52

The Wash

A15

Holbeach

A1

N

0 10 20 30 40 miles

0 10 20 30 40   60 km

89

1   FRAMPTON MARSH

RSPB RESERVE
170 ha (420 acres)
Frampton Marsh lies 6 km (4 miles) south-east of Boston, and comprises salt marsh and mud flats on the shores of the Wash. The mud flats from autumn through to spring attract all the typical waders of the Wash.

A visit between autumn and spring arriving two hours before high tide will provide the best birding. The marsh lies between the River Witham (The Haven) and the River Welland. The Haven Bank and sea banks give good views across the marshes.

KEY BIRDS
ALL YEAR: Black-headed Gull, Redshank, Oystercatcher, Barn Owl.
SPRING AND AUTUMN: Passage waders plus estuarine waders and wildfowl as for winter.
SUMMER: Marsh Harrier, Black-headed Gull colony, Common Tern, Reed Bunting, Meadow Pipit, Skylark.
WINTER: Dunlin, Grey Plover, Curlew, Golden Plover, Bar-tailed Godwit, Knot, Dark-bellied Brent Goose, Wigeon, Teal, Shelduck, Hen Harrier, Short-eared Owl, Merlin, Peregrine, Linnet, Twite, chance of Lapland Bunting.

ACCESS
OS MAP: 131 REF: TR 364 385
From A16 south-east of Boston, turn off for Frampton where the marshes are signposted.

2   FREISTON SHORE

RSPB RESERVE
700 ha (1730 acres)
Just east of Boston this reserve is north of the RSPB's Frampton Marshes reserve, and encompasses a similar salt marsh and mud flat habitat. As a result similar species can be found.

A recent interesting development at this reserve has been the reclamation of agricultural land to salt marsh. A visit at, or a little before high tide is likely to be most productive, particularly in autumn and winter.

KEY BIRDS
ALL YEAR: Redshank, Oystercatcher, Ringed Plover, Corn Bunting, Tree Sparrow.

SPRING AND AUTUMN: Variety of passage waders, possible Little and Mediterranean Gulls, Little Egret, plus a chance of Gannet, skuas and terns offshore, and passerine migrants such as Redstart and Pied Flycatcher in autumn in areas of cover.
SUMMER: Avocet, Little Ringed Plover plus non-breeding waders such as godwits.
WINTER: Dark-bellied Brent Goose, Wigeon, Teal, Shelduck, estuarine waders, Short-eared Owl, Hen Harrier, Merlin, Twite, Lapland Bunting.

ACCESS
OS MAP: 131 REF: TF 397 424
From the A52 east of Boston, turn off to Freiston Shore at Haltoft End, and follow signs. There are two car parks.

3   GIBRALTAR POINT

NNR / LINCOLNSHIRE WILDLIFE TRUST
430 ha (1,063 acres)
Located on the northern shore of the Wash, much of the reserve's dunes are covered in sea buckthorn scrub. Freshwater pools, marsh and salt marsh are further habitats attracting birds. Gibraltar Point is one of the east coast's prime migration watchpoints.

To witness migrational movements, the right conditions are needed, and an early morning visit is ideal. Poor visibility and easterly or south-easterly winds can produce falls, which might include drift migrants. During April and early May a diverse array of migrants may be seen. During autumn, migration is more protracted, lasting from August through to November. Gibraltar Point attracts rarities annually.

Winter provides plenty of interest – waders use the spit as a high-tide roost, notably Knot, along with various other estuarine species.

KEY BIRDS
SPRING: Migrants include warblers, flycatchers and chats. Pipits, hirundines and thrush movements; rarer visitors in suitable weather conditions include Bluethroat and Red-backed Shrike. Waders in the Wash.
SUMMER: Little Tern breed. Returning waders visiting the mere may include Spotted Redshank, Wood Sandpiper and Curlew Sandpiper.
AUTUMN: As for spring with scarce drift migrants on easterlies such as Wryneck, Icterine Warbler, Barred Warbler, Bluethroat and Red-breasted

Flycatcher. Skuas, gulls, wildfowl and waders
in the Wash.
WINTER: Estuarine waders with large numbers of
Knot, Hen Harrier and Short-eared Owl, Twite,
Snow Bunting, divers, grebes and seaduck.

⛵ ACCESS
OS MAP: **122** REF: **TF 556 580**
Open from dawn to dusk, and signposted from
Skegness town centre. Take the coast road
alongside the golf course to the car park at the
end.

🏠 FACILITIES
Reserve centre and toilets. Field centre offers
courses and accommodation. Details from
Gibraltar Point Field Station, Skegness,
Lincolnshire PE24 4SU. Wheelchair access is
possible in the vicinity of the visitor centre.

4   TETNEY MARSHES

RSPB RESERVE
1,274 ha (3,150 acres)
Close to the mouth of the Humber, Tetney
Marshes is an area of inter-tidal sand flats, salt
marsh and buckthorn covered dunes. Estuarine
wildfowl and waders plus the chance of hunting
raptors are the winter attractions. A few passage
waders and migrants may be seen, while in
summer there is a large colony of Little Tern and
a variety of breeding waders.

Visitors should view only from the sea wall on
this reserve to avoid undue disturbance,
particularly during the breeding season.

🦜 KEY BIRDS
ALL YEAR: Cormorant, Shelduck, Oystercatcher,
Ringed Plover, Redshank, Skylark, Meadow Pipit.
SPRING AND AUTUMN: Passage waders.
SUMMER: Common Tern, Little Tern.
WINTER: Red-throated Diver, Dark-bellied Brent
Goose, Common Scoter, Red-breasted
Merganser, Wigeon, Teal, Golden and Grey
Plovers, Knot, Dunlin, Curlew, Bar-tailed
Godwit, chance of Snow Bunting.

⛵ ACCESS
OS MAP: **113** REF: **TA 345 025**
South of Cleethorpes, the reserve is reached by
turning off the A1031 to Tetney Lock and entering
via the entrance gate to the east of Tetney Lock.

5   SPURN HEAD

YORKSHIRE WILDLIFE TRUST / BIRD OBSERVATORY
112 ha (277 acres)
A sand peninsula covered in sea buckthorn and
marram grass stretching south into the Humber
estuary for 5.3 km (3½ miles), Spurn Head is
renowned as one of Europe's top migration
watchpoints.

The Neck is a good spot to view visible
migration as migrants get funnelled along to this
thin strip of land. Early mornings are best.
However, on really good days, migrants may be
on the move throughout the day. If a fall occurs
the peninsula can be heaving with birds, easterly
winds usually being the catalyst to provoke these
mass arrivals. Seawatching can be good in
autumn with the chance of Leach's and European
Storm Petrels and often in late autumn Little
Auks. In winter the Humber estuary and North
Sea sides of the spit have offshore divers, grebes
and seaduck.

Just before the entrance gate, a hide overlooks
a scrape attractive to passage waders, and there is
a hide overlooking a high-tide wader roost at
Chalk Bank, which is two-thirds of the way
along the spit.

🦜 KEY BIRDS
SPRING AND AUTUMN: Migrants may include
Osprey, Wryneck, Nightingale, Bluethroat, chats,
thrushes, various warblers, Goldcrest, Firecrest,
flycatchers, finches and annually a bagful of
rarities. Passing seabirds, Whimbrel, Greenshank,
in autumn, passage waders and Jack Snipe.
North-east to north-westerly winds in autumn
may produce petrels, Sooty Shearwater, skuas,
auks and Little Auk.
WINTER: In the Humber and offshore, divers,
grebes, wildfowl and estuarine waders.

⛵ ACCESS
OS MAP: **113** REF: **TA 417 151**
Take the 1033 from Hull to Patrington, then the
B1445 to Easington. A minor road then takes
you to Spurn.

🏠 FACILITIES
The bird observatory, and information centre are
open weekends, Bank Holidays and school
holidays except Fridays. There are two hides and
toilets, and limited disabled access.

6 BLACKTOFT SANDS

RSPB RESERVE

202 ha (500 acres)

A tidal reed bed, lagoons and grazing marsh at the head of the Humber, Blacktoft is best in autumn when it attracts a good variety of waders. A visit at high tide is recommended as many of the birds feed out on the Humber at low water.

Reed-bed specialities include Bearded Tit, and recently Bitterns have made a comeback. Wildfowl numbers build up in winter, and Pink-footed Geese are often seen flying overhead.

KEY BIRDS

ALL YEAR: Bittern, Shelduck, Gadwall, Shoveler, Barn Owl, Water Rail, Redshank, Bearded Tit.
SPRING AND AUTUMN: Occasional Garganey, Marsh Harrier (breeds), Hobby, estuarine and passage waders, Little Gull, Common and Black Terns, Yellow Wagtail, Whinchat and Wheatear.
SUMMER: Grasshopper, Sedge and Reed Warblers, Avocet, Short-eared Owl.
WINTER: Wildfowl, Hen Harrier, Peregrine, Merlin, good variety of waders.

ACCESS

OS MAP: 112 REF: SE 843 232

Open daily from 9am. Take the A161 east from Goole to Swinefleet, turn left for Reedness and continue to Ousefleet, the reserve is 2.5 km (1½ miles) beyond the village, on the left.

FACILITIES

Six hides, visitor reception; wheelchair access.

7 FAIRBURN INGS

RSPB RESERVE

275 ha (680 acres)

Nestled below the village of Fairburn, this reserve comprises lakes formed through mining subsidence, bordered by deciduous woodland, pools and grazing marsh.

During passage periods a few waders and passerines pass through, whilst various species of tern and Little Gull are regular. A good range of breeding birds can be found in summer, whilst in winter, main interest surrounds waterfowl with regular visits by Whooper Swan and in cold weather the chance of sawbills such as Smew.

KEY BIRDS

ALL YEAR: Great Crested and Little Grebes, Kingfisher, wildfowl, Snipe.
SPRING AND AUTUMN: On passage, Garganey, Osprey, Common, Arctic and Black Terns, Little Gull, Yellow Wagtail, Redstart, Whinchat and Wheatear; passage waders.
WINTER: Occasional visits from rarer grebes, divers and sawbills. Whooper Swans roost, Goosander, Wigeon, Teal, Pintail, Goldeneye, Ruddy Duck, Redpoll and Siskin; gull roost.

ACCESS

OS MAP: 105 REF: SE 452 277

Easily reached off the A1 at Fairburn north of M62 junction.

FACILITIES

Three main parking areas, an information centre and hides open from 10am to 5pm at weekends and Bank Holidays. There is some wheelchair access.

8 WHELDRAKE INGS – LOWER DERWENT VALLEY

NNR / YORKSHIRE WILDLIFE TRUST

The Lower Derwent Valley has in recent years become one of the north's prime birding locations. A series of meadows, pasture and woodland with the former seasonally flooded ensures a wide diversity of birds. Thousands of wildfowl winter in the valley, whilst in summer a variety of waders breed.

Peak times for a visit are between December and March when large numbers of birds use the floods, or in May and early June for breeding species. Other sites in the valley worth visiting include Duffield Carrs, where there are two hides, and Bank Island.

KEY BIRDS

ALL YEAR: Gadwall, Curlew, Lapwing, Snipe, Redshank, Goshawk, Barn Owl plus common grassland and woodland species.
SPRING AND SUMMER: Breeding wildfowl and waders including Garganey and Ruff. Corncrake, Spotted Crake and Quail are sometimes heard.
WINTER: Bewick's and Whooper Swans, Greylag Goose, Shoveler, Wigeon, Teal, Golden Plover, Curlew, Snipe, occasional Jack Snipe, Short-eared Owl, large gull roost.

ACCESS
OS MAP: **105** REF: **SE 691 444**

Nine kilometres (6 miles) south-east of York, the valley runs for 18.5 km (12 miles). Travel east through the village of Wheldrake, and after a sharp right-hand bend, take a minor road on the left that leads to a small car park and bridge across the river.

OS MAP: **105** REF: **SE 691 448**

Bank Island car park is 0.8 km (½ mile) south-east of Wheldrake on the Wheldrake Thorganby road.

OS MAP: **105** REF: **SE 697 367**

North Duffield Carrs is about 1.6 km (1 mile) east of North Duffield off the A163.

FACILITIES
There are six hides at Wheldrake. Two hides at North Duffield have wheelchair access. Bank Island has two hides and a viewing platform.

9 HORNSEA MERE

LNR

235 ha (580 acres)

This large shallow lake just a mile from the Yorkshire coast is known for its wintering wildfowl and passage migrants.

In winter, seaduck, divers and grebes are regular visitors, particularly after bad weather. Passage migrants are varied and include plenty of passerines in the surrounding woodland and scrub, and regularly over the pool are Black Tern and Little Gull.

A footpath along the southern shore and a boating area on the eastern shore are the two best access points from which to view.

KEY BIRDS
ALL YEAR: Great Crested and Little Grebe, Shoveler, Ruddy Duck, Gadwall, Kingfisher.
SPRING: Passage migrants include Garganey, Marsh Harrier, Osprey, various waders, Little Gull, Common, Arctic and Black Terns, Yellow Wagtail, Whinchat, Wheatear.
SUMMER: Hirundines and Swift, Reed and Sedge Warblers, Little Gull.
AUTUMN: As for spring with Little Gull peaking in August.
WINTER: Occasional divers, rarer grebes and seaduck. Smew, Goldeneye, Goosander, and sometimes white-winged gulls. Low chance of Bearded Tit and Bittern in reeds.

ACCESS
OS MAP: **107** REF: **TA 200 450**

The mere is just east of Hornsea village beside the B1242. The footpath along the south side starts in Hull Road.

FACILITIES
Wheelchair users can view the Mere from the boating area car park.

10 ANGLERS COUNTRY PARK AND WINTERSETT RESERVOIR

COUNTRY PARK

These adjacent sites share the same birds with much interchange between them. The centrepiece to the country park is its lake. Both sites are at their best in winter when various wildfowl can be seen. There is also a large gull roost that regularly attracts white-winged gulls and Mediterranean Gulls.

A pleasant 2.5 km (1½ mile) walk takes you around the lake in the country park. There are various access points from which to view Wintersett. From the northern edge, right of the sailing club compound, follow the path to a bridge, which is another good vantage point.

KEY BIRDS
ALL YEAR: Grebes, Cormorant, Grey Heron, Tufted Duck, Kingfisher, Green and Great Spotted Woodpeckers, Lesser Spotted Woodpecker is very scarce, various other common woodland birds.
SPRING AND AUTUMN: A few passage waders, occasional Garganey, Osprey, Marsh Harrier, Common, Arctic and Black Terns, Wheatear.
SUMMER: Little Ringed Plover, Redshank, Lapwing, Cuckoo, warblers.
WINTER: Occasional divers and rarer grebes, Wigeon, Gadwall, Teal, Pintail, Pochard, Tufted Duck, Goldeneye, Goosander, Ruddy Duck, occasional Smew, Water Rail, Snipe, Jack Snipe Golden Plover, large gull roost including chance of Glaucous, Iceland and Mediterranean Gulls.

ACCESS
OS MAP: **110/111** REF: **SE 380 160**

Located south-east of Wakefield, leave the A638 on minor roads towards Ryhill. The sites are well signposted.

11 FLAMBOROUGH HEAD

Jutting 9 km (6 miles) out into the North Sea, Flamborough Head is one of Yorkshire's top birding spots. The heads, woods, hedgerows, fields and scrub attract migrants and rarities. The head itself is one of the best seawatching sites on the east coast with an enviable list of rare seabird records.

Key areas attractive to migrants include South Landing, a wooded valley on the south side of the head, and North Landing on the northern side which is overlooked by a cliff-top path. Further back down the headland, Danes Dyke, the wooded remains of an ancient line of fortification, runs north to south across the entire headland. The hedgerows, fields and scrub close to the headland, with Old Fall Hedgerow and Old Fall Plantation being further productive sites for passerine migrants.

Autumn is usually far more productive than spring. However, there are occasional falls that can bring with them scarce migrants such as Bluethroats and Red-back Shrikes among the chats, pipits, flycatchers and warblers. Seawatching in spring can be excellent with movements of divers, seaduck, skuas, terns, gulls and auks flying north.

The cliffs at the head have a few cliff-nesting seabirds in summer, whilst offshore on summer evenings Puffins, Guillemots and various other species can be watched passing on route to the big colonies at Bempton Cliffs nearby. From late July seabird passage starts to pick up. During August and September, shearwaters, skuas, petrels, terns, gulls and auks will all be on the move. From late October, if there are northerly gales, there are few better places to see Little Auks. These can occur in their hundreds.

In autumn, scarce and rare birds may include Yellow-browed and Pallas's Warblers. Later in the season, thrushes and finches arrive in large numbers.

🐦 KEY BIRDS
SPRING AND AUTUMN: Offshore divers, grebes and seaduck, both on the sea and moving offshore. Movements of Pomarine, Arctic and Great Skuas with Long-tailed in autumn. Little Gull, terns, auks, plus in autumn Sooty Shearwater and possible Cory's and Great Shearwaters, Manx Shearwater, Leach's and European Storm Petrels,

Sabine's Gull and from late October Little Auk. Passerine migrants include wagtails, hirundines, chats, flycatchers, warblers. On easterly winds chance of scarce drift migrants such as Bluethroat and Wryneck in spring, and in autumn Icterine, Barred and Yellow-browed Warblers, Red-breasted Flycatcher, Richard's and Tawny Pipits, Red-backed Shrike. Finches and thrushes in late autumn.
SUMMER: Breeding seabirds on the cliffs include Guillemot, Razorbill, Puffin, Fulmar, Shag and Kittiwake.
WINTER: Offshore divers grebes and seaduck. Seabird movements offshore from February. Purple Sandpiper on rocks.

🌲 ACCESS
OS MAP: **101** REF: **TA 250 700**
Flamborough is just north of Bridlington, the B1259 takes you to the head. Seawatching is best from below the lighthouse. North Landing is reached on a minor road from Flamborough village and is well signposted.

South Landing can also be reached from Flamborough Village. There is a car park here and various paths – this is one of the best spots for migrants and rarities in autumn. Alternatively, South Landing can be reached from the head by walking along Old Fall Hedgerow and continuing on while checking the plantation on route. Old Fall Hedgerow is set a little back from the head. A footpath leads south off the B1259.

12 BEMPTON CLIFFS

RSPB RESERVE
212 ha (524 acres)
At 4.8 km (3 miles) long, Bempton's high chalk cliffs are an impressive sight at any time of year, but visit in spring and summer and they swarm with seabirds. There is a large Gannet colony, the only one on the English mainland, and a colony of Kittiwakes. Guillemots, Razorbills and Puffins all nest. A cliff top walk takes you to various observation decks.

🐦 KEY BIRDS
SPRING AND SUMMER: Fulmar, Gannet, Shag, Kittiwake, Herring Gull, Guillemot, Razorbill, Puffin, plus migrants in spring.
AUTUMN: Chance of migrants.

ACCESS
OS MAP: **101** REF: **TA 197 738**
Bempton Cliffs are located on the northern side of Flamborough Head. From the B1229 at Bempton, turn down Cliff Lane. The reserve is well signposted, and is open at all times.

FACILITIES
A visitor centre opens daily in breeding season; viewing platforms, some with wheelchair access.

13 FILEY BRIGG BIRD OBSERVATORY

BIRD OBSERVATORY
416 ha (1,028 acres)
Filey Brigg is the next headland up the coast from Flamborough. Like Flamborough, it is a good seawatching point, and you can expect to see the same species. This goes for migrants, too.

The brigg itself is a natural breakwater of shelving slabs of rock that become covered at high tide. At low tide the brigg attracts waders, gulls and terns resting on the rocks, while offshore from autumn to spring assemblages of grebes, divers and seaduck occur and there is always a chance of a rarer gull.

Back from the brigg, the North Cliff Country Park and Arndale and Church Ravines are the key spots for migrants. Easterly winds are best for passerine migrants, which include scarce drift migrants and rarities. For seawatching, a northerly aspect to the wind is best.

KEY BIRDS
SPRING AND AUTUMN: Passing offshore, divers, grebes, seaduck, waders, gulls, terns, skuas and auks, plus in autumn shearwaters, petrels, chance of Sabine's Gull, Long-tailed Skua, and from late October Little Auk. Passerine migrants include chats, wagtails, warblers, pipits, flycatchers, finches and thrushes. Chance of scarce drift migrants in easterly winds such as Bluethroat and Wryneck, plus in autumn Barred and Yellow-browed Warblers and Red-breasted Flycatcher.
WINTER: Offshore, seaduck, divers and grebes.

ACCESS
OS MAP: **101** REF: **TA 118 811**
Signposted from Filey. Parking facilities in the country park.

14 TEESMOUTH

NNR
355 ha (828 acres)
This large area incorporates a collection of excellent birding sites, and just recently English Nature has started to develop a number of these in terms of improving habitats. The area is particularly good for waders with a reputation for turning up rarities in Autumn. Saltholme Pools and especially nearby Dorman's Pool are two of the best sites. Cowpen Marsh has a public hide and attracts roosting waders from Seal Sands, which is best visited on a rising tide for waders, whilst at high tide diving ducks can be seen in Greatham Creek. Haverton Hole to the west is an area of freshwater pools and a shallow scrape and attracts a good variety of species.

KEY BIRDS
ALL YEAR: Little Grebe, Shelduck, Teal, Shoveler, Pochard, Tufted Duck, Grey Partridge, Water Rail, Snipe, Dunlin, Redshank, Curlew.
SPRING AND AUTUMN: Garganey, Marsh Harrier, passage waders, Mediterranean Gull, terns, rarities.
SUMMER: Little Ringed Plover, Yellow Wagtail, Whinchat, various warblers.
WINTER: Wigeon, Goldeneye, Peregrine, Merlin, Golden Plover, chance of Jack Snipe, Short-eared Owl; chance of grey geese, Scaup and white-winged gulls.

ACCESS
OS MAP: **93** REF: **NZ 530 260**
The areas of interest lie north of the River Tees. Saltholme Pools lie beside the A178, 1½ km (1 mile) north of Port Clarence. Dorman's Pool is reached by turning east off the A178, 69 m (75 yds) south of Saltholme Pools on to the private ICI road; cross the level crossing and then turn left. Reclamation Pond, often used by gulls, lies next door and is worth checking. Cowpen Marsh is accessed off the A178, 1½ km (1 mile) north of Seal Sands roundabout. Seal Sands is reached by taking the track east along the south bank of Greatham Creek, which is 274 m (300 yds) north of the Cowpen Marsh car park. Haverton Hole is reached off the A1046 at Haverton Hill. Turn north at the lights onto the B1275 and continue straight ahead into Cowpen Bewley Road. Take the rough track on the right at the end of the village.

15 DRURIDGE BAY

NORTHUMBERLAND WILDLIFE TRUST

130 ha (320 acres)

Druridge Bay is a long sandy bay stretching for around 9 km (6 miles), backed by sand dunes, behind which are a series of pools, patches of scrub, hedgerows and fields. Birding is good throughout the year.

The bay itself offers divers, grebes and seaduck in winter.

Behind the dunes, working from south to north the pools offer interest throughout the year. Cresswell Pond is at its best in spring and autumn, when passage waders feed along the ponds margins. Druridge Pools, 2.5 km (1½ miles) to the north, is another good site for waders, and has a long list of rarities to its name. Just to the south of the main pool is an area of wet fields with shallow scrapes and rank vegetation, favoured by a wide variety of wildfowl and waders, too. Whilst wader numbers in Druridge Bay are never high, there are a good variety present.

To the north of Druridge Pools are East Chevington Pools and Ladyburn Lake.

At the northern end of the bay is Hauxley Nature Reserve, with as its central feature a freshwater pool. During summer the pool is used by bathing terns, predominantly Sandwich, Common and Arctic Terns, but Roseates also visit. At other times wildfowl and passage waders are a feature.

🐦 KEY BIRDS

ALL YEAR: Grebes, Shelduck, Teal, Grey Partridge, Ringed Plover, Lapwing, Redshank, Rock Pipit, Tree Sparrow, Corn Bunting.
SPRING AND AUTUMN: Passage Black Tern and Little Gull, passage waders on the pools in spring include Greenshank, Ruff, Whimbrel, Green and Common Sandpipers, chance of Temminck's Stint. In autumn Little Stint, Wood Sandpiper, Spotted Redshank, Curlew Sandpiper, Black-tailed Godwit, chance of rarities; offshore, passage of terns and skuas; passerine migrants include chats, flycatchers, warblers, wagtails, pipits plus drift migrants maybe Yellow-browed Warbler or Red-backed Shrike. In late autumn chance of arriving Long-eared Owl, Woodcock and influxes of thrushes.
SUMMER: Breeding warblers plus a few wildfowl and waders. Terns including Roseate.

WINTER: Divers, grebes, seaduck offshore; Merlin, Peregrine, Hen Harrier and Short-eared Owl hunting in dunes and over fields. Geese including Pink-footed Goose and Brent Goose, Golden Plover, Grey Plover, Sanderling, Dunlin, Ruff, Jack Snipe, Bar-tailed Godwit, Curlew, Turnstone, Snow Bunting, Twite, Shorelark and a chance of Lapland Bunting.

🚲 ACCESS

OS MAP: 81

The whole area lies east of the A1068 and just south of Amble. Hauxley reserve is approached from a track leading from the High to Low Hauxley road. Ladyburn Lake and East Chevington Pools are accessed off the A1068, clearly signposted opposite the village of Broomhill. The southern sites, including Cresswell Pond and Druridge Pools, are reached from the Cresswell coast road. Druridge Pools can be accessed from a coastal track off this road at a sharp left-hand bend.

🏛 FACILITIES

At Hauxley there is a visitor centre and hides, of which one is accessible to wheelchairs. Some of the other sites have hides.

16 COQUET ISLAND

RSPB RESERVE

22 ha (54 acres)

Offshore from Amble this low, flat-topped island is the British stronghold for the Roseate Tern. Common, Arctic and Sandwich Terns breed too, along with Eider and Puffin. Landing is not allowed, however boat trips from Amble allow good opportunities to view the birds.

The River Coquet meets the sea at Amble, and it is worth checking the sandbanks and mud flats viewable from Amble Braid for terns, gulls and in winter wildfowl and waders.

🐦 KEY BIRDS

SPRING AND SUMMER: Eider, Puffin, Roseate, Common, Arctic and Sandwich Terns.

🚲 ACCESS

OS MAP: 81 REF: NU 294 046

Boat trips around the island in spring and summer depart from Amble and are advertised in the town.

17 LINDISFARNE

NNR
4,000 ha (9,884 acres)
Perched on a large rock, Lindisfarne Castle looks out from Holy Island across the vast expanse of mud flats and dunes that is Lindisfarne National Nature Reserve (NNR). This reserve is outstanding for birds from autumn through to spring.

During winter thousands of wildfowl and waders use this large area of mud to feed. Wigeon can number in excess of 20,000, while virtually the entire British wintering population of the Svalbard Light-bellied Brent Goose is found here. Offshore species such as Eider and Red-breasted Merganser can be found.

To reach Holy Island a causeway has to be crossed which becomes impassable two hours either side of high tide. Therefore, a visit to the island needs to be planned. However, in winter the causeway is one of the best vantage points for viewing the waders and wildfowl. The dunes in winter hold Snow Buntings and Twites, whilst at passage times migrants can be discovered.

The key site for migrants is Holy Island. There is a lake overlooked by a hide. On the approach to Holy Island the area known as the Snook, reached from the car park in the dunes, can be particularly productive for migrants.

To the south of Holy Island is Budle Bay, not far from the picturesque village of Bamburgh. The bay is a good place for wildfowl and waders, and Budle Point at the mouth of the bay is a good vantage point for seaduck, grebes and divers in winter.

KEY BIRDS
ALL YEAR: Fulmar, Shag, Eider, Shelduck, Oystercatcher, Ringed Plover, Rock Pipit.
SPRING AND AUTUMN: Passage waders plus migrant passerines including chats, warblers, flycatchers, finches and thrushes with scarce migrants that annually include Bluethroat, Wryneck, Shorelark, Black Redstart and frequently Red-breasted Flycatcher and Yellow-browed Warbler in autumn.
SUMMER: Eider plus a few terns and waders.
WINTER: Red-throated and less regularly Black-throated and Great Northern Divers, Slavonian and Red-necked Grebes, Whooper Swan, Light- and Dark-bellied Brent Geese, Pink-footed and Greylag Geese, Wigeon, Teal, Pintail, Scaup, Long-tailed Duck, Common and Velvet Scoters, Goldeneye, Red-breasted Merganser, Merlin, Peregrine, more rarely Hen Harrier, Lapwing, Golden Plover, Grey Plover, Knot, Sanderling, Purple Sandpiper (scarce), Dunlin, Bar-tailed Godwit, Curlew, Redshank, Twite, Snow and Lapland Buntings, occasional Shorelarks.

ACCESS
OS MAP: 75 **REF: NU 090 430**
North of Bamburgh, the causeway to Holy Island is signposted off the A1. Budle Bay is found on the coast road just north of Bamburgh, the point can be reached by taking a road to the golf course from Bamburgh.

FACILITIES
There is a visitor centre in the village on Holy Island, plus a hide on the island with wheelchair access.

18 CAMPFIELD MARSH

RSPB RESERVE
222 ha (550 acres)
Situated on the south bank of the Solway estuary the reserve has salt marsh, wet grassland and open water. The reserve hosts the largest wader roost on the Solway, along with a good selection of wildfowl in winter. During summer various species of wader and wildfowl breed.

KEY BIRDS
ALL YEAR: Lapwing, Redshank, Snipe, Tree Sparrow.
SPRING AND AUTUMN: Passage waders, and large numbers of wintering estuarine species.
WINTER: Roosting waders include Oystercatcher, Curlew, Golden and Grey Plovers, Lapwing, Knot, Dunlin, Bar-tailed Godwit, Redshank, Turnstone, wildfowl include Barnacle Goose, Pink-footed Goose, Shoveler, Scaup, Peregrine, Merlin and Barn Owl.

ACCESS
OS MAP: 85 **REF: NY 207 620**
Take the B3057 from Carlisle west, turning off north for Bowness on Solway. The reserve is 5 km (3 miles) west of Bowness on a minor road following the coast. Wader roosts can be viewed from laybys, and there is a 2.5 km (1½ mile) trail.

FARNE ISLANDS

THE NATIONAL TRUST (28 islands)

As a bird spectacle, the Farne Islands are hard to beat. Thousands of seabirds breed on these low-lying islands situated between 2.5 km (1½ miles) and 7.3 km (4½ miles) off the Northumberland coast. No other seabird sites in Britain offer such intimate encounters with their birds as here – the Farnes are a bird photographers paradise.

Viewing is so good with species such as Arctic Tern and Puffin within touching distance that binoculars are obsolete. Boat trips run daily from Seahouses Harbour on the mainland during spring and summer, taking you around the islands and landing on two. A full day trip, which will encompass a landing on Staple Island during the morning and Inner Farne in the afternoon, is recommended.

Staple Island has a large Puffin colony, with much of the grassy inner island riddled with burrows. One of the best points to get close to Puffins is around the landing stage on the northern side, where many off duty and non-breeding birds rest on the rocks. Shags are another feature of Staple Island, often nesting on or just inches from the paths. A boardwalk looks out over a large colony of auks, mostly Guillemots but with Razorbills too,

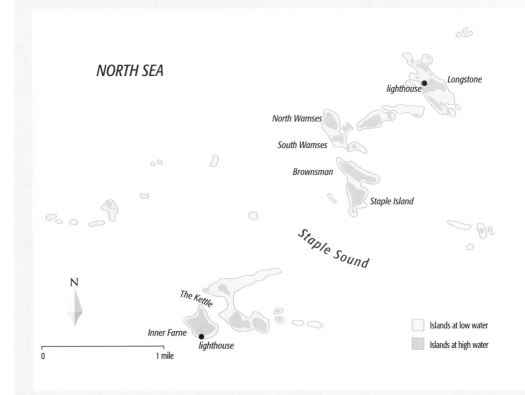

and there are plenty of Kittiwakes both here and on just about any suitable cliff face.

Inner Farne has the same species found on Staple Island plus a large colony of mainly Arctic Terns. After landing, visitors have to run the gauntlet of terns nesting right by the path that rise into the air to mob visitors as they disembark from the boats. Eiders nest here too, particularly around the chapel. The Farne's most notable inhabitant was St Cuthbert who lived on Inner Farne in the seventh century. He protected the birds, providing special care for the Eider ducks which are such a feature of the islands today.

Common and Sandwich Terns also nest on Inner Farne and each year at least one pair of Roseate Terns attempt to nest. The wardens can usually point you in the direction of this rarity. The islands attract passage migrants, and each spring and autumn a good selection of birds turn up. There are no trees and limited cover so birds often do not linger long, particularly in spring. Rarities occur and there have been some impressive falls, particularly in autumn.

For a visit to see the seabirds, the period from mid-May to late July is best. Remember to take a hat, as the terns can draw blood if an exposed scalp is on show. The islands also have a large Grey Seal colony, which is visited during boat excursions to the islands.

Inner Farne has the added historical attraction of a chapel dating back to 1370, whilst on Longstone Island, the lighthouse was made famous by Grace Darling, who with her father undertook the rescue in 1838 of the stricken crew of *The Forfarshire*.

KEY BIRDS
SPRING AND SUMMER: Fulmar, Cormorant, Shag, Eider, Ringed Plover, Oystercatcher, Black-headed, Lesser Black-backed and Herring Gulls, Kittiwake, Sandwich, Roseate, Common and Arctic Terns, Guillemot, Razorbill, Puffin and Rock Pipit. Passage migrants in spring. Turnstones in late summer.
AUTUMN: Passage migrants plus arrival of wintering waders.

ACCESS
OS MAP: 75 REF: NU 230 370
The islands are reached by boat from Seahouses Harbour on the mainland, from April to September, weather permitting. Boats depart from 10am. To join the all-day excursions landing at both islands, it is best to book in advance as the islands are very popular in summer and at weekends. If faced with a shorter time, then Inner Farne will give the best overall experience, offering a variety of birds, close encounters with terns and the islands' historical interest.

FACILITIES
Staple Island is only open to visitors from 10.30am to 1.30pm. Inner Farne is open in the afternoons. Information centre on Inner Farne. Charges for landing on both islands are made to non-members of The National Trust.

Arctic Tern
Sterna paradisaea

Visit Inner Farne in summer and Arctic Terns will visit you. They rise in attack at intruders close to their nests, and as they often nest 2.5–5 cm (1–2 in) from the paths, they are continually mobbing visitors.

Arctic Terns experience more daylight in their lives than any other living animal. This is due to their remarkable migration, the longest of any bird, which takes them in autumn from their breeding grounds in the northern hemisphere, to their wintering grounds in the southern hemisphere in Antarctica.

20 GELTSDALE

RSPB RESERVE

5,000 ha (12,355 acres)

Geltsdale is primarily an area of heather moorland with steep-sided wooded valleys and tumbling streams. Situated in the northern end of the Pennines, the reserve is home to the typical upland species of the area.

Access to the moorland is prohibited, but some of the area can be adequately covered from public bridleways.

KEY BIRDS

ALL YEAR: Tufted Duck, Sparrowhawk, Buzzard, Merlin, Peregrine, Red Grouse, Black Grouse, Short-eared Owl, Dipper, Raven, common resident woodland birds.
SPRING AND SUMMER: Golden Plover, Lapwing, Curlew, Redshank, Common Sandpiper, Tree Pipit, Whinchat, Wheatear, Ring Ouzel, Redstart, Wood Warbler, Pied Flycatcher.
AUTUMN AND WINTER: Chance of Whooper Swan on Tarn, Wigeon, Teal, Goldeneye, Hen Harrier.

ACCESS

OS MAP: 86 REF: NY 550 655

Geltsdale is east of Carlisle. The reserve lies to the south of Brampton between the A69 and the B6413. Access is from the B6413, 5 km (3 miles) south of Brampton where there is wheelchair access, or from the west side off the A69, where Tindale Tarn can be viewed.

21 ST BEES HEAD

RSPB RESERVE

22 ha (55 acres)

Stretching for 5 km (3 miles) and rising to 90 metres (300 feet), the red sandstone cliffs of St Bees Head mark Cumbria's most westerly point. Breeding seabirds are the main attraction, including England's only breeding Black Guillemots, which although low in numbers are relatively easy to see.

There are three viewpoints overlooking the seabird colony. The path to these viewpoints is steep, and a walk there and back is likely to take a couple of hours.

KEY BIRDS

SPRING AND SUMMER: Fulmar, Cormorant,

Guillemot, Razorbill, Puffin, Black Guillemot, Kittiwake, Herring Gull, Rock Pipit, Raven.
AUTUMN AND WINTER: Chance of a few migrants in autumn, and offshore, chance of petrels and shearwaters, and in winter divers and seaduck.

ACCESS

OS MAP: 89 REF: NX 962 118

From St Bees village take the minor road to St Bees Beach from where the footpath climbs the cliffs; walk north.

22 HAWESWATER

RSPB RESERVE

This lakeland reserve has long been the site for a nesting pair of Golden Eagles. If you visit for the eagles then avoid days with low cloud or rain, as the chances of a sighting are remote. However, the reserve has much more to offer with a good range of upland birds present. The woodlands of oak and birch support Redstart, Wood Warbler and Pied Flycatcher. Outside of spring and summer, bird interest is reduced, so the ideal time for a visit is in late spring and early summer.

KEY BIRDS

SPRING AND SUMMER: Golden Eagle, Peregrine, Buzzard, Sparrowhawk, Ring Ouzel, Curlew, Redshank, Snipe, Common Sandpiper, Red-breasted Merganser, Wheatear, Pied Flycatcher, Wood Warbler, Tree Pipit, Redstart.

ACCESS

OS MAP: 90 REF: NY 470 108

Haweswater is west of Shap. Take minor roads to the village of Bampton, then follow the road to the southern end of the lake, where there is an eagle observation point at Riggindale, which is a moderate walk from the car park.

23 HODBARROW

RSPB RESERVE

This lagoon beside the Duddon Estuary attracts waders and wildfowl from autumn to spring, and in summer there is a tern and gull colony.

KEY BIRDS

ALL YEAR: Tufted Duck, Red-breasted Merganser, Peregrine.
SPRING AND SUMMER: Little Gull and Black Tern, chance of Garganey and passage waders.

Breeding terns predominantly Sandwich Tern, Black-headed Gull, Eider.

AUTUMN: Passage waders and migrant passerines.

WINTER: Chance of divers, rarer grebes and seaduck. Regulars include Goldeneye, Wigeon, Teal, Pochard, Golden Plover, Dunlin, godwits.

ACCESS
OS MAP: 96 REF: SD 174 791
Beside the Duddon Estuary on the outskirts of Millom, follow signs via Mainsgate.

FACILITIES
The hide is accessible to wheelchairs.

24 WALNEY ISLAND

CUMBRIA WILDLIFE TRUST
93 ha (230 acres)
Situated on the southern tip of Walney Island this reserve of sand dunes, salt marsh and a lagoon hosts a large colony of gulls and has breeding Eider. During passage periods migrants and occasional rarities are found, while in winter, interest is maintained with wildfowl and waders both on the lagoon and offshore.

Seabird passage in autumn can be excellent, the ideal conditions being a westerly or south-westerly gale, which usually produces Leach's Storm Petrels.

A circular trail allows all the habitats of the reserve to be experienced. Hides along the trail allow views over the gull colony and out to sea, ideal for seawatching. There is a hide overlooking the spit that attracts waders and in summer it is a good spot for terns.

KEY BIRDS
ALL YEAR: Cormorant, Shelduck, Eider, Oystercatcher, Ringed Plover, Redshank, Black-headed, Greater Black-backed, Lesser Black-backed and Herring Gulls, Stonechat.

SPRING: Gannet, Fulmar, Arctic Skua, Yellow Wagtail, Whinchat, Wheatear, passage waders, warblers and flycatchers.

SUMMER: Large breeding colony of Herring and Lesser Black-backed Gulls, Sandwich, Common and Little Terns.

AUTUMN: As for spring plus Redstart, Black Redstart, Pied Flycatcher. Offshore Manx Shearwater, Leach's Storm Petrel.

WINTER: Red-throated Diver, Red-necked Grebe, Wigeon, Teal, Pintail, Shoveler, Scaup, Eider,

scoters, Goldeneye, Red-breasted Merganser, Merlin, Peregrine, estuarine waders, possible Twite and Snow Bunting.

ACCESS
OS MAP: 96 REF: SD 215 620
Go to Walney Island from Barrow-in-Furness, drive south past Biggar village to the South End caravan park. Take the track past South End Farm. The reserve is open from 10am to 5pm, but is closed on Mondays except Bank Holidays.

FACILITIES
Hides with one accessible to wheelchairs.

25 MORECAMBE BAY

RSPB RESERVE
31,080 ha (76,800 acres)
This vast area of mud flats backed by salt marsh and shingle beaches supports large numbers of waders and wildfowl from autumn through to spring. The RSPB reserve at Hest Bank is easily accessible and gives a flavour of what the bay has to offer. Arrival a couple of hours prior to high tide is ideal, as this is when the incoming tide pushes birds feeding out on the mud closer to the shore and eventually to high-tide roosts, one of which is on the salt marsh at Hest Bank.

KEY BIRDS
ALL YEAR: Cormorant, Grey Heron, Shelduck, Oystercatcher, Ringed Plover, Redshank.

SPRING AND AUTUMN: Golden Plover, Little Stint, Curlew Sandpiper, Whimbrel, Ruff, Greenshank plus arriving and departing winter birds.

SUMMER: A few waders and wildfowl, non-breeders plus returning autumn migrants from mid-July.

WINTER: Red-throated Diver, Great Crested Grebe, Greylag Goose, Wigeon, Teal, Pintail, Shoveler, Scaup, Eider, Common Scoter, Goldeneye, Long-tailed Duck, Red-breasted Merganser, Merlin, Peregrine, Grey Plover, Knot, Sanderling, Dunlin, Bar-tailed Godwit, Curlew, Turnstone, Kingfisher, gulls.

ACCESS
OS MAP: 96 REF: SD 468 667
Hest Bank is 3 km (2 miles) north of Morecambe. From the town take the A5105 towards Carnforth. Turn off to Hest Bank, cross the level crossing and park by the shore.

LEIGHTON MOSS

RSPB RESERVE (161 ha/398 acres)

Leighton Moss lies within a limestone valley, close to the shores of Morecambe Bay. The reserve's large reed bed, one of the biggest in Britain, is surrounded by willow and alder scrub, while within the reeds are shallow pools and dykes.

The reed bed supports breeding Bittern, Bearded Tit and, a recent colonist, the Marsh Harrier. Bitterns can be heard booming in spring, their deep rhythmic call can carry a considerable distance. Catching sight of a Bittern can be difficult, however, you have a good chance of seeing one in flight, in summer, when they are busy feeding young and may commute between favoured feeding sites and the nest.

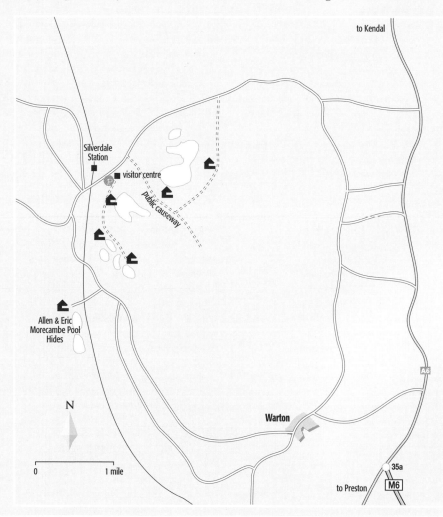

Otherwise, in cold winters, Bitterns are often forced out into the open to feed.

Avocet bred for the first time in 2001, and occasionally Mediterranean Gulls appear within the Black-headed Gull colony. Other interesting breeding species include Grasshopper Warbler and, in the surrounding woodlands, all three species of woodpecker and the elusive Hawfinch.

A variety of passage species occur, with early spring bringing the chance of a Garganey lurking on the edge of one of the pools, while in May, Black Terns occasionally drop in. Autumn visitors include a variety of passage waders that favour the muddy margins and pools. In autumn, the reed bed is used as a safe roost site by a variety of species, including wagtails and hirundines; while in winter, Starlings roost in their thousands, performing an impressive aerial ballet as the arriving flocks swoop and rise over the reed bed prior to dusk.

The open water attracts a variety of wildfowl during winter, including Goldeneye and Goosander. Hunting raptors are another feature of winter with Hen Harrier and Merlin joining the resident species.

KEY BIRDS

ALL YEAR: Bittern, Gadwall, Teal, Shoveler, Pochard, Tufted Duck, Buzzard, Peregrine, Water Rail, Barn Owl, Green, Great Spotted and Lesser Spotted Woodpeckers, Kingfisher, Bearded Tit.
SPRING: Garganey, Marsh Harrier, Osprey, Black Tern, Little Gull, Hobby, passage waders.
SUMMER: Marsh Harrier, Black-headed Gull, occasional Mediterranean Gull, Common Tern, Avocet, Yellow Wagtail, a wide variety of warblers including Grasshopper Warbler.
AUTUMN: As for spring, plus Little Stint, Ruff, Spotted Redshank, Wood Sandpiper, Greenshank, Green and Common Sandpipers. Roosts in reeds of Starlings, wagtails and hirundines.
WINTER: Pintail, Wigeon, Goldeneye, Goosander, Hen Harrier, Merlin, Redwing, Fieldfare and Yellowhammer.

ACCESS

OS MAP: 97 REF: SD 478 750
Open daily from 9am. The reserve is very close to Silverdale Railway Station, reached by leaving the M6 at junction 35 and continuing on the A6. Turn off for Yealand Redmayne and Silverdale.

FACILITIES

Wheelchair access to a number of hides. The visitor centre opens from 10am to 5pm except Christmas Day.

Bearded Tit
Panurus biarmicus

The Bearded Tit is dependant on reed beds, and Leighton Moss is a great site in which to find the species. They are easily identified, being predominantly a tawny brown in colour with a long tail. The male has a striking black moustache. They are best located by listening for their pinging call, a distinctive sound that cannot be confused.

Bearded Tits live on average for just two to three years and are social, usually found in small flocks. They breed between April and August and can be prolific, often having two or even three broods in a season. In some winters, population pressure can cause some birds to leave reed beds. These departures are known as irruptions.

27 HEYSHAM NATURE RESERVE

**THE WILDLIFE TRUST FOR LANCASHIRE,
MANCHESTER AND NORTH MERSEYSIDE**
10 ha (25 acres)
This harbour on a small promontory on the southern side of Morecambe Bay is best known for its seawatching opportunities. It is one of the most reliable sites on mainland Britain for connecting with Leach's Petrel in autumn.

A visit in September or October, after or during a sustained period of westerly winds, may produce not only Leach's Petrels but species such as Sabine's Gull, Grey Phalarope and various other commoner seabirds. The birds are pushed into Moercambe Bay, and then struggle back out to sea along this part of the coast. A visit at, or around, high tide is best.

The power station outfalls are always worth checking for gulls and terns, whilst offshore in winter there may be a variety of divers, grebes and seaduck. An area of scrub attracts migrants and there have been a number of rarities discovered during passage periods.

KEY BIRDS
SPRING: Passage migrants, passerines include chats, and warblers. Seabird passage includes Arctic Terns in April and May.
SUMMER: Various warblers breeding.
AUTUMN: Seabird passage after gales may include Leach's and European Storm Petrels, Sabine's Gull, Grey Phalarope plus skuas, terns including Black Tern, Little Gull and auks. Passerine migrants with the chance of a rarity.
WINTER: Offshore, divers, grebes and seaduck plus auks, Little Gull, Purple Sandpiper.

ACCESS
OS MAP: 97/102 REF: SD 404 596
Heysham is south of Morecambe. From the A589 south through Heysham, turn right at the traffic lights for Heysham Harbour, then turn left at the next set of lights into Moneyclose Lane. The next right takes you to the observation tower. Continue straight on for the outflow.

28 MARTIN MERE

WWT
147 ha (363 acres)
Thousands of wintering wildfowl, which inhabit the grazing marsh, pools and scrapes, are Martin Mere's main attraction.

Hides overlook this area, which, during passage periods, attracts waders, and in summer, a range of breeding birds. Whooper and Bewick's Swans can be watched just a few yards away from the hides, whilst out in the fields thousands of Pink-footed Geese graze in winter.

During winter, various activities include wild-bird feeds, and the chance to view swans and ducks under floodlight from a heated observatory. To check on days and times for these, visit the trust website or contact Martin Mere. There is a good collection of captive wildfowl, along with a range of facilities that make this a site for a good family day out.

KEY BIRDS
ALL YEAR: Grey Heron, feral Greylag, Barnacle and Canada Geese, Shelduck, Mandarin, Gadwall, Shoveler, Pochard, Ruddy Duck, Grey Partridge, Redshank, Barn and Little Owls, Corn Bunting and Tree Sparrow.
SPRING: Garganey, Black-tailed Godwit, Green, Common and Wood Sandpipers, Ruff, Spotted Redshank, Dunlin, Lapwing, Snipe, Whimbrel, Curlew, Marsh Harrier, Yellow Wagtail.
SUMMER: Marsh Harrier, Black-tailed Godwit, Little Ringed Plover, warblers, Spotted Flycatcher.
AUTUMN: As for spring plus Little Stint, Greenshank, Pink-footed Goose start to return in September.
WINTER: Whooper and Bewick's Swans, Pink-footed Goose which sometimes attract other species such as Bean and White-fronted Geese, Wigeon, Teal, Pintail, Tufted Duck, Goldeneye, Hen Harrier, Merlin, Peregrine, Golden Plover, Lapwing, Ruff, Snipe.

ACCESS
OS MAP: 108 REF: SD 428 145
Martin Mere is north of Liverpool. Turn off the A59 at Burscough Bridge just after the hump-back bridge over the railway line. The reserve is a little way along this road on the left. It is open from 9.30am to 5.00pm, November to February and from 9.30am to 5.30pm for the rest of the year.

FACILITIES
Wheelchair access and a wide range of facilities including restaurant, shop, gardens, a captive wildfowl collection and hides.

29 | HILBRE

WIRRAL BOROUGH COUNCIL

5 ha (12 acres)

Situated at the entrance to the Dee Estuary off the north-west tip of the Wirral, these small rocky islands are famed for their migrant birds and in particular their wader roosts, which are the main attraction.

The islands comprise Hilbre, the largest at 5 ha (12 acres), with grassland and a few bushes. The others, Little Eye and Little Hilbre, have less cover and are smaller. They can be reached only at low tide and with extreme caution.

KEY BIRDS

SPRING AND AUTUMN: Passage waders plus migrant passerines including warblers, chats, wagtails and hirundines, particularly in spring. Autumn seawatching may produce Leach's Petrel, skuas, gulls including Little Gull, occasional Sabine's Gull.
WINTER: Impressive wader roosts of estuarine species including Knot, Dunlin, Grey Plover, Oystercatcher, Ringed Plover, Curlew, Redshank and godwits. Purple Sandpipers on the rocks. Peregrine and occasional Merlin; seaduck offshore.

ACCESS

OS MAP: **108** REF: **SJ 184 880**
Walk out over the sands from West Kirby. Best to set out from the end of Dee Lane (brown signs to Dee Lane and Marine Lake), head for the left-hand side of the left-hand island (Little Eye). Make sure to set off at least 3½ hours before high tide. Visitors must stay on the island until two hours after high tide.

30 | GAYTON SANDS

RSPB RESERVE

2,040 ha (5,041 acres)

Sited on the English side of the Dee Estuary, Gayton Sands is an area of extensive mud flats and salt marsh. Best viewing is on spring tides when birds are pushed close to shore. Winter is the peak season for estuarine wildfowl and wader species, along with hunting raptors.

KEY BIRDS

SPRING AND AUTUMN: Passage waders include Spotted Redshank, Curlew Sandpiper, Ruff,

Greenshank, Black-tailed Godwit. All the wintering species will be present.
WINTER: Shelduck, Wigeon, Teal, Pintail, Scaup, Red-breasted Merganser, Hen Harrier, Merlin Peregrine, Oystercatcher, Ringed Plover, Grey Plover, Knot, Sanderling, Dunlin, Curlew, Twite, Redshank, Turnstone, Short-eared Owl, Kingfisher.

ACCESS

OS MAP: **117** REF: **SJ 275 785**
The best viewing is from Parkgate on the B5135 reached from the A540 that runs along the western side of the Wirral.

31 | MARSHSIDE

RSPB RESERVE

2,182 ha (5,392 acres)

Close to Southport and the Ribble Estuary this reserve of grazing marsh and lagoons attracts thousands of Pink-footed Geese in winter along with wildfowl and waders. Large numbers of Golden Plover and Black-tailed Godwit are present too. Passage periods see a few migrants, whilst in summer interest is maintained by breeding waders and a few wildfowl.

The Ribble Estuary, close by, is one of Britain's most important estuaries for wildfowl and waders. There are various access points, close to Marshside, from which to view the area.

KEY BIRDS

ALL YEAR: Shoveler, Teal, Tufted Duck, Redshank, Snipe, Lapwing, Black-tailed Godwit.
SPRING AND AUTUMN: A few passage migrants, Garganey.
SUMMER: Marsh Harrier, Common Tern, Yellow Wagtail.
WINTER: Pink-footed Goose, Bewick's Swan, Whooper Swan, Pintail, Wigeon, Golden Plover, Ruff, Short-eared Owl, Hen Harrier, Merlin, Peregrine.

ACCESS

OS MAP: **102** REF: **SD 355 202**
Viewing from the roads running along the south eastern part of the reserve. Access to trails and hides via Marine Drive, 1.6 km (1 mile) north of Southport centre.

FACILITIES

Hides with wheelchair access.

32 PENDLE HILL

LANCASHIRE COUNTRYSIDE SERVICE
891 ha (2,200 acres)
This tall isolated hill rises 557 metres (1,827 feet) and is 9 km (6 miles) east of Clitheroe. The summit is a grassy moor with sparse areas of heather. From mid-April Dotterel may start to arrive, with a peak in early May before departure by the middle of the month.

KEY BIRDS
SPRING: Dotterel, Twite, Wheatear, chance of Ring Ouzel and Whinchat.

ACCESS
OS MAP: 103 REF: **SD 815 416**
From Clitheroe take minor roads towards Barley. Park at the above grid reference by the track to Pendle House Farm, walk past the farm and take the left-hand track across the slope of the hill to reach the summit ridge.

33 SEAFORTH

THE WILDLIFE TRUST FOR LANCASHIRE, MANCHESTER AND NORTH MERSEYSIDE
30 ha (74 acres)
Seaforth lies within Liverpool Docks and comprises fresh and salt-water lagoons. The site is of interest in winter for gulls and a few wildfowl, and at passage periods for migrant gulls and terns. Annually during April, Little Gulls appear and can be watched at close quarters as they hawk over the lagoons. Terns in spring regularly include Black and Little Terns and often Roseate Tern. Common Terns nest on artificial rafts.

Seaforth has an impressive list of rare gulls to its name with three records of Ross's Gull, about half a dozen Bonaparte's Gulls and there is always a chance of a Mediterranean or Glaucous Gull.

KEY BIRDS
SPRING AND AUTUMN: Little Gull (spring), Black Tern, Roseate Tern and Little Tern, chance of rare gulls.
SUMMER: Common Tern.
WINTER: Shelduck, Red-breasted Merganser, Goldeneye, Tufted Duck, Gadwall, Scaup, Pochard, Redshank, Golden Plover, Black-tailed Godwit, Dunlin, Knot and chance of rare gulls such as Glaucous and Mediterranean Gull.

ACCESS
OS MAP: 108 REF: **SJ 315 970**
Access is on foot through the entrance to Liverpool Docks just south of Crosby.

34 FRODSHAM AND THE WEAVER BEND

CHESHIRE WILDLIFE TRUST
15 ha (36 acres)
Of most interest for passage waders and wintering wildfowl. Bordering the River Mersey this is an area of embanked lagoons, fields and a meander with mud banks in the River Weaver – the Weaver Bend.

Passage waders in autumn often include good numbers of Little Stints and Curlew Sandpipers, and with regularity rarities are found, particularly American species. During winter, wildfowl use the lagoons, and raptors hunt over the area.

Although waders are likely to be present in the lagoons at all times of the day, high-tide visits can be beneficial as birds are pushed off the mud flats of the Mersey.

KEY BIRDS
ALL YEAR: Little Grebe, Lapwing, Dunlin, Redshank.
SPRING: Garganey, Ringed and Little Ringed Plovers, Common Sandpiper, Sanderling, Ruff, Greenshank, Spotted Redshank, Whimbrel.
SUMMER: Returning waders from mid-July.
AUTUMN: As for spring plus Black-tailed Godwit, Curlew Sandpiper, Little Stint, Knot, chance of Little Gull and Black Tern, Hobby, chance of a rare wader.
WINTER: Regular Pink-footed Geese overhead, chance of other species of grey geese and wild swans in hard weather, Wigeon, Teal, Pintail, Pochard, Tufted Duck, Goldeneye, occasional Smew and Scaup, Peregrine, Merlin, Short-eared Owl, chance of Hen Harrier, Golden Plover, Ruff, Black-tailed Godwit, Little Stint over winters.

ACCESS
OS MAP: 117 REF: **SJ 513 778**
Pass through the main shopping area in Frodsham heading south, then turn right down Marsh Lane, which leads over the motorway. Take the right-hand fork to the Weaver Bend. Proceed on the path.

35 SANDBACH FLASHES

This series of pools lies close to the Trent and Mersey Canal. They are of most interest for wintering wildfowl and passage waders; a number of rare waders have also put in appearances.

KEY BIRDS

ALL YEAR: Grebes, Ruddy Duck, Shelduck, Sparrowhawk, Lapwing, Little Owl, Willow Tit, Reed Bunting.
SPRING AND AUTUMN: A few passage waders, Whinchat, Wheatear.
SUMMER: Little Ringed Plover, various warblers.
WINTER: Wigeon, Teal, Pintail, Shoveler, Water Rail, Snipe, Green Sandpiper.

ACCESS

OS MAP: 118 REF: SJ 720 590
Sandbach Flashes are close to Sandbach. If travelling north turn off the A533 just north of Sandbach station and go over a humpback bridge.
OS MAP: 118 REF: SJ 730 614
For Fodens Flash, turn right immediately at the bridge and view the flash from the roadside.
OS MAP: 118 REF: SJ 728 608
For Watch Lane Flash, take the other fork from the bridge, turn left into Red Lane and continue to Watch Lane on the right. Park at the end of Watch Lane. Elton Hall Flash is **REF: SJ 716 595**.

36 PENNINGTON FLASH

WIGAN COUNCIL
400 ha (988 acres)
Centre stage in this park is the 1.6 km (1 mile) long flash resulting from mining subsidence. The surrounding area attracts a good range of farmland, woodland and water birds.

A few migrants pass through on passage, particularly waders – whilst not in large numbers, annual records indicate a good variety. Common Tern and Little Ringed Plover breed. During winter there is a chance of roosting Long-eared Owls. The winter feeding station viewable from Bunting Hide can be very productive with Willow Tit and Water Rail regular visitors.

KEY BIRDS

ALL YEAR: Great Crested Grebe, Kingfisher, Willow Tit and various other resident woodland and farmland species.

SPRING AND AUTUMN: A few passage waders, may include Greenshank, Curlew, Dunlin, Common and Green Sandpipers, with often more unusual species. Terns, notably in spring, include Common, Arctic and on occasions Black Tern.
SUMMER: Common Tern, Oystercatcher, Ringed and Little Ringed Plovers, various warblers.
WINTER: Tufted Duck, Pochard, Gadwall, Shoveler, Teal, Goldeneye, Ruddy Duck, gulls, chance of Long-eared Owl, feeding station birds.

ACCESS

OS MAP: 109 REF: SJ 640 990
Pennington Flash is west of Manchester and close to Leigh. The main entrance is off the A572 St Helens Road north of Lowton Common.

FACILITIES

Hides accessible to wheelchairs.

37 CALF OF MAN BIRD OBSERVATORY

BIRD OBSERVATORY
250 ha (618 acres)
Perched off the south-west tip of the Isle of Man, this small island boasts nine species of breeding seabird and in addition Chough, one of the Isle of Man's star birds. It is also an excellent site for spring and autumn migration with a good range of species. Seabird movements off the Isle are best in autumn.

KEY BIRDS

ALL YEAR: Hen Harrier, Stonechat, Chough, Raven.
SPRING AND AUTUMN: A range of passerine migrants, with the chance of rarities. In autumn seabird passage.
SUMMER: European Storm Petrel, Cormorant, Manx Shearwater, Fulmar, Shag, Guillemot, Razorbill, Eider, Peregrine, Water Rail, Wheatear.

ACCESS

OS MAP: 95 REF: SC 155 655
For visiting see website or contact Manx National Heritage, Manx Museum, Douglas, Isle of Man IMI 3LY.

FACILITIES

There is accommodation available for eight people between April and October.

SCOTLAND

Specialist bird communities and dramatic scenery are two ingredients that make Scotland popular with birders. The habitats to be found in the region are diverse, from fertile islands, havens for tens of thousands of wintering geese, to rugged mountain tops – the domain of Arctic-alpine specialists such as Ptarmigan.

One of its most valuable habitats are the old Caledonian pinewoods, just remnants of what once was, but nonetheless vital to Crested Tit, Capercaillie and Britain's only official endemic bird – the Scottish Crossbill.

The offshore islands are also important sites for birding in Scotland. West coast islands, such as Tiree and North Uist, resonate to calling Corncrakes in summer. Travel west into the Atlantic and you meet the majestic sea stacks of St Kilda. To the north lies fertile Orkney, contrasting with the bleak moors of our most northerly outpost, Shetland. Summer here sees sea cliffs teeming with birds. In autumn, eyes turn to Fair Isle, a legendary island that rarely fails to excite with migrants and vagrants.

In winter, Scotland's far north is bleak, with few birds, but, in summer, it offers teeming seabird cliffs, such as the remote and dramatic Cape Wrath. Inland is the vast Flow Country – extensive peatland of bogs and moor, home to some of Britain's rarest breeding birds such as the Greenshank and Common Scoter. Inverpolly National Nature Reserve, situated on the west coast, is a landscape of pools, bogs and mountains; this is the realm of the Golden Eagle and a breeding stronghold of the Black-throated Diver.

The mountain tops attract few birds in summer, but those that do exist here are true specialists. Ptarmigan, Dotterel and Snow Bunting are three such species that occur at a number of sites in the region, but are most easily found in the Cairngorm mountains.

48 *St Kilda*

Beir (

Uib (S

Ming

KEY

1) Caerlaverock	21) Inversnaid	38) Cairngorm
2) Mereshead	22) Loch of the Lowes	39) Culbin Sands
3) Loch Ken/Dee Marshes	23) Montrose Basin	40) Glen Affric
4) Wigtown Bay	24) Fowlsheugh	41) Loch Fleet
5) Wood of Cree	25) Sands of Forvie and Ythan	42) Flow Country
6) Mull of Galloway	Estuary	43) Dunnet Head
7) Loch Ryan	26) Loch of Strathbeg	44) Clo Mor
8) Lochwinnoch	27) Banff Harbour	45) Handa Island
9) Barons Haugh	28) Spey Bay	46) Inverpolly
10) St Abb's Head	29) Glen Tanar	47) Beinn Eighe
11) Musselburgh	30) Glen Muick and	48) St Kilda
12) John Muir Country Park	Lochnagar	49) Monach Islands
13) Bass Rock	31) Insh Marshes	50) Isle of Rum
14) Aberlady Bay	32) Abernethy including Loch	51) Balranald
15) Craigleath	Garten	52) Glenborrodale
16) Isle of May	33) Loch An Eilean	53) Coll
17) Loch Leven/Vane Farm	34) Findhorn Valley	54) Tiree
18) Largo Bay	35) Loch Ruthven	55) Mull
19) Eden Estuary	36) Fairy Glen	56) Islay
20) Loch of Kinnordy	37) Udale Bay	

ESTERN
ISLES

Isle of Lewis

Gallan Head

Port Nis
(Port of Ness)

Steornabhagh
(Stornoway)

Eye Peninsula

Hushinish Point

Harris

*hist a Tuath
orth Uist)*

Tairbeart
(Tarbert)

Rodel

Uig

Loch nam Madadh
(Lochmaddy)

*Isle of
Skye*

*Deas
ist)*

*Gaoghla
ula)*

Creagorry

Loch Baghasdail
(Lochboisdale)

Canna

Rum

Bagh a Chaisteil
(Castlebay)

Muck

Coll

Tiree

Isle of Mull

Oban

Colonsay

Jura

Islay

Arran

Ardrossan

Campbeltown

*Mull of
Kintyre*

Girvan

Stranraer

Newton
Stewart

*Luce
Bay*

N

HIGHLAND

Tain

*Tarbat
Ness*

Alness

Dingwall

Inverness

Nairn

Forres

Elgin

MORAY

Peterhead

Aberdeen

Stonehaven

Brechin

Montrose

Forfar

Arbroath

Blairgowrie

Dundee

Perth

St Andrews

Fife Ness

Kinross

FIFE

Stirling

Dunfermline

EDINBURGH

Dunbar

Falkirk

Eyemouth

Greenock

Clydebank

GLASGOW

Hamilton

Paisley

East Kilbride

Lesmahagow

Biggar

Galashiels

Selkirk

Kilmarnock

Ayr

Cumnock

M74

Hawick

Jedburgh

Moffat

ENGLAND

Lockerbie

Langholm

Dumfries

DUMFRIES
AND GALLOWAY

ARGYLL
AND BUTE

Fort William

Pitlochry

Crieff

Duncansby Head

Thurso

Noss Head

Wick

Fraserburgh

Banff

Loch Ness

0 10 20 30 40 miles

0 20 40 60 80 km

1 CAERLAVEROCK

WWT

524 ha (1,295 acres)

Caerlaverock is located on the north side of the Solway. During the winter, spectacular flocks of Barnacle Geese and close views of Whooper Swans are two highlights you can expect from a visit to this reserve.

The entire Svalbard population of Barnacle Geese winter in the inner Solway, with the lion's share using Caerlaverock's fields, salt marsh and shore on which to feed. They start to arrive in late September and peak in November when more than 25,000 may be present. Pink-footed Geese are more numerous in late winter.

A network of 20 hides big and small overlook the reserve and range from small, two to three person hides to a large tower hide and a heated observatory. The observatory overlooks a lake where Whooper Swans along with a range of other wildfowl are tempted in by daily feeds. Views of the birds here are tremendous.

Waders are of interest too, with both large numbers of wintering birds and a good range of passage species.

KEY BIRDS

ALL YEAR: Shelduck, Teal, Shoveler, Sparrowhawk, Peregrine, Buzzard, Snipe, Redshank, Barn Owl.
SPRING AND AUTUMN: Passage waders.
WINTER: Whooper Swan, Bewick's Swan (a few), Barnacle Goose, Pink-footed and Greylag Geese, Pintail, Teal, Gadwall, Wigeon, Tufted Duck, Pochard, Hen Harrier, Peregrine, Merlin, Black-tailed Godwit, Golden Plover, Oystercatcher, Lapwing.

ACCESS

OS MAP: 84/85 REF: NY 051 656

The reserve is 12 km (8 miles) south-east of Dumfries, signposted from the A75, via the B725. Open daily except Christmas Day.

FACILITIES

There are 20 hides including tower hides and a heated observatory. There is also wheelchair access.

2 MERESHEAD

RSPB RESERVE

243 ha (600 acres)

A reserve of wet grassland, farmland, salt marsh and mud flats on the north Solway shore, Mereshead is most productive in winter. Barnacle Geese are one of the main attractions. A small woodland adds interest.

KEY BIRDS

ALL YEAR: Lapwing, Curlew, Redshank, Skylark and resident woodland birds.
SPRING AND AUTUMN: Passage waders.
SUMMER: Breeding waders, summer visitors to wood.
WINTER: Barnacle Goose, Pink-footed Goose, Shelduck, Teal, Wigeon, Pintail, estuarine waders, Peregrine, Hen Harrier, Merlin.

ACCESS

OS MAP: 84 REF: NX 925 560

The reserve is off the A710, just east of Caulkerbush.

FACILITIES

There is a visitor centre, hide and trails.

3 LOCH KEN / DEE MARSHES

RSPB RESERVE

This site stretches for over 14 km (9 miles) and encompasses a shallow loch and bordering marshes. When the loch is low, large areas of mud appear, particularly in the south-west corner which helps attract a few passage waders in late summer.

Winter is the best time to visit, a small wintering flock of Greenland White-fronted Geese being one of the main attractions. Roads surrounding the loch allow good access. The RSPB own a number of plots of land, and there is a hide at Mains of Duchrae. Woodlands support species such as Redstart and Pied Flycatcher.

KEY BIRDS

ALL YEAR: Goosander, Teal, Shoveler, Buzzard, Red Kite, Peregrine, Snipe, Redshank, Barn Owl, Kingfisher, Willow Tit.
SPRING AND SUMMER: A few passage waders, Common Tern, Grasshopper Warbler, Wood Warbler, Redstart, Pied Flycatcher.

AUTUMN: A few passage waders, wildfowl arrive.
WINTER: Whooper Swan, Greenland White-fronted Goose, Greylag Goose, Wigeon, Pintail, Teal, Goosander, Goldeneye, Hen Harrier.

ACCESS
OS MAP: 77/84 REF: **NX 699 684**
Access to the Mains of Duchrae RSPB reserve is off the C50, which is off the B795 west of Glenlochar Bridge. Surrounding roads give good access, and there are a number of footpaths.

4 WIGTOWN BAY

LNR
2,845 ha (7,030 acres)
Wigtown Bay's mud flats and salt marsh are of most interest in winter for wildfowl and waders. From late December, up to 10,000 Pink-footed Geese use the bay. A flood at Wigtown harbour attacts passage waders, and Garganey are an annual visitor.

KEY BIRDS
SPRING AND AUTUMN: Garganey, passage waders.
WINTER: Greylag and Pink-footed Geese, Shelduck, Pintail, Wigeon, estuarine waders, Hen Harrier, Merlin and Peregrine.

ACCESS
OS MAP: 83 REF: **NX 465 545**
View from the A75. A minor road at Creetown that loops back on to the A75 is worth taking for the Pink-footed Geese in late winter.

5 WOOD OF CREE

RSPB RESERVE
266 ha (657 acres)
A sessile oak, birch and hazel woodland, and encompassing a river and meadows, this reserve is best visited in spring and early summer. Typically for this type of wood, Pied Flycatcher, Redstart and Wood Warbler are present, along with a good supporting cast of woodland birds.

KEY BIRDS
ALL YEAR: Buzzard, Sparrowhawk, Woodcock, Barn Owl, Dipper, Grey Wagtail, Great Spotted Woodpecker, Willow Tit.
SPRING AND SUMMER: Common Sandpiper, Pied Flycatcher, Redstart, Wood Warbler, Tree Pipit.

ACCESS
OS MAP: 77 REF: **NX 382 708**
Located 6 km (4 miles) north-west of Newton Stewart. From Minnigaff take the minor road north that runs parallel with the A714. Park by the road and take the trail up into the wood.

6 MULL OF GALLOWAY

RSPB RESERVE
This is a rocky headland with 80 m (260 ft) high granite cliffs. The reserve is best visited in summer for its breeding seabirds. During passage periods a few migrants may be encountered and seawatching in autumn can produce impressive numbers of passing Manx Shearwaters.

KEY BIRDS
SPRING AND SUMMER: A few passerine migrants; breeding seabirds include Fulmar, Shag, Cormorant, Kittiwake, Guillemot, Black Guillemot, Razorbill, offshore, Gannet and possibility of Puffin; Stonechat, Twite.
AUTUMN: Manx Shearwater offshore and chance of passerine migrants on headland.

ACCESS
OS MAP: 82 REF: **NX 156 304**
Follow the A716 south of Stranraer, then take the B7041 towards the lighthouse.

7 LOCH RYAN

This deep sea loch stretching for 12 km (8 miles) to the sea attracts seaduck and divers in winter, when there can often be white-winged gulls present, too.

KEY BIRDS
WINTER: Red-throated and often Black-throated and Great Northern Divers, grebes include Slavonian and Black-necked, Light-bellied Brent Goose, Red-breasted Merganser, Eider, Scaup, Long-tailed Duck, Common Scoter, Goldeneye, Black Guillemot, a few waders.

ACCESS
OS MAP: 82 REF: **NX 055 655**
Viewing is good from the surrounding A77 and A718 roads that run along the shore.

8 LOCHWINNOCH

RSPB RESERVE
158 ha (264 acres)
Cut in half by the A760, Aird Meadow on the
northern side of the road is an area of marsh and
shallow water and woodland, whilst on the
southern side Barr Loch is a more extensive area
of open water. Various species of wildfowl, and
Grasshopper Warbler breeds. Wintering wildfowl
include Whooper Swan.

KEY BIRDS
SPRING AND SUMMER: Great Crested and Little
Grebes, Teal, Shoveler, Pochard, Tufted Duck,
Black-headed Gull, Grasshopper Warbler.
AUTUMN AND WINTER: Passage waders
(dependent on water level), Whooper Swan,
Greylag Goose, Teal, Wigeon, Shoveler,
Goldeneye, Goosander.

ACCESS
OS MAP: 63 REF: NS 358 582
The reserve lies 29 km (18 miles) south-west of
Glasgow on the A760 east of Lochwinnoch village.

9 BARONS HAUGH

RSPB RESERVE
107 ha (264 acres)
Just south of the centre of Motherwell in the
Clyde Valley, this is a reserve of marsh, woodland
and meadows. It is home to a typical array of
marshland birds. In autumn, passage waders are a
feature, and in winter, wildfowl are of interest.

KEY BIRDS
ALL YEAR: Little Grebe, Grey Heron, Teal,
Shoveler, Water Rail, Redshank, Grey Wagtail,
Kingfisher, Willow Tit.
SPRING AND SUMMER: Common Sandpiper,
Whinchat, Grasshopper Warbler.
AUTUMN: Passage waders.
WINTER: Whooper Swan, Shoveler, Goldeneye,
Water Rail.

ACCESS
OS MAP: 64 REF: NS 755 552
The reserve is due south of the centre of
Motherwell along the banks of the River Clyde.

Adele Street opposite Motherwell Civic Centre
leads to North Lodge Avenue and the reserve.

10 ST ABB'S HEAD

NNR / SCOTTISH WILDLIFE TRUST
78 ha (192 acres)
Situated about 21 km (13 miles) north of the
border between Scotland and England at the
southern edge of the Firth of Forth. The dramatic
cliffs on this reserve rise to about 100 m (330 ft)
and echo to the cries of Kittiwakes and auks
during summer. In autumn, interest is diverted to
a sheltered valley behind the cliffs, where trees
and shrubs surround a small loch. This oasis of
cover attracts migrants and annually rarities.
Easterly winds with poor visibility are the best
conditions. Seawatching in spring and
particularly autumn can be good too, with north
to easterly winds being best.
    You can walk from Northfield Farm where
there is a visitor centre, up to the cliffs and then
back along an inland route, a total of around
5 km (3 miles). Alternatively, it is possible to
drive up to the lighthouse.

KEY BIRDS
ALL YEAR: Little Grebe, Gannet, Fulmar, Shag,
Tufted Duck.
SPRING: Migrant chats, warblers, flycatchers, plus
annually Red-backed Shrike, Wryneck, Black
Redstart and Bluethroat. Offshore sea passage
includes Gannet, wildfowl.
SUMMER: Breeding seabirds include Kittiwake,
Guillemot, Razorbill, Puffin, Herring Gull, plus
Rock Pipit, Wheatear and Raven.
AUTUMN: Offshore Manx Shearwater, chance of
rarer shearwaters in favourable conditions, skuas.
Passerine migrants include crests, thrushes, chats,
flycatchers and warblers. Scarce species as in
spring with the added chance of Yellow-browed
Warbler and Red-breasted Flycatcher which are
annual.
WINTER: Seaduck and divers offshore. Wildfowl
such as Goldeneye and Wigeon on the loch.

ACCESS
OS MAP: 67 REF: NT 914 693
Signposted off the A1, follow the A1107 to
Coldingham, and then St Abb's.

Wheldrake Ings' floods in winter are a haven for wildfowl.

Above: Morecambe Bay attracts large wintering flocks of Knot.

Above: A reed-fringed dyke at Leighton Moss.

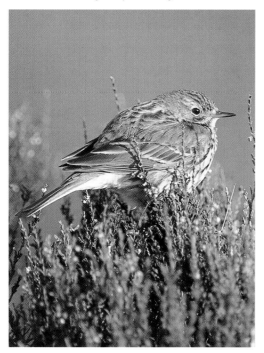

Above: Meadow Pipits are common on upland reserves in summer.

Above: A Lapwing in autumn.

Above: Goldcrests can arrive in large numbers along the east coast in late autumn.

Above: Breeding seabirds on Brownsman Island in the Farnes.

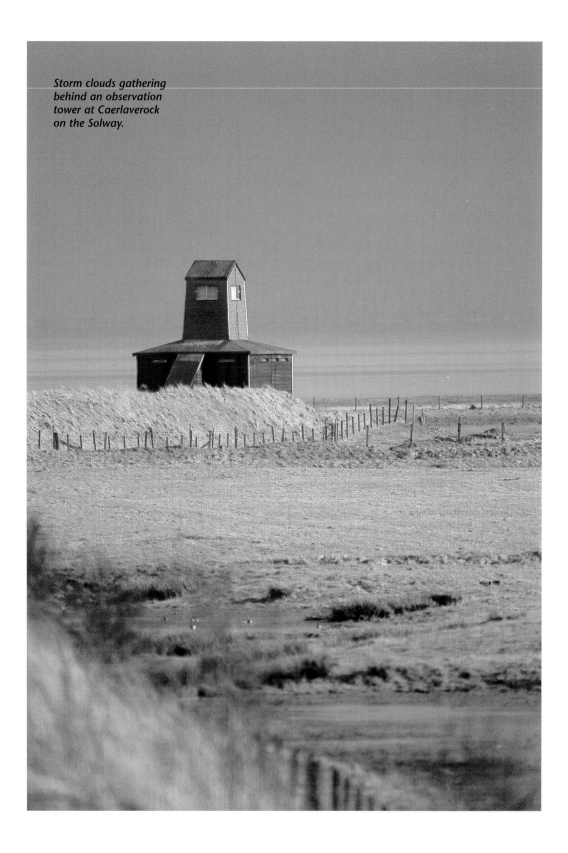

Storm clouds gathering behind an observation tower at Caerlaverock on the Solway.

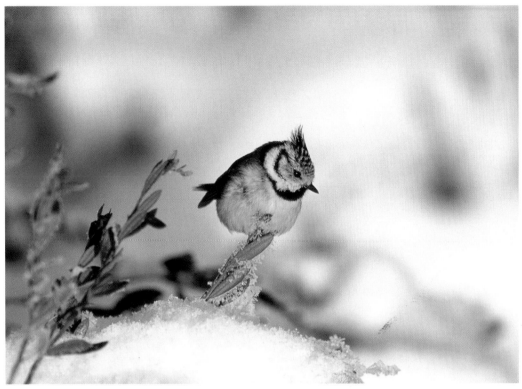

Above: Crested Tits are a sought-after speciality, restricted to Scotland.

Above: Abernethy RSPB reserve in winter.

Above: Gannets cover the Bass Rock in the Firth of Forth.

Above: A view along Lairhig Ghru in the Cairngorm mountains.

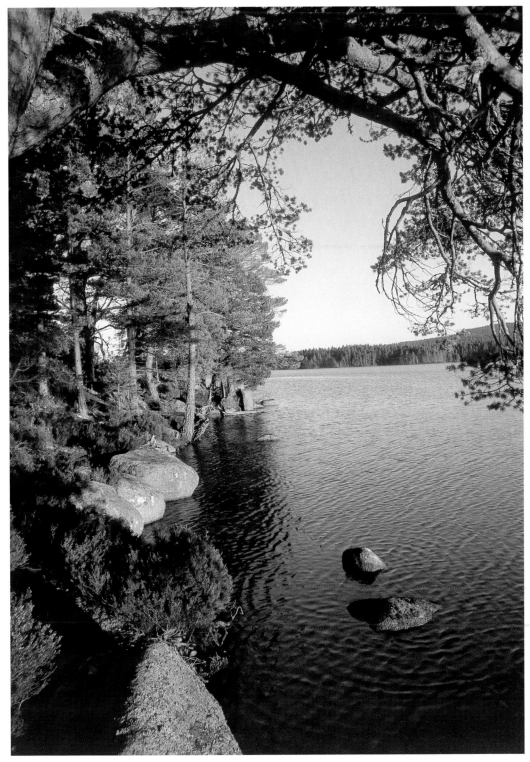

Above: The shoreline of Loch Garten.

Above: Snow Buntings can be found in the Cairngorms throughout the year.

Above: The Machair ablaze with colour on the Balranald reserve.

FACILITIES

There is a visitor centre open daily between April and October.

11 MUSSELBURGH

Just east of Edinburgh, Musselburgh may not be the most scenic of birding sites, but this is made up by some quality birding, particularly in winter. Seaduck are present in numbers and variety, along with divers and the rarer grebes. Large numbers of gulls congregate in the area notably around the mouth of the Esk. Wintering waders are of interest, whilst during passage periods wader scrapes attract migrants, and there is a wader roost on the lagoons.

KEY BIRDS

SPRING: Departing seaduck, divers and grebes offshore, Sandwich and Common Terns, Common Sandpiper and estuarine waders, Wheatear.
SUMMER: Terns offshore, loafing gulls, waders returning by mid-July.
AUTUMN: Estuarine waders plus Ruff, Whimbrel, Spotted Redshank, Little Stint, Curlew Sandpiper, Common, Sandwich and occasional Black Tern, Little Gull, occasional skuas offshore.
WINTER: Grebes, divers and seaduck, estuarine waders, auks, Twite, chance of Peregrine, Merlin and Short-eared Owl.

ACCESS

OS MAP: 66 REF: NT 345 736
The sea and Esk River mouth can be viewed from an embankment, reached by turning off the main road at the eastern end of Musselburgh, signed to the racecourse, then right. The western end can be accessed through Levenhall Links Leisure Park, west of the racecourse. Parking is by the sailing lake from where the wader scrape can be accessed.

12 JOHN MUIR COUNTRY PARK

COUNTRY PARK
700 ha (1,730 acres)
Lying west of Dunbar this country park incorporates the estuary of the River Tyne, and includes salt marsh, sand dunes, grassland and scrub. Wintering and passage wildfowl and waders are the main attraction. During passage periods the scrub may hold a few migrants, and in late summer Goosander may be present.

KEY BIRDS

ALL YEAR: Eider, Ringed Plover, Oystercatcher.
SPRING AND AUTUMN: Estuarine waders, passerine migrants such as Wheatear, Whinchat and Redstart.
SUMMER: Gannet, Kittiwake, Great and Arctic Skuas, Goosander.
WINTER: Divers, seaduck, estuarine waders, gulls.

ACCESS

OS MAP: 67 REF: NT 645 785
Turn off the A1 on to the A1087, 1.6 km (1 mile) west of Dunbar. After 0.8 km (½ mile) take the minor road on the left to Linkfield car park. A second car park, the South Shore car park in Dunbar, can be reached off the A1087 through West Barns. A footpath runs between the two.

13 BASS ROCK

Lying in the Firth of Forth, this spectacular looking lump of volcanic rock towers out of the sea. Viewed from North Berwick it appears covered in whitewash, until a closer inspection reveals the white is a living mass of Gannets. As one of the most spectacular Gannet colonies in the world, a visit either sailing around the island by boat, or landing on the rock itself is not to be missed.

KEY BIRDS

SPRING AND SUMMER: Gannet, Shag, Razorbill, Guillemot, Puffin, Kittiwake, Herring Gull.

ACCESS

OS MAP: 67 REF: NT 602 873
A boat trip often runs twice a day from North Berwick. It is possible to land on the rock for a hefty landing fee of £20. Boat times can be obtained from the tourist office in North Berwick (see page 171 for details), and are advertised at the quay.

ABERLADY BAY

LNR (582 ha/1,438 acres)

Nestled on the south shore of the Firth of Forth, Aberlady Bay has much to offer the birder throughout the year. Winter birding is excellent with a big range of species on offer, from divers and grebes offshore to large numbers of geese, ducks and waders on the mud flats and salt marsh. During spring and autumn, passage waders along with a wide range of migrants pass through, and often include rare or scarce species.

Aberlady is flanked by Gosford and Gullane Bays, both are worthy of coverage particularly from autumn through to spring. Gosford Bay is outstanding for grebes, notably Red-necked Grebes that peak in August to September and February to March

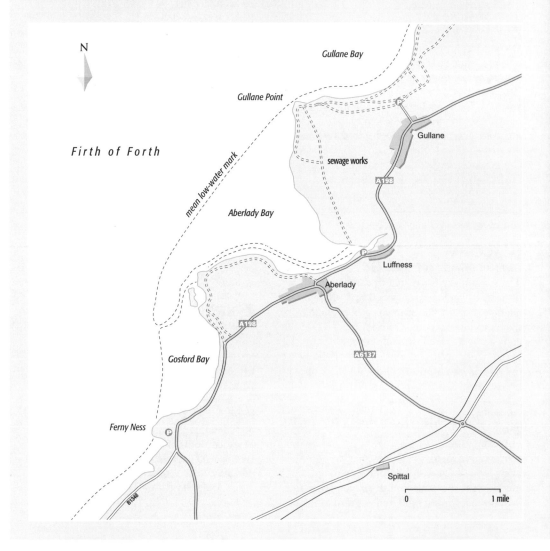

with often more than 50 present. During the winter large numbers of Slavonian Grebes congregate and can number more than 100. Viewing is best from Ferny Ness. Gullane Bay attracts Red-throated Divers in some numbers, along with rafts of scoters, eiders and mergansers.

The mud flats of Aberlady in winter throng with waders, with all the expected estuarine species present. At dawn, Pink-footed Geese leave their roost site in the bay to feed in surrounding fields before returning at dusk. They peak in November when more than 15,000 may be present. Whooper Swans roost too, though in small numbers.

A path leads from the small car park across a bridge to Gullane Point, leading through scrub and grassland. Passerine migrants can be searched for here and out towards the point. During passage periods a variety of waders travel through. During summer, apart from the breeding birds, there are always terns feeding offshore. In autumn, they become targets for marauding skuas. During north or north-easterly winds, seabirds offshore can be interesting and in late autumn/early winter it is worth looking for Little Auks.

🪶 KEY BIRDS

SPRING: Red-necked Grebe present into May, passage waders and migrant passerines plus terns in the bay and offshore.
SUMMER: Returning waders by mid-July. Breeding birds include Little Grebe, Greylag Goose, Shelduck, Eider, Ringed Plover, Lapwing, Redshank, Snipe, Sedge Warbler and Lesser Whitethroat.
AUTUMN: Red-necked Grebe, Red-throated Diver, Common and Velvet Scoters, Greenshank, Spotted Redshank, Wood Sandpiper, Little Stint, terns and skuas, Little Gull, chance of Black Tern, passerine migrants. Seabirds offshore including Little Auk in late autumn.
WINTER: Red-necked and Slavonian Grebes, divers, Whooper Swan, Pink-footed, Greylag and Brent Geese, Common and Velvet Scoters, Red-breasted Merganser, Eider, Wigeon, Teal, Goldeneye, Long-tailed Duck, Short-eared and Long-eared Owls, Peregrine, Merlin, Twite, Snow and Lapland Buntings, Shorelark.

🪶 ACCESS

OS MAP: 66 REF: NT 471 805
The bay is just east of Aberlady village off the A198. Viewing is possible from the car park and the roadside just north of the car park. See map opposite for access to Gullane and Gosford Bays.

🏛 FACILITIES

Disabled can view from a vehicle at various points along the A198.

Red-necked Grebe
Podiceps grisegena

Occasionally attempting to breed in Britain, the Red-necked Grebes that congregate off Aberlady Bay have originated from the continent. They nest in reed-fringed ponds and lakes often surrounded by forest. Once breeding is over, Red-necked Grebes disperse to open waters particularly estuarine and coastal areas.

Although easy to identify in summer with their striking red neck, in winter this is lost, and identification becomes a little more difficult. However, these are large grebes, and in winter they are separated from the Slavonian and Black-necked Grebes by their larger size, less white, and the distinctive yellow base to their straight dagger-like bill, which they use to catch fish and crustaceans when on the sea.

They often congregate in loose social flocks in winter when on the coast. Individuals or pairs may turn up inland on reservoirs or lakes on occasion.

15 CRAIGLEATH

This small island just off North Berwick has a wide variety of breeding seabirds, and can be viewed as with the Bass Rock by boat or occasionally in very calm sea conditions by landing.

KEY BIRDS
SPRING AND SUMMER: Cormorant, Shag, gulls, Kittiwake, Puffin, Razorbill, Guillemot.

ACCESS
OS MAP: 66 REF: NT 553 870
By boat from North Berwick, trips run by the same boatman as Bass Rock (see page 113). Boat times can be obtained from the tourist office in North Berwick, and are advertised at the quay.

16 ISLE OF MAY

NNR
57 ha (140 acres)
Lying 9 km (6 miles) off Fife Ness in the Firth of Forth, the Isle of May is home to a bird observatory. Its cliffs hold large numbers of breeding seabirds with plenty of Puffins. The island is best known as a site for migrants. When easterly or south-easterly winds combine with poor visibility, spectacular falls can occur. Each year a range of scarce and rare species are found.

KEY BIRDS
SPRING: Passerine migrants with the chance of a rarity. Offshore, Manx Shearwater and both Great and Arctic Skuas.
SUMMER: Breeding seabirds include Fulmar, Shag, Puffin, Razorbill, Guillemot, Common and Arctic Terns, Herring and Lesser Black-backed Gulls, Eider, Rock Pipit, Wheatear.
AUTUMN: Passerine migrants include chats, flycatchers, warblers, crests and thrushes. Offshore, a chance of shearwaters, skuas, European Storm Petrel and in late autumn Little Auk.

ACCESS
OS MAP: 59 REF: NT 655 995
Day trips are possible from Anstruther, contact 01333 310103. The observatory offers hostel style accommodation; you take your own food and sleeping bag. Contact Mike Martin, 2 Manse Park, Uphall, West Lothian, EH52 6NX.

17 LOCH LEVEN/VANE FARM

RSPB RESERVE
1,597 ha (3,946 acres)
Impossible to miss if travelling on the M90, this large shallow loch is a haven for wildfowl. Over 1,000 pairs of duck nest annually on St Serf's Island. A tern colony and breeding waders are also of interest.

This site is best visited in autumn and winter. The loch acts as an autumn staging post for arriving Pink-footed Geese, the majority of which disperse to other wintering sites. A few thousand Greylag Geese winter, as do a number of species of duck. Vane Farm offers the best opportunities for close views and a good variety of birds.

KEY BIRDS
ALL YEAR: Great Crested Grebe, Cormorant, Wigeon, Gadwall, Teal, Mallard, Shoveler, Pochard, Tufted Duck, Ruddy Duck, Sparrowhawk, Lapwing, Snipe, Curlew.
SPRING AND SUMMER: Shelduck, Common Sandpiper, Common Tern, Ringed Plover, Wheatear, Tree Pipit.
AUTUMN AND WINTER: A few passage waders, geese start to arrive late September. Pink-footed and Greylag Geese with chance of other species such as White-fronted Goose, Whooper and small numbers of Bewick's Swans, Goldeneye, Goosander, chance of Smew and Long-tailed Duck, Short-eared Owl.

ACCESS
OS MAP: 58 REF: NT 160 993
Vane Farm is the best access point around the loch, at others birds are often very distant. The reserve is easily reached off the M90 at junction 5, then take the B9097 towards Glenrothes for 3 km (2 miles).

FACILITIES
There is an observation room with wheelchair access, a shop and coffee shop, plus hides and trails.

18 LARGO BAY

Largo Bay is a wintering site for a variety of grebes, divers and seaduck and is an annual wintering site for Surf Scoter, best searched for in late winter. In years when Little Auks are numerous, this species is likely to be found in the bay.

The bay attracts white-winged gulls and a few wintering waders. During summer, terns are a feature and a few seaduck appear in late summer.

KEY BIRDS
WINTER: Red-throated and Black-throated Divers, Slavonian and Red-necked Grebes, Red-breasted Merganser, Long-tailed Duck, Eider, Goldeneye, Common and Velvet Scoters, chance of Surf Scoter, Little Auk, white-winged gulls, a few estuarine waders.
SUMMER: Terns, Little Gull, Eider, scoters and Red-breasted Merganser.

ACCESS
OS MAP: 59 REF: NO 420 010
Various points allow good views of the bay, two of the best are from the free car park at the east end of Lower Largo, and Ruddon's Point, which is reached by leaving the A917 near Kilconqhar Loch, 1.6 km (1 mile) before Elie, and following the minor road through Shell Bay Caravan Park to the point. Gates to the caravan park are closed between 4pm and 9am.

19 EDEN ESTUARY

LNR
891 ha (2,200 acres)
Stretching north from St Andrews, the Eden Estuary incorporates sand dunes, salt marsh and mud flats. It is important for its wintering populations of waders and wildfowl. Seaduck congregate offshore, including flocks of Long-tailed Ducks and Velvet Scoter.

In spring and autumn, passage waders are of interest. There are a number of access points. A sandy spit at Outhead gives good views to the outer estuary, whilst the inner estuary can be viewed from both Coble Shore and Guardbridge.

KEY BIRDS
SPRING AND AUTUMN: Passage waders.
SUMMER: Terns congregate, Red-breasted Mergansers and Arctic Skua, plus returning waders.
WINTER: Red-throated Diver, sometimes rarer grebes, Greylag Goose, sometimes Whooper Swan, Brent Goose, Pintail, Teal, Shoveler, Wigeon, Goldeneye, Red-breasted Merganser, Goosander, Long-tailed Duck, Scaup, Eider, Common and Velvet Scoters, estuarine waders plus Greenshank and Black-tailed Godwit. Short-eared Owl, Peregrine and Merlin, Snow Bunting.

ACCESS
OS MAP: 59 REF: NO 470 196
From St Andrews, Outhead is reached by taking the coast road from the town to West Sands, park at the end of the road. Coble Shore is reached off the A91, 5.6 km (3½ miles) east of Guardbridge. At Guardbridge, a layby is immediately east of the bridge.

20 LOCH OF KINNORDY

LNR
81 ha (200 acres)
A freshwater loch with surrounding marsh and scrub. Historically, Black-necked Grebes bred here, but have recently ceased. A variety of wildfowl breed along with a large Black-headed Gull colony. Ospreys are regular visitors in late summer. Greylag Geese roost in winter.

KEY BIRDS
SPRING AND SUMMER: Possible Black-necked Grebe, Wigeon, Gadwall, Shoveler, Water Rail, Osprey, Marsh Harrier, Black-headed Gull, Snipe, Redshank, Curlew, Sedge Warbler.
AUTUMN AND WINTER: A few passage waders, Greylag and Pink-footed Geese, Wigeon, Shoveler, Gadwall, Hen Harrier, Short-eared Owl.

ACCESS
OS MAP: 54 REF: NO 351 539
The reserve is 1.6 km (1 mile) west of Kirrimuir on the B951.

FACILITIES
There are hides with disabled access.

21 INVERSNAID

RSPB RESERVE

374 ha (924 acres)

Tucked in along the eastern shore of Loch Lomond, Inversnaid's habitats of loch shore, woodland, and moorland ensure birding here is rewarding at any season.

Spring and early summer is a prime time for a visit. The oakwoods resonate to the trilling songs of Wood Warblers, whilst those other two western oakwood specialists, the Pied Flycatcher and Redstart, can be found too. Out on the loch Red-breasted Mergansers can be enjoyed, and it is worth keeping an eye out for a passing Golden Eagle.

A trail leads through the main habitats of the reserve, giving an excellent view of Loch Lomond at a viewpoint.

KEY BIRDS

ALL YEAR: Goosander, Golden Eagle (scarce), Buzzard, Black Grouse, Woodcock, Great Spotted Woodpecker, Dipper, Grey Wagtail, Raven, Siskin.
SPRING AND AUTUMN: Red-breasted Merganser, Common Sandpiper, Tree Pipit, Whinchat, Redstart, Wood Warbler, Pied and Spotted Flycatchers.
WINTER: Wildfowl including Goldeneye.

ACCESS

OS MAP: 56 REF: NN 337 088

Take the B829 west from Aberfoyle, after 20 km (12 miles) take a left turn to the Inversnaid Hotel. From the hotel car park, walk north along the West Highland Way to the reserve.

22 LOCH OF THE LOWES

SCOTTISH WILDLIFE TRUST

135 ha (325 acres)

Loch of the Lowes is a shallow, reed-fringed loch much visited in summer for its breeding pair of Ospreys. Good views of the nest are possible from a hide. There is a good cross section of marsh and woodland birds breeding in summer, and in autumn Greylag Geese roost. Wildfowl including Goosander in winter.

KEY BIRDS

SPRING AND SUMMER: Great Crested Grebe, Osprey, Sedge Warbler, Spotted Flycatcher.

AUTUMN AND WINTER: Greylag Goose, Goldeneye, Wigeon, Goosander.

ACCESS

OS MAP: 52 REF: NO 042 435

The reserve is signposted off the A923, just east of Dunkeld and 25 km (16 miles) north of Perth.

FACILITIES

Visitor centre and hide. Limited disabled access.

23 MONTROSE BASIN

SCOTTISH WILDLIFE TRUST

1,012 ha (2,500 acres)

The Montrose Basin is a large enclosed river estuary, that is rich in birdlife throughout the year. Thousands of wildfowl and waders occur on passage and winter. Summer brings return wader passage from July, and there is a healthy breeding population of wildfowl and waders including Eider. The late summer gathering of terns can number in their thousands.

During autumn Pink-footed Geese arrive, and by November more than 30,000 may be roosting before numbers fall off. They roost in the central part of the basin and are best viewed from the railway station and Rossie Island. Greylag Geese roost too, whilst a good variety of other wildfowl species are likely on a typical winter visit.

Thousands of waders winter, notably Knot and Oystercatcher, and a good variety pass through on autumn passage.

A visitor centre is a good starting point to explore the basin, which is located at Rossie Braes. Directions to hides and various vantage points around the basin can be obtained from here.

KEY BIRDS

ALL YEAR: Eider, Sparrowhawk, Oystercatcher, Redshank, Ringed Plover, Lapwing, Reed Bunting.
SPRING AND AUTUMN: Passage waders notably in autumn include Spotted Redshank, Ruff, Wood Sandpiper. Terns on passage and autumn gatherings include Common, Arctic, Little and Sandwich.
SUMMER: Breeding birds, returning passage waders and terns.
WINTER: Pink-footed Goose, Greylag Goose, Shelduck, Wigeon, Pintail, Teal, Shoveler,

Goosander, Red-breasted Merganser, occasional
Scaup, Peregrine, Merlin, Short-eared Owl,
estuarine waders.

ACCESS
OS MAP: 54 REF: **NO 702 565**
The basin is immediately inland of the town of
Montrose. The visitor centre is on the southern
side of the basin on the A92.

FACILITIES
There is a visitor centre open from 10.30am to
5pm from April to October, and open at
weekends only from 10.30am to 4pm from
November to March. There are hides, too.

24   FOWLSHEUGH
RSPB RESERVE
This has to be one of the best mainland seabird
breeding cliffs, for viewing birds at close quarters.
The crumbly red sandstone cliffs that stretch for
2.5 km (1½ miles) have indentations allowing good
views of a range of cliff-nesting species. Due to
the nature of these cliffs, extreme care should be
taken. A visit between May and mid-July is best.

KEY BIRDS
SPRING AND SUMMER: Shag, Fulmar, Eider,
Razorbill, Guillemot, Puffin, Herring Gull,
Kittiwake.

ACCESS
OS MAP: 45 REF: **NO 879 800**
There is a cliff-top car park at Crawton off the
A92 Inverbervie to Stonehaven road, 5 km
(3 miles) south of Stonehaven

25   SANDS OF FORVIE AND YTHAN ESTUARY
NNR
1,018 ha (2,516 acres)
Nineteen kilometres (12 miles) north of
Aberdeen, the Sands of Forvie encompasses
coastal moorland and impressive sand dunes. The
adjacent Ythan Estuary is long and thin, being
around 350 metres (380 yards) wide. Large
numbers of Eiders reside year round, the
moorland hosts Britain's largest concentration of
this species. Terns are a feature too, with a mixed
colony of four species.

The Ythan is an important staging post for
migrating wildfowl and waders, most prominent
are the large flocks of geese that stop off here at
both seasons. Pink-footed Geese can number in
their thousands with lesser numbers of other
species. The scarcer passage waders such as Little
Stint join far more numerous estuarine species
both migrating and arriving for the winter. A
typical winter visit will bag an excellent array of
wildfowl and waders, plus hunting raptors and
Snow Buntings.

KEY BIRDS
ALL YEAR: Eider, Oystercatcher, Curlew, Ringed
Plover, Stonechat.
SPRING AND AUTUMN: Migrant geese include
Pink-footed, Greylag, Brent, Barnacle and
White-fronted Geese. Passage waders include
Whimbrel, Little Stint, Curlew Sandpiper,
Spotted Redshank.
SUMMER: Common, Arctic, Little and Sandwich
Terns, Great and Arctic Skuas in estuary mouth
in late summer.
WINTER: Red-throated Diver, Pink-footed and
Greylag Geese, Whooper Swan, Wigeon, Teal,
Goldeneye, Red-breasted Merganser, Long-tailed
Duck, Common and Velvet Scoters, Short-eared
Owl, Merlin, Peregrine, Snow Bunting, Twite,
and estuarine waders.

ACCESS
OS MAP: 38 REF: **NK 034 289**
From Aberdeen take the A90 north, turning off
on to the A975 to Newburgh. There are various
access points worthy of attention. The outer
estuary, particularly the concentrations of Eider,
can be viewed from Newburgh golf course,
reached by taking the right-hand turn by the
Ythan Hotel, you can drive to the edge of the
estuary. Waterside Bridge, where the A975 crosses
the Ythan, provides views of the inner estuary.
Waulkmill Hide overlooks mud flats
frequented by waders and wildfowl and is
upstream from the bridge, reached by taking the
left-hand turn, after the bridge to Ellon. After
2.5 km (1½ miles) and just before a right-hand
bend, take a track to the left to the hide.
Finally Forvie visitor centre and the moorland
is just before the village of Collieston.

FACILITIES
There is a visitor centre and hides.

26 LOCH OF STRATHBEG

RSPB RESERVE
1,012 ha (2,500 acres)
Just a short strip of dunes separates this shallow
loch from the sea. Surrounded by willow scrub,
dunes and farmland there is much bird interest
throughout the year. The site is important as a
staging post and wintering site for wildfowl.
Wildfowl counts can exceed 30,000 birds,
underlining the importance of the reserve.

Pink-footed and Greylag Geese are prominent
in the winter. Whooper Swans peak in November.
The summer sees activity on the loch with
Sandwich and Common Terns breeding. By
mid-July, wader passage is in full swing with many
species likely in August.

KEY BIRDS
SPRING: Garganey, Wood Sandpiper and
Temminck's Stint are regular.
SUMMER: Shelduck, Shoveler, Teal, Tufted Duck,
Eider, Water Rail, Marsh Harrier, Black-tailed
Godwit, Sandwich and Common Terns.
AUTUMN: Ruff, Greenshank, Black-tailed
Godwit, Green Sandpiper, Spotted Redshank,
Curlew Sandpiper, Little Stint. Wildfowl arrive.
WINTER: Pink-footed, Greylag, Barnacle Geese,
Whooper Swan, Mute Swan, Teal, Wigeon,
Pochard, Tufted Duck, Goldeneye, Red-breasted
Merganser, Goosander, Smew.

ACCESS
OS MAP: 30 REF: **NK 057 581**
Accessed via the A952 Peterhead to Fraserburgh
road at Crimond.

FACILITIES
There is a visitor centre and hides.

27 BANFF HARBOUR

Located on Grampian's north coast, Banff
Harbour and surrounds is a top winter location
for divers, seaduck and white-winged gulls. This
is a good site for looking for Little Auks in years
when they are in the North Sea in large
numbers.

KEY BIRDS
WINTER: Divers, seaduck, Purple Sandpiper,
Glaucous and Iceland Gulls.

ACCESS
OS MAP: 29 REF: **NJ 695 645**
Check the harbour and surrounding coast, many
vantage points. River mouth for gulls.

28 SPEY BAY

Spey Bay is a large shallow bay, stretching from
Buckie to Lossiemouth. Hundreds of Red-throated
Divers, scoters and Long-tailed Ducks, winter.
Snow Buntings are numerous along the shoreline,
particularly on the Lossiemouth side of the bay.

Lossie Forest holds both Crested Tit and
Scottish Crossbill. A visit in late summer and
autumn is likely to yield a few passage waders at
the mouth of the Spey, and terns congregate in
the bay in summer.

KEY BIRDS
ALL YEAR: Eider, Crested Tit, Scottish Crossbill.
SPRING: Sandwich Tern, Osprey, a few passage
waders, wildfowl disperse.
SUMMER: Goosander, Sandwich Tern, Osprey.
AUTUMN: Passage waders, arrival of winter visitors.
WINTER: Red-throated and Great Northern
Divers, Black-throated Diver is scarce, grebes,
Long-tailed Duck, Red-breasted Merganser,
Common and Velvet Scoters, Goldeneye, Eider,
Scaup, Purple Sandpiper, Glaucous and Iceland
Gulls, Snow Bunting.

ACCESS
OS MAP: 28 REF: **NJ 335 658**
There are various access points. Boar's Head
Rock (NJ 285 678) is a good site for viewing
seaduck offshore and is reached through Lossie
Forest. Take the B9013 from Lossiemouth. After
3 km (2 mile) park, and take the forest track just
after the bridge over the river. Two minor roads
run parallel with the river to the river mouth.
Buckie is a good site for white-winged gulls.

29 GLEN TANAR

NNR
4,185 ha (10,340 acres)
Caledonian forest, moorland and mountain top
combine to make this one of Deesides top
birding spots. Surprisingly, the Crested Tit is
absent, however, the other Scottish specialities
of Scottish Crossbill, Capercaillie and
Ptarmigan are all present.

A good starting point for exploring the area is the visitor centre, where information is readily available on the various trails that can be taken.

🐦 KEY BIRDS
ALL YEAR: Golden Eagle, Buzzard, Hen Harrier, Merlin, Ptarmigan, Scottish Crossbill, Capercaillie, Black Grouse, Red Grouse, Woodcock, Dipper, Grey Wagtail, Siskin.

⛵ ACCESS
OS MAP: 44 REF: **NO 481 965**
From the A93 at Aboyne turn south on to the B976 towards Ballater, after 2.5 km (1½ miles) take the minor road on the left to Braeloine and Glen Tanar House, the information centre is along here.

🏠 FACILITIES
Visitor centre open from April to September.

30 GLEN MUICK AND LOCHNAGAR

SCOTTISH WILDLIFE TRUST
2,570 ha (6,350 acres)
As part of the Balmoral Estate, Loch Muick lies to the south-east of the mountain plateau of Lochnager. Typical species of the area include Ptarmigan, Dotterel and Golden Eagle.

Ptarmigan can be found on the plateau, and in winter on the scree slopes lower down. A visit from spring to mid-summer is ideal.

🐦 KEY BIRDS
ALL YEAR: Golden Eagle, Peregrine, Merlin, Hen Harrier, Ptarmigan, Black and Red Grouse.
SPRING AND SUMMER: Golden Plover, Dotterel, Dunlin, Common Sandpiper, Short-eared Owl.

⛵ ACCESS
OS MAP: 44 REF: **NO 300 850**
Reached west from Ballater on the B976, then left at Glen Muick. The visitor centre and car park are at the end of this road, a further 12 km (8 miles) along.

🏠 FACILITIES
A visitor centre with information on various trails that can be taken.

31 INSH MARSHES

RSPB RESERVE
850 ha (2,100 acres)
The Insh marshes stretch for 8 km (5 miles) along the floodplain of the River Spey, between Kingussie and the village of Insh.

Breeding birds include wildfowl, waders and the nationally rare Spotted Crake. The latter is impossible to see, but can often be heard calling between midnight and 2am. One of the best places to listen, being from the B1952 south-west of the Highland Wildlife Park. Loch Insh, at the northern end of the reserve, is a regular site for fishing Osprey.

Winter visitors include wildfowl such as Whooper Swans, and raptors such as Hen Harriers are regularly seen. Paths allow exploration through patches of birch woodland and along the edge of the marsh, and there are hides to assist viewing.

🐦 KEY BIRDS
ALL YEAR: Greylag Goose, Wigeon, Teal, Shoveler, Tufted Duck, Goldeneye, Snipe, Redshank, Water Rail, Spotted Crake, Great Spotted Woodpecker.
SPRING AND SUMMER: Osprey, Black-headed Gull, Tree Pipit, Redstart, Pied Flycatcher, Wood Warbler.
AUTUMN AND WINTER: Pink-footed and Greylag Geese stop off on autumn migration, Whooper Swan, Hen Harrier, Short-eared Owl.

⛵ ACCESS
OS MAP: 35 REF: **NN 775 999**
From Kingussie take the B970 past Ruthven Barracks to the RSPB car park, where there are trails and hides. For further viewpoints across the reserve, continue along this road, and then back to Kingussie from Insh on the B9152. An RSPB leaflet obtained from the information point gives details for various places to stop along this route.

🏠 FACILITIES
There are hides, trails and an information point.

32 ABERNETHY INCLUDING LOCH GARTEN

RSPB RESERVE

12,500 ha (30,890 acres)

Encompassing Loch Garten, the Abernethy reserve covers a vast area of Caledonian forest, bogs, moorland, lochs and mountain plateau. Loch Garten is best know for its breeding pair of Ospreys, which can be viewed from a well-equipped observation room. Crested Tit and Scottish Crossbill lurk in the surrounding forest, and occasionally Capercaillie are seen from the observation room. Capercaillie have become increasingly difficult to see on other parts of the reserve in recent years. However, there is always the chance of discovering one close to the road early in the morning.

Across the road from the Ospreys, Loch Garten attracts Goldeneye in summer, while in winter Goosander is likely. During early winter Greylag Geese roost. The path to Loch Mallachie is a good route for seeing Crested Tits and Crossbills.

Forest Lodge, nearby, has two tracks offering longer walks, with the chance of all the specialities including Parrot Crossbill. The area around the car park is often productive for Scottish Crossbill, and the track leading to Forest Lodge is a good place to try for Capercailie early in the morning.

🦅 KEY BIRDS

ALL YEAR: Goosander, Goldeneye, Capercaillie, Black Grouse, Woodcock, Dipper, Crossbill, Scottish Crossbill, Parrot Crossbill, Crested Tit.
SPRING AND SUMMER: Osprey, Common Sandpiper, Redstart, Tree Pipit, Whinchat.
AUTUMN AND WINTER: Roosting Greylag Goose, roosting gulls.

🛶 ACCESS

OS MAP: 36 REF: NH 981 184
Not far from the village of Boat of Garten, Loch Garten is signposted off the B970. This reserve is sensitive to disturbance, so keep to the tracks at all times. Forest Lodge is reached by turning left out of the Loch Garten Osprey car park, turn right at the next junction, and after about 2 km (1 mile) you will see a track on your right, which leads to the car park.

It is worth noting that the Osprey observation hide does not open as soon as the birds return in spring. A settling down period is allowed first. Therefore, if you are planning to visit in early spring before the start of May, it would be wise to check with the Aviemore tourist board office first.

📷 FACILITIES

The Osprey observation room is well equipped with telescopes, closed-circuit TV on the nest, and volunteers on hand to answer questions. There is a shop, and good disabled access.

33 LOCH AN EILEAN

Popular with tourists in summer, an early morning visit to beat the crowds can be a good idea here. Very scenic, the loch lies at the base of the Cairngorms and is surrounded by pine forest. Crested Tit and Scottish Crossbill are regular here, with Crested Tit most likely along the far shore. A good path runs around the loch.

🦅 KEY BIRDS

ALL YEAR: Goldeneye, Scottish Crossbill, Crested Tit, Siskin.
SPRING AND SUMMER: Red-throated Diver, Redstart.

🛶 ACCESS

OS MAP: 36 REF: NH 897 087
From Aviemore take the Colyumbridge (Cairn Gorm) road and turn right at Inverdruie on to the B970, after approximately 0.8 km (½ mile) there is a turning to the loch on the left.

📷 FACILITIES

A visitor centre with a recent sightings board.

34 FINDHORN VALLEY

A single track road runs for 14 km (9 miles) along the scenic Findhorn Valley. Golden Eagles are often seen patrolling the mountain ridges. The river is frequented by Dipper.

Where the road ends, there is a small parking

area. From here you can walk along a track further into the valley; this is a worthwhile route, particularly for Ring Ouzel in spring.

After 8 km (5 miles), a single track road off to the right to Farr is also worth exploration. The moorland this road crosses is also good for eagles, and both Golden Plover and Red Grouse.

KEY BIRDS
ALL YEAR: Golden Eagle, Buzzard, Peregrine, Merlin, Goosander, Golden Plover, Red Grouse, Dipper, Grey Wagtail, Raven.
SPRING AND SUMMER: Osprey, Oystercatcher, Common Sandpiper, Common Tern, Ring Ouzel.

ACCESS
OS MAP: **35** REF: **NH 711 182**
The valley road is reached from Tomatin, by leaving the A9, 24 km (15 miles) south of Inverness. The access track at the head of the valley should not be walked during the grouse and stalking seasons, from August to February.

35 LOCH RUTHVEN

RSPB RESERVE
85 ha (210 acres)
Loch Ruthven is best visited in spring or early summer for its speciality the Slavonian Grebe. This is the most important breeding site for this species in Britain, and good views of the birds can be enjoyed at the eastern end of the loch, where there is a trail and hide.

A few species of wildfowl breed, and in winter there is a chance of Smew.

KEY BIRDS
ALL YEAR: Black Grouse (scarce), Tufted Duck, Teal, Wigeon, Peregrine, Hen Harrier, Raven, Reed Bunting, Siskin, Redpoll.
SPRING AND SUMMER: Slavonian Grebe, Red-breasted Merganser, Osprey, Sedge and Willow Warblers.

ACCESS
OS MAP: **26** REF: **NH 638 281**
From the A9 turn west on to B851, 10 km (6 miles) from Inverness. Fork right at East Croachy on to a minor road, where there is a car park.

36 FAIRY GLEN

RSPB RESERVE
2.4 ha (6 acres)
This small woodland reserve lies in a steep-sided valley on the Black Isle north of Inverness. There is a stream and waterfalls attractive to Dipper and Grey Wagtail. The reserve is of interest throughout the year for a good range of woodland species, too.

KEY BIRDS
ALL YEAR: Buzzard, Dipper, Grey Wagtail, common woodland species.

ACCESS
OS MAP: **27** REF: **NH 735 578**
The reserve has a car park located off the A832 on the northern edge of Rosemarkie (on a corner opposite some houses).

37 UDALE BAY

RSPB RESERVE
Udale Bay encompasses intertidal mud flats on the south shore of the Cromarty Firth. Wintering and passage wildfowl and waders are of key interest, so a visit from autumn through to spring is best.

KEY BIRDS
SPRING AND AUTUMN: Passage waders, arriving and departing wildfowl.
WINTER: A few seaduck, divers and grebes in Cromarty Firth, in bay estuarine waders and wildfowl including Greylag Goose, Wigeon and Teal. Peregrine and Merlin.

ACCESS
OS MAP: **27** REF: **NH 715 650**
Udale Bay is on the Black Isle, best viewed from the B9163 west of Cromarty. There is a layby just west of Jemimaville, and from a parking area east of Jemimaville, and from Newhall Point reached on a minor road from Balblair.

CAIRNGORM
NNR / RSPB RESERVE (41,440 ha/102,400 acres)

This is the highest mountain plateau in Britain rising to over 1,300 metres (4,265 ft) at Ben Macdui. Its barren, boulder-strewn landscape supports few birds, however, those it does are true specialists of this Arctic-type environment: more snow falls here than anywhere else in Britain. Ptarmigan, Snow Bunting and Dotterel are the three key species to search for, although Dotterel is just a summer visitor.

Dotterel arrive from mid- to late May and care should be taken not to disturb this rare breeding bird at or near the nest. Dotterel can be tricky to locate, as they are well camouflaged and often very confiding.

Ptarmigan, too, are cryptically camouflaged, being white in winter and grey in summer, and like Dotterel will often sit tight making locating them tricky. However, Ptarmigan have a distinctive croaking call that can often be heard. One of the best methods for finding both Dotterel and Ptarmigan is to stop every few paces and thoroughly scan the

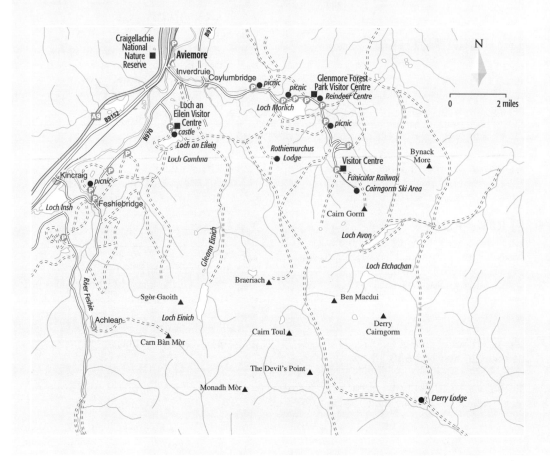

ground ahead. In winter, Ptarmigan often gather in the corries, sometimes in flocks numbering 40 or 50 birds. One of the best sites to find this species in winter is in the corries below Ben Macdui, easily reached from the funicular railway car park.

Snow Buntings can be found at various sites across the plateau in summer, and congregate in flocks at the bottom of the chair-lifts and around the funicular car park in winter. To access this area of the Cairngorms, you need to take the footpath leading from the car park. To undertake this walk, a reasonable level of fitness is required, and care should be taken particularly in winter, when the weather can change suddenly.

Alternatively, Carn Bàn Mòr to the west attracts fewer people and is a good walk. It will produce all the specialities and there is a better chance of a passing Golden Eagle. This walk entails ascending 700 metres (2,297 ft), so a reasonable level of fitness is once again required. Care should be taken on all routes up on to Cairngorm not to stray off paths, both to limit disturbance to birds and trampling of fragile plant communities. It is also very easy in poor weather to become disorientated and lost. The weather at these altitudes can change dramatically within minutes and, during winter, white-out conditions can occur, even during what appears to be calm, settled weather.

Much of the base and lower slopes of the Cairngorms are cloaked in Caledonian pine forest and heather. These habitats hold many of the typical species of the area, including Capercaillie, Black and Red Grouse, Crested Tit and Scottish Crossbill.

KEY BIRDS

ALL YEAR: Golden Eagle, Peregrine, Ptarmigan, Red Grouse, Black Grouse, Capercaillie, Crested Tit, Scottish Crossbill, Snow Bunting.
SPRING AND SUMMER: Dotterel.

ACCESS

OS MAP: 36 REF: NH 989 060
From Aviemore take the Colyumbridge road past Loch Morlich to the car parks below the ski lifts and Funicular railway. A path at the main car park by the railway station leads up through the corries to the plateau.
OS MAP: 36 REF: NN 852 975
For Carn Bàn Mòr, from the B970 at Feshiebridge take the road to Lagganlia, and follow this for 8 km (5 miles) to the end at Achlean. The track from here leads up to the summit.

Ptarmigan
Lagopas mutus

In Britain, Ptarmigan are restricted to mountainous areas in Scotland. They feed on shoots, buds, berries and seeds, while in the breeding season their diet is supplemented with insects. Beautiful in their winter white plumage, the species can prove hard to find when on snow. Males are easily separated from females by the red patch above their eye.

The Cairngorms offer one of the more accessible locations in Scotland in which to find the species. During summer, they frequent the high tops. However, once the weather starts to close in during early winter, they descend, often forming quite large flocks on scree slopes and in corries.

39 CULBIN SANDS

RSPB RESERVE

Just west of Nairn on the south side of the Moray Firth, Culbin Sands is best visited in winter for wildfowl and waders. Offshore seaducks, particularly scoters and Long-tailed Ducks congregate, whilst the sands attract flocks of Knot and Bar-tailed Godwits. Various species of raptor hunt over the area, which includes salt marsh and large shingle and sand bars.

KEY BIRDS

AUTUMN AND WINTER: Red-breasted Merganser, Long-tailed Duck, Velvet and Common Scoters, Eider and divers are all regular offshore, Hen Harrier, Merlin, Peregrine, Bar-tailed Godwit, Knot, Oystercatcher.
SPRING AND SUMMER: Oystercatcher, Ringed Plover and Common Tern breed; Eider offshore.

ACCESS

OS MAP: 27 REF: NH 900 580
The reserve can be reached by travelling 0.8 km (½ mile) east of Nairn on the A96, and turning off at the sign for the East Beach car park.

40 GLEN AFFRIC

FOREST ENTERPRISE

Glen Affric is one of the best known glens in the Highlands, with its Caledonian pine woods supporting Capercaillie, Crested Tit and Scottish Crossbill. The rivers and streams support typical species such as Dipper, whilst in summer the lochs occasionally attract Black-throated Divers. It is always worth keeping an eye on the sky here, for passing Golden Eagles.

The glen covers a large area, and there are various trails that allow exploration. Most start at designated parking areas along the road through the glen. A good route runs for a little over 16 km (10 miles) around Loch Affric, shorter routes that are often productive include the path to Dog Falls and Coire Loch, both at the Cannich end of the glen.

KEY BIRDS

ALL YEAR: Golden Eagle, Buzzard, Osprey (occasional), Black Grouse, Capercaillie, Dipper, Grey Wagtail, Crested Tit, Common Crossbill, Scottish Crossbill, Siskin, Redpoll.

SPRING AND SUMMER: Black-throated and occasional Red-throated Divers, Red-breasted Merganser, Goosander, Redstart, Tree Pipit.

ACCESS

OS MAP: 25 REF: NH 240 240
Take the A831 west from Loch Ness. At Cannich, take the minor road down the glen past Fasnakyle.

41 LOCH FLEET

SCOTTISH WILDLIFE TRUST
1,163 ha (2,874 acres)
A tidal basin bordered by dunes, pinewoods, and an area of alder carr at the back of the fleet are the main habitats. Large areas of mud become exposed at low tide attracting estuarine waders in winter, although in modest numbers, whilst during passage periods a variety of species occur.

The fleet and the sea area between Golspie in the north and Embo in the south is best known for the wildfowl the area attracts from autumn through to spring. On the sea, divers, grebes and seaduck gather, with autumn and late spring being best. During late May, up to 2,000 Long-tailed Ducks congregate before moving north to breed. During some years King Eiders and Surf Scoters occur. The fleet attracts dabbling ducks, Whooper Swans and Greylag Geese.

During summer the pinewoods support Redstarts and Scottish Crossbills. These can be reached by taking a minor road south from Golspie to Little Ferry, there are access points along this road. The sea and fleet mouth can be viewed by parking at Little Ferry and walking east. Embo Pier is another good site for viewing seaduck, and can be reached by going through the caravan site at Embo to its south eastern corner. Finally, one of the best spots for passage waders is the Mound Pool, reached where the A9 crosses the head of the fleet, the pool is on the left.

KEY BIRDS

ALL YEAR: Eider, Buzzard, Scottish Crossbill.
SPRING: Long-tailed Duck, various wildfowl, Greenshank.
SUMMER: Fulmar, Shelduck, Osprey, Arctic Tern, Redstart.
AUTUMN: Passage waders. Seaduck arrive offshore.

WINTER: Offshore, divers, Slavonian and Red-necked Grebes, Common and Velvet Scoters, Long-tailed Duck, Goldeneye, Red-breasted Merganser, in and around the fleet Whooper Swan, Greylag Goose, Wigeon, Teal, Peregrine, Short-eared Owl, a few waders, Twite and Snow Bunting.

ACCESS
OS MAP: **21** REF: **NH 794 965**
Loch Fleet is on the A9 just south of Golspie.

42 FLOW COUNTRY

RSPB RESERVE
7,000 ha (17,297 acres)
Forsinaird lies in the Flow Country a vast area of blanket bog. The area is characterised by a mosaic of pools and spaghnum dominated vegetation. Spring into early summer is the best time to visit, outside of the breeding season there is little bird interest.

Breeding bird density is low, so the chances of seeing many of the specialists such as Greenshank are limited. However, the reserve at Forsinaird is a good introduction to the Flow Country. There is a trail here, through lochans and blanket bog, that allows the habitat to be experienced, if not the birds.

KEY BIRDS
SPRING AND SUMMER: Red-throated and Black-throated Divers, Common Scoter, Wigeon, Ptarmigan, Hen Harrier, Golden Eagle, Merlin, Peregrine, Golden Plover, Curlew, Dunlin, Greenshank, Short-eared Owl, Dipper, Wheatear, Twite, Raven.

ACCESS
OS MAP: **10** REF: **NC 890 425**
Forsinaird is midway along the A897, which runs between the A836 on the north coast and the A9 on the east coast. This is a lonely route that winds its way through the peatlands, so frequent stops may produce birds. Alternatively, the reserve is on the Inverness to Thurso railway line.

FACILITIES
The reserve centre is in the railway station, and there is a trail and guided walks. The centre is open from April to October from 9am to 6pm.

43 DUNNET HEAD

Dunnet Head is the most northerly headland on mainland Britain. The sea cliffs here support a range of breeding seabirds, found on the north and eastern sides of the headland. In winter, Dunnet Bay is worth checking for white-winged gulls as well as divers and seaduck.

KEY BIRDS
ALL YEAR: Rock Dove, Twite, Raven.
SPRING AND SUMMER: Great Skua, Fulmar, Kittiwake, Guillemot, Razorbill, Black Guillemot, Puffin.
WINTER: Divers, seaduck, white-winged gulls in the bay.

ACCESS
OS MAP: **12** REF: **ND 203 767**
Dunnet Head lies a short distance east of Thurso. From the village of Dunnet, take the minor road to the lighthouse.

44 CLO MOR

Six kilometres (4 miles) east of Cape Wrath in Scotland's north-west corner, lies Clo Mor. Spectacular cliffs rising to almost 300 metres (1,000 ft), the highest on mainland Britain, are home to a variety of breeding seabirds.

KEY BIRDS
SPRING AND SUMMER: Golden Eagle, Peregrine, Red Grouse, Ptarmigan, Greenshank, Fulmar, Kittiwake, Guillemot, Razorbill, Black Guillemot, Puffin, Rock Dove.

ACCESS
OS MAP: **9** REF: **NC 293 727**
Due to its remoteness, this sites requires a fair amount of walking to reach. Take the ferry across the Kyle of Durness (no motor vehicles). A connecting minibus service to Cape Wrath can be taken; ask to be dropped off at the Kearvaig track. Walk to the cliffs at Kearvaig, then follow the cliffs back east for 5 km (3 miles), before cutting back to the track at Inshore, where you can meet the minibus by prior arrangement.

45 HANDA ISLAND

SCOTTISH WILDLIFE TRUST

364 ha (900 acres)

Just a few hundred yards off the Sutherland coast, this island is bordered by high sea cliffs on three sides. Cliff-nesting seabirds are the main attraction along with both Arctic and Great Skuas breeding on the boggy moorland interior.

A 5 km (3 mile) circular route allows exploration; the Great Stack in the north-west of the island is particularly good for viewing the cliff-nesting species. The Great Skuas on Handa are very tolerant of visitors, allowing close views.

KEY BIRDS

SPRING AND SUMMER: Red-throated Diver, Eider, Shelduck, Oystercatcher, Ringed Plover, Fulmar, Shag, Guillemot, Razorbill, Puffin, Kittiwake, Great and Arctic Skuas, Rock Dove, Wheatear, chance of Black-throated Diver offshore or in the Sound of Handa.
WINTER: Barnacle Goose, Great Northern Diver in the sound.

ACCESS

OS MAP: 9 REF: NC 147 476

Approximately 64 km (40 miles) north of Ullapool, take a minor road to Tarbet off the A894. Boats leave from here from 9.30am to 2.30 pm from April to September. The last boat back is at 5pm.

46 INVERPOLLY

NNR

10,855 ha (26,825 acres)

Mountains, bogs, lochs, rushing streams; scenically, Inverpolly is hard to beat. This large reserve lies on the coast of north-west Scotland. Birds are relatively few, due to the environment, but those that do live here are some of our most sought after. There are few easier places to find Golden Eagle on mainland Britain than here. Ptarmigan inhabit the mountains, whilst the bogs and lochs are the refuge of Greenshank and Black-throated Diver.

Walking in this landscape is hard work, and needs the proper gear. However, the following sites allow good coverage of the reserve. The Knockan Cliff famed for its geology is a good vantage point for scanning for Golden Eagles,

and the lochs below may have divers on them.

The River Kirkaig is a popular route for walkers, and allows good access. The route takes you past some impressive waterfalls, a good site for Dippers, before reaching the bogs and moorland below the impressive summit of Suilven.

KEY BIRDS

ALL YEAR: Golden Eagle, Ptarmigan, Red Grouse, Dipper, Raven, Snow Bunting.
SPRING AND SUMMER: Black-throated and Red-throated Divers, Red-breasted Merganser, Goosander, Wigeon, Greylag Goose, Buzzard, Merlin, Peregrine, Golden Plover, Greenshank, Ring Ouzel, Wood Warbler, Twite. Fulmar, Shag and Eider breed on the coast.

ACCESS

OS MAP: 15 REF: NC 166 054

The reserve lies to the west of the A835. Much of the reserve can be viewed by taking the road west off the A835 at Drumrunie and following this to Lochinver, stopping frequently on route to view.

The Knockan Cliff is midway between Drumrunie and Elphin on the A835.

The River Kirkaig is near Inverkirkaig on the minor road south of Lochinver.

47 BEINN EIGHE

NNR

4,800 ha (11,860 acres)

This is a reserve of Caledonian pine forest, dwarf shrub heath, mountain top and loch shore. Redstart, Wood Warbler, Crossbill and Scottish Crossbill inhabit the woods, whilst the high ground supports Ptarmigan, and in the skies above, Golden Eagle. Loch Maree holds both Red and Black-throated Divers.

The reserve can be explored along two nature trails, a short 1.6 km (1 mile) woodland route, and a 6 km (4 mile) upland trail.

KEY BIRDS

ALL YEAR: Golden Eagle, Buzzard, Red Grouse, Ptarmigan, Goosander, Dipper, Scottish and Common Crossbills, Raven.
SPRING AND SUMMER: Black-throated and Red-throated Divers, Red-breasted Merganser, Common Sandpiper, Tree Pipit, Whinchat, Wheatear, Redstart, Wood Warbler.

ACCESS
OS MAP: **19** REF: **NG 019 630**
The reserve lies between the A896 and A832.
Loch Maree is easily viewed along its south shore
from the A832.
OS MAP: **19** REF: **NH 000 650**
The two nature trails leave from a car park (grid
reference above) 5 km (3 miles) north-west of
Kinlochewe.

FACILITIES
Reserve centre with leaflets on trails, located
5 km (3 miles) north west of Kinlochewe off the
A832.

48　ST KILDA

NATIONAL TRUST FOR SCOTLAND / NNR
853 ha (2,107 acres)
With some of the best cliff and sea stack scenery
in the world, huge seabird colonies, and a
remarkable human history, it is easy to
understand why the archipelago was made a
World Heritage Site in 1987.

St Kilda supports more than 60,000 pairs of
Gannets the majority on sea stacks that tower
out of the ocean, huge numbers of Puffins and
rarer breeding seabirds such as Leach's Storm
Petrel breed. The main island of Hirta supports
the St Kilda Wren, a subspecies that is greyer and
a third larger than its common mainland relative.
Apart from the seabirds, the islands attract
vagrants, mostly North American species in
autumn. Severely underwatched due to the
problems of reaching the islands, it is anyone's
guess as to the vagrant potential these islands
have.

KEY BIRDS
SPRING AND SUMMER: Eider, Manx Shearwater,
Fulmar, Gannet, Guillemot, Black Guillemot,
Razorbill, Puffin, gulls, Kittiwake, Leach's and
European Storm Petrels, Great Skua, Wheatear,
St Kilda Wren, Snipe.

ACCESS
OS MAP: **18** REF: **NF 102 991**
Only accessible during the summer and only by
boat. Due to the uncertainties of the Atlantic
weather, there are never any guarantees that St
Kilda will be reached. There are various charter
companies who run tours out to the islands

during the summer months, with most leaving from
Oban.

49　MONACH ISLANDS
This low-lying chain of 5 islands, 9 km (6 miles) off
the North Uist coast have some of the best
examples of Machair left in Britain.

Rarely visited, various species of tern nest, and
due to the lack of ground predators species such as
Fulmar and Buzzard nest on the ground. There is a
healthy population of Black Guillemot. In winter
Barnacle Geese use the islands.

KEY BIRDS
SPRING AND SUMMER: Fulmar, Shag, Cormorant,
Eider, Buzzard, Common, Arctic, Little and
sometimes Sandwich Terns, Black Guillemot,
Ringed Plover, Dunlin, Wheatear, Twite. In offshore
waters, Manx Shearwater and European Storm
Petrel.
AUTUMN AND WINTER: Barnacle Goose.

ACCESS
OS MAP: **22** REF: **NF 643 617**
There are no regular boat services to the islands,
however, charters heading to St Kilda often stop at
the islands.

50　ISLE OF RUM
NNR
10,684 ha (26,400 acres)
Home to the largest Manx Shearwater colony in the
world, the island also supports both Golden and
White-tailed Eagles. Seabirds nest on some of the
cliffs on the south and north-east coasts.

KEY BIRDS
ALL YEAR: Golden Eagle, White-tailed Eagle, Raven.
SPRING AND SUMMER: Manx Shearwater, Red-
throated Diver, Fulmar, Kittiwake, Guillemot, Black
Guillemot, Merlin, Eider, Golden Plover.

ACCESS
OS MAP: **39** REF: **NM 407 992**
A passenger ferry service runs from Mallaig, reached
on the A830, north from Fort William.

BALRANALD
RSPB RESERVE (658 ha/1,626 acres)

Balranald is situated on the western tip of North Uist in the Outer Hebrides. The reserve encompasses machair, a habitat created by wind-blown sand mixing with the underlying peat. Rich in wild flowers, the reserve is dotted with freshwater lochs, boggy areas and rough pasture, as well as cultivated and uncultivated machair.

The reserve proves attractive to Corncrakes, with Balranald being not only one of the Scottish strongholds, but also one of the easier places to see this notoriously difficult species. A visit in May is the optimum time for seeing Corncrakes, as they return in late April from their winter quarters, but the vegetation on the reserve, particularly the iris beds that they favour, will not have grown enough to conceal them fully. By June and July, vegetation will have grown sufficiently to make tracking down a calling bird an exasperating experience.

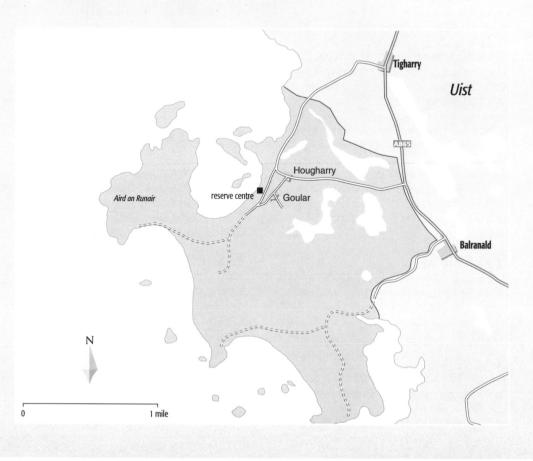

The machair attracts waders to breed and is particularly attractive to Corn Buntings, which are very common in summer. Aird an Runair is a rocky headland on the reserve, which in spring and autumn is a good point for seawatching. During spring, westerly and north-westerly winds may produce a passage of Long-tailed and Pomarine Skuas, with mid-May being the peak time. During autumn, both Leach's and European Storm Petrels, Grey Phalarope, auks, skuas and gulls can occur, the best conditions being strong westerly winds. Autumn seawatching is, however, normally more productive from Rubha Ardvule, a headland on South Uist.

A circular trail around the reserve starts at the car park and reserve centre that, incidentally, is one of the best spots from which to see Corncrakes.

The lochs and marshes on the reserve are favoured by breeding wildfowl: Teal and Mallard predominate, though Shoveler, Gadwall, Wigeon and Tufted Duck are present in smaller numbers. A recent campaign to remove introduced Hedgehogs will hopefully restore the breeding wader populations that the reserve is important for. Dunlin, Redshank, Ringed Plover, Lapwing and Oystercatcher all breed here.

There are a number of other sites close to Balranald on the Uists. One worthy of exploration is Loch Druidbeg, a National Nature Reserve covering 1,677 hectares (4,144 acres). The loch is worth checking for wildfowl and waders, and is a good spot from which to scan for raptors such as Golden Eagle.

⚡ KEY BIRDS

SPRING: Red-throated Diver (overhead and on sea), lingering Great Northern Diver, skuas on passage.
SUMMER: Teal, Shoveler, Gadwall, Wigeon, Tufted Duck, Lapwing, Redshank, Oystercatcher, Ringed Plover, Dunlin, Corn Bunting, Twite, Corncrake.
AUTUMN: Petrels, auks, skuas, gulls offshore.
WINTER: Whooper Swan, Greylag Goose, various dabbling ducks, offshore divers and grebes, Purple Sandpiper, Snow Bunting.

⚓ ACCESS

OS MAP: 18 REF: NF 705 707
The reserve is on the western side of North Uist, off the A865.

Loch Druidbeg is easily found alongside the A865 Lochboisdale to Benbecula road.
OS MAP: 22 REF: NF 712 298
Rubha Ardvule is on South Uist.

Corncrake
Crex crex

Its distinctive rasping 'crex crex' call and skulking habits can make searching for the Corncrake a frustrating business. Often sounding as if it is at your feet, the Corncrake has the uncanny ability to throw its voice. Searching for a calling bird in an overgrown field can be a fruitless exercise.

As mentioned above, the trick is to arrive before the vegetation has had a chance to grow. Then, with patience, the calling bird is relatively easy to see. The Corncrake was in serious decline, until the late 80s and early 90s when measures were taken to introduce Corncrake-friendly farming regimes in its strongholds on islands off the west coast of Scotland. This has been a big success, and in recent years the population at many localities has started to recover.

52 GLENBORRODALE

RSPB RESERVE

100 ha (247 acres)

Situated on the Ardnamurchan Peninsula, Glenborrodale is a coastal oak woodland bordering the shore of Loch Sunart. A good range of woodland birds may be found, including Wood Warbler, Redstart and in the more open areas Whinchat breed. Golden Eagle are occasionally seen overhead. A nature trail allows access through the reserve.

KEY BIRDS

ALL YEAR: Buzzard, woodland birds.

SPRING AND SUMMER: Offshore Eider, feeding terns, Common Sandpiper, Tree Pipit, Redstart, Wood Warbler, Wheatear, Whinchat, Stonechat.

ACCESS

OS MAP: 40 REF: NM 611 611

The peninsula is west of Fort William. The reserve can be found 1.6 km (1 mile) west of Glenborrodale on the B8007.

53 COLL

RSPB RESERVE

1,221 ha (3,017 acres)

Coll is best visited in spring and summer for its Corncrakes and breeding waders. The reserve is located at the western end of the island and comprises machair, sand dunes, hay meadows and moorland.

KEY BIRDS

SPRING AND SUMMER: Red-throated Diver, Greylag Goose, Eider, Teal, Arctic Skua, Little, Common and Arctic Terns, Corncrake.

WINTER: Greenland White-fronted Goose, Barnacle Goose, Greylag Goose, offshore, divers and seaduck.

ACCESS

OS MAP: 46 REF: NM 154 546

By ferry from Oban. The reserve is reached by taking the B8070 to Arileod at the islands southern end, then turn left here, keeping right at the turn off to the castle. Park after the cattle grid. Alternatively, at Arileod turn right to Totronald where there is a information point and a car park.

54 TIREE

8,400 ha (20,757 acres)

Similar to nearby Coll in birds and habitat, machair and low moorland predominate. Corncrakes thrive here and there are breeding waders typical of this type of habitat.

KEY BIRDS

ALL YEAR: Greylag Goose, dabbling ducks, Eider, Red-breasted Merganser, Buzzard, Peregrine, Ringed Plover, Lapwing, Dunlin, Snipe, Curlew, Redshank, Rock Dove, Stonechat, Raven, Twite.

SPRING AND SUMMER: Corncrake, Common, Arctic and Little Terns, Arctic Skua.

AUTUMN AND WINTER: Whooper Swan, (autumn congregation), Greenland White-fronted Goose, Barnacle Goose, shore waders, divers and seaduck, wildfowl on lochs. Merlin and Peregrine.

ACCESS

OS MAP: 46 REF: NM 050 457

Ferry from Oban, and flights from Glasgow. There is no public transport on Tiree, and a car is a big advantage due to the size of the island.

55 MULL

Mountainous, with wooded glens, moorland and lochs. Raptors are a main ingredient with Golden Eagles and White-tailed Eagles easier to see here than at many other west coast sites. Mull's moorland and plantations are favoured by Short-eared Owls and Hen Harriers.

There are a number of sites around the island worth concentrating on, such as the Mishnish Lochs, Loch Na Keal, and for upland species particularly raptors try Glen More.

Off Mull there are the Treshnish Isles, popular with bird photographers, the islands support big populations of auks, especially Puffins. Day trips can be arranged from Ulva Ferry.

KEY BIRDS

ALL YEAR: Red-throated Diver, Eider, Red-breasted Merganser, Hen Harrier, Buzzard, Golden Eagle, White-tailed Eagle, Merlin, Peregrine, Red Grouse, Ptarmigan, Greenshank, Guillemot, Black Guillemot, Razorbill, Rock Dove, Short-eared Owl, Dipper, Crossbill.

SPRING AND SUMMER: Great Northern Diver, Goldeneye, Manx Shearwater, Corncrake, Golden

Plover, Kittiwake, Common and Arctic Terns, Tree Pipit, Whinchat, Wheatear, Redstart, Ring Ouzel.
AUTUMN: Passage waders, passage seabirds.
WINTER: Great Northern, Black-throated and Red-throated Divers, Slavonian Grebe, Whooper Swan, Greylag, Barnacle and Greenland White-fronted Geese, various ducks, white-winged gulls, Purple Sandpiper.

ACCESS
OS MAP: 47, 48, 49
Caledonian MacBrayne operate ferries to Mull from Oban, Lochaline and Kilchoan.

Mishnish Lochs is just south of Tobermory on the B8073 and Loch Na Keal is on the western end of the island, on the B8035. Glen More is reached via the A849 west of Strathcoil.

56 ISLAY

RSPB RESERVE
Spectacular numbers of geese decend on Islay each autumn. Thousands remain through the winter with in excess of 30,000 Barnacle and 15,000 Greenland White-fronted Geese.

Choughs are easily seen throughout the year. Golden Eagles hunt over the island.

Although just about anywhere on the island is good for birds, there are a few sites listed below that should not be missed.

LOCH GRUINART is an RSPB reserve. Large numbers of geese congregate here on their arrival in October. The loch attracts wintering and passage waders, whilst the reserve in summer is important for both breeding wildfowl and waders, and there is the chance of a calling Corncrake. The reserve has a visitor centre and a small hide. From Bridgend take the B8017 to Gruinart.

ARDNAVE LOCH is reached by following the minor road up the western side of Loch Gruinart. It is a favourite spot for Chough, and there can be waders around the loch shore.

MACHAIR BAY is one of the most reliable sites for Chough. Before reaching the church at Kilchonan, take the lane to the sea and walk through the dunes.

BRIDGEND in the centre of the island has productive mud flats at the head of Loch Indaal,

with viewing from various points along the A847 and A846. Barnacle Geese roost in the bay.

LOCH INDAAL can also be viewed from Bowmore Pier in Bowmore. This is a good vantage point in winter for viewing divers, grebes and seaduck.

THE OA RSPB reserve is found by taking a minor road from Port Ellen, and heading towards the American Monument. Seabirds breed on the cliffs, which are a good site for Chough in summer, along with Golden Eagle, Raven and Peregrine.

The most westerly point on Islay is **RUBHA NA FAING** reached by the A847. This can be a good seawatching point. Sooty Shearwaters pass offshore from early August to mid-September. Petrels and auks pass, with a westerly bias in the winds necessary.

JURA supports Golden Eagle, Red-throated Diver and the most southerly colony of breeding Arctic Skuas. In winter the bays support similar species to Islay, with seaduck, divers, grebes and Black Guillemot.

KEY BIRDS
ALL YEAR: Red-throated Diver, Red-breasted Merganser, Eider, Common Scoter, Golden Eagle, Buzzard, Merlin, Peregrine, Hen Harrier, Short-eared Owl, Barn Owl, Black Guillemot, Twite, Chough, Raven.
SPRING AND SUMMER: Corncrake (scarce), Fulmar, Shag, Kittiwake, Black Guillemot, Guillemot, Razorbill, Hen Harrier, Wood Warbler, Whinchat.
AUTUMN AND WINTER: Passage and wintering estuarine waders. Whooper Swan (mainly passage), Barnacle and Greenland White-fronted Geese, a few Pink-footed and Greylag Geese, almost annually vagrant Snow and small race Canada Geese, divers and Slavonian Grebe, seaduck, Scaup, Goldeneye, Wigeon, white-winged gulls, Purple Sandpiper.

ACCESS
OS MAP: 60
Caledonian MacBrayne operates a ferry service from Kennacraig on the mainland. There are flights from Glasgow.

ORKNEY

With more than 70 islands lying off the northern tip of Britain, Orkney is a green and fertile archipelago. Its lengthy coastline ranges from towering cliffs to long sandy beaches: habitats rich in birdlife.

Spring and summer are when many birders visit. The sea cliffs buzz with seabirds, and this is one of Orkney's big attractions. Areas such as Marwick Head and Westray, both RSPB reserves, offer spectacular sights. Many islands support maritime heath, a now rare habitat, attracting nesting Arctic Terns, which in turn encourage both Arctic and Great Skuas to nest nearby. Many areas of moorland conceal lochs and lochans, favoured breeding sites for Red-throated Divers, whilst the moors themselves are important habitat for Hen Harriers and Short-eared Owls.

Passage periods on Orkney bring an air of anticipation. Migrant hotspots such as North Ronaldsay produce exciting birding with drift migrants in both seasons and the lure of vagrants in autumn.

Winter is a season of plenty on Orkney, too. Scapa Flow of World War One fame hosts outstanding numbers of divers, grebes and seaduck. Inland on mainland Orkney, Loch Harray boasts impressive winter wildfowl flocks. Orkney's fields get probed by wintering Curlews, whilst the rocky shorelines of many islands support large numbers of Purple Sandpipers.

North Ronaldsay, however, is the lure that brings many to Orkney in both spring and autumn, but it is the latter season that has produced some outstanding rarities, often eclipsing Fair Isle, which has traditionally been the island for autumn rarities.

Great birding can be enjoyed at whatever season you decide to visit. With good air links and a regular ferry service from the mainland, various travel options are possible. Summer is a popular time to visit, as it is possible to take a round trip if you have a car, visiting Shetland, followed by Orkney, and then taking the ferry to Scrabster and driving back through the Flow country.

KEY

1) The Loons	8) Hoy
2) Marwick Head	9) Westray: Noup Head
3) Birsay and Cottascarth	10) Pappa Westray: North Hill
4) Loch of Harray and Loch of Stenness	11) Copinsay
5) Scapa Flow	12) Rousay and Egilsay
6) Stromness and Kirkwall Harbours	13) Sanday
7) Binscarth Wood	14) Eday
	15) Stronsay
	16) North Ronaldsay

10 Papa Westray

16 North Ronaldsay

9 ○Pierowall
Westray

Sanday
13

Rousay
12

14
Eday ○Backaland

2
Twatt ○
1

A967

3

A966

7
4 ○Finstown

Mainland

Stromness ○ 6
Houghton ○

Scapa
Flow

5

8
Lyness ○
Hoy
Flotta

Longhope ○

A967

South Ronaldsay

○Burwick

Island of
Stroma

○Whitehall
Stronsay
15

Shapinsay

○Kirkwall 6

11

Orkney

Burray

N

0   10 miles

0   10   20 km

1 THE LOONS

RSPB RESERVE

73 ha (180 acres)

Overlooked by a roadside hide, this mainland marsh attracts breeding wildfowl and waders in summer, and wintering wildfowl.

KEY BIRDS

SPRING AND SUMMER: Red-breasted Merganser, Shoveler, Wigeon, Pintail, Teal, Tufted Duck, Arctic Tern, Kittiwake, Snipe, Redshank, Curlew. **AUTUMN AND WINTER:** Various wildfowl including small flock of Greenland White-fronted Geese.

ACCESS

OS MAP: 6 REF: HY 246 242

Just north of Twatt on the A986 take a left turn on to a minor road, the hide is approximately 2.5 km (1½ miles) along on the left.

FACILITIES

The hide on the west side of the reserve is the best point to view from. There is no access to the remainder of the reserve.

2 MARWICK HEAD

RSPB RESERVE

The red sandstone cliffs of Marwick Head extend for more than 1.6 km (1 mile) and rise to 1000m (328 feet). Thousands of cliff-nesting seabirds breed. Care should be taken here as there are overhangs and crumbly areas along the cliff top. The bay below the cliff attracts Eider, whilst Twite and Rock Dove occur in the fields. The cliff scenery here is some of the best in Orkney, with good vantage points to enjoy the long sweep of cliffs and rows and rows of attendant birds on their ledges.

KEY BIRDS

SPRING AND SUMMER: Fulmar, Kittiwake, Eider, Guillemot, Razorbill, Puffin (elusive here), Rock Dove, Twite, Raven.

ACCESS

OS MAP: 6 REF: HY 229 242

Close to the Loons, continue past this site to the B9056, turn right and then left to Marwick Bay. Park here and proceed up onto the cliff top.

3 BIRSAY AND COTTASCARTH

RSPB RESERVE

2,340 ha (5,782 acres)

Moorland, bogs, grassland and small lochs attract waders, skuas, raptors and Red-throated Divers to breed. A visit from spring to mid summer is best. There is limited bird interest in winter.

A hide at Cottascarth is a good vantage point for finding Hen Harriers and Short-eared Owls. A further hide at Burgar Hill overlooks a loch, and is particularly good for Red-throated Divers and some of the other typical breeding birds.

KEY BIRDS

SPRING AND SUMMER: Red-throated Diver, Red-breasted Merganser, Wigeon, Teal, Merlin, Short-eared Owl, Hen Harrier, Golden Plover, Dunlin, Curlew, Artic and Great Skuas, Twite, Wheatear, Stonechat.

ACCESS

OS MAP: 6 REF: HY 324 236

Viewing of the reserve is possible from the B9057, and from a minor road off this running along the Burn of Hillside. The hide at Cottascarth is reached by turning left off the A966, 5 km (3 miles) north of Finstown, then the first turning on the right signposted to Cottascarth. Drive to the farm at the end, from here there is a short walk to the hide at the bottom of a hillside. The hide at Burgar Hill is reached by taking a track off to the left off the A966, 0.8km (½ mile) after the B9057 junction. Look for the wind generators that are next to the car park.

FACILITIES

There is wheelchair access to the hide at Burgar Hill.

4 LOCH OF HARRAY AND LOCH OF STENNESS

RSPB RESERVE

These two lochs are the largest in Orkney. Loch Harray is a freshwater loch attracting huge numbers of wintering wildfowl. During winter Loch of Harray can hold more than 10,000 wildfowl, being of major importance in Britain for wintering Pochard, whilst Loch Stenness is tidal, attracting seaducks and grebes. Surrounding roads and tracks provide good vantage points across the lochs. A good place to start is at the car park at the Ring of Brodgar, a very impressive stone circle.

KEY BIRDS
AUTUMN AND WINTER: Slavonian Grebe, Whooper Swan, Greylag Goose, Tufted Duck, Pochard, Scaup, Long-tailed Duck.
SPRING AND SUMMER: A few wildfowl and fields contain breeding waders such as Curlew and Oystercatcher.

ACCESS
OS MAP: 6 REF: HY 116 135
The lochs are 6 km (4 miles) east of Stromness off the A966. Look for signs to Ring of Brodgar.

FACILITIES
The surrounding roads allow good views for the disabled.

5 SCAPA FLOW

RSPB RESERVE
Famous for its wartime history, this large area – encompassing Waulkmill Bay, part of the RSPB reserve at Hobbister – supports large numbers of divers, grebes and particularly seaduck in winter. The Hobbister reserve also supports a range of moorland species. Flocks of Long-tailed Ducks can exceed 2,000 in number. Whilst many birds are likely to be in the distance, there are various vantage points for viewing. Waulkmill Bay and the Churchill Barriers both provide excellent viewing. Additionally, there are vantage points on the islands of Hoy, Burray and South Ronaldsay.

KEY BIRDS
WINTER: Great Northern, Black-throated (scarce) and Red-throated Divers, Slavonian Grebe, Eider, Red-breasted Merganser, Scaup, Long-tailed Duck, scoters, Black Guillemot.

ACCESS
OS MAP: 6
Various vantage points overlooking Scapa Flow as detailed above. The Churchill Barriers are crossed by the A961, which leads to South Ronaldsay. Hobbister reserve is reached off the A964, 2.5 km (1½ miles) east of Orphir.

6 STROMNESS AND KIRKWALL HARBOURS
Both Stromness and Kirkwall Harbours attract gulls in winter, particularly Glaucous and Iceland Gulls. A few wildfowl are likely to be present too, including Goldeneye and Long-tailed Duck.

ACCESS
OS MAP: 6
The roads allow good views for the disabled.

7 BINSCARTH WOOD
This sycamore and conifer wood is the largest stand of trees on Orkney, and so frequently holds migrants during passage periods. Long-eared Owls roost in winter.

ACCESS
OS MAP: 6 REF: HY 348 140
Access is from the A965, 1.6 km (1 mile) west of the town of Finstown. Turn right down to Binscarth Farm until the road becomes a track. At the sharp left turn, park and enter the woodland.

8 HOY

RSPB RESERVE

3,926 ha (9,701 acres)

Hoy is rugged with vast expanses of moorland and dramatic cliff scenery. The reserve encompasses Britain's most famous sea stack, the Old Man of Hoy, which stands at 150 m (492 ft) high. The reserve includes high cliffs, boggy and dry moorland, and Britain's most northerly woodland at Berriedale, providing shelter for migrants.

Great and Arctic Skuas nest on the moorland, and are seen on the walk out to the Old Man of Hoy and cliffs, which takes around 45 minutes from Rackwick (a circular route can be taken from Moaness Pier). On summer evenings in Rackwick Bay, Manx Shearwaters may be visible sitting on the sea. Other species of interest in summer include raptors and waders breeding on the moorland. In spring and autumn, passerine migrants may be encountered – at these times the woodland at Berriedale should be checked.

KEY BIRDS

SPRING AND SUMMER: Red-throated Diver, Great and Arctic Skuas, Fulmar, Shag, Razorbill, Manx Shearwater, Puffin, Guillemot, Black Guillemot, Kittiwake, Short-eared Owl, Hen Harrier, Merlin, Peregrine, Buzzard, Rock Dove, Red Grouse, Golden Plover, Snipe, Dunlin, Curlew, Wheatear, Twite, Raven. A few passage migrants in spring.
AUTUMN AND WINTER Migrant passerines possible, Snow Bunting, Raven, Rock Dove.

ACCESS

OS MAP: 7 REF: HY 210 025

A car ferry runs from Houten on mainland Orkney to Lyness. There is a foot passenger ferry service from Stromness to Moaness Pier.

9 WESTRAY: NOUP HEAD

RSPB RESERVE

Centrepoint of this reserve are the 2.5 km (1½ miles) of cliffs packed with seabirds. This is one of the most densely packed seabird sites in Britain. Guillemots and Kittiwakes predominate with tens of thousands of pairs. Inland, maritime heath attracts both Arctic Terns and Arctic Skuas to nest. A visit from mid-May to July is best to experience the seabird colony at its height.

Outside of the breeding season, passage migrants may be found, particularly in the vicinity of the lighthouse. Some outstanding rarities have been found.

Away from the Noup, Westray has a number of other good birding sites. These include Loch of Burness. Waders are attracted to the margins, and the loch is worth checking for wildfowl at any time of year.

KEY BIRDS

SPRING AND SUMMER: A few passage migrants. Breeding birds include Eider, Oystercatcher, Ringed Plover, Arctic Skua, gulls, Arctic Tern, Shag, Fulmar, Kittiwake, Guillemot, Razorbill, Puffin, Black Guillemot, Rock Dove, Raven.
AUTUMN: Migrants and chance of rarities.

ACCESS

OS MAP: 5 REF: HY 392 500

There are daily ferries and daily flights with Loganair from Kirkwall. Take the track to the lighthouse from Pierowall.
OS MAP: 5 REF: HY 428 481

Loch of Burness is immediately west of Pierowall.

10 PAPA WESTRAY: NORTH HILL

RSPB RESERVE

Papa Westray is a small island close to Westray, and the North Hill reserve encompasses the northern end of the island. The reserve's maritime heath supports breeding Arctic Terns, Arctic Skuas and waders. Fowl Craig on the east coast of the island is the tallest section of cliff and one of the best spots for observing nesting seabirds. Seawatching can be good from the island's northern tip during autumn.

KEY BIRDS

SPRING AND SUMMER: Fulmar, Shag, Eider, Curlew, Snipe, Arctic Skua, Arctic Tern, Kittiwake, Guillemot, Black Guillemot, Puffin.
AUTUMN: Chance of migrants, seawatching may produce skuas, petrels and shearwaters.

ACCESS

OS MAP: 5 REF: HY 496 538

The reserve is at the northern end of the island's main road. Daily ferry service from Westray in summer. Flights from Kirkwall by Loganair, six days a week, and flights from neighbouring Westray.

11 COPINSAY

RSPB RESERVE

15 ha (37 acres)

Lying 3 km (2 miles) off east mainland, Copinsay is a small island with impressive seabird cliffs on the south-eastern side. Although the seabirds are the big attraction, during passage periods, particularly on easterly winds, migrants are likely.

KEY BIRDS

SPRING AND SUMMER: Fulmar, Shag, Eider, Guillemot, Black Guillemot, Puffin, Razorbill, Kittiwake, Great Black-backed Gull, Rock Dove, Twite, Raven.
AUTUMN: Migrants.

ACCESS

OS MAP: 6 REF: HY 610 010

The boatman based in SIkail in Deerness takes trips across to the island in summer. Contact the boatman S. Foubister on tel: 01856 741252.

12 ROUSAY AND EGILSAY

These two islands are situated next to each other. Egilsay has breeding Corncrakes and its lochs support various species of duck. Many Turnstones and Purple Sandpipers winter here.

Rousay's breeding birds include Red-throated Diver, Hen Harrier, Merlin, Short-eared Owl, Arctic and Great Skua, Arctic Tern and Golden Plover. Its cliffs hold many typical cliff nesting seabirds. Trumland RSPB reserve, grid reference HY 430280, covers over 400 ha (988 acres) of moorland in the south of the island.

ACCESS

OS MAP: 6

Both islands can be reached by ferry from Tingwall.

13 SANDAY

Sanday encompasses dunes, machair and a small area of moorland. Spring and autumn migrants are of most interest, however, a summer visit will reveal a reasonable variety of birds. The islands supports a few pairs of Corncrakes and Corn Buntings, and there are large numbers of breeding Ringed Plovers and various Arctic Tern colonies. Wildfowl breed around the shallow lochs, which attract a few wintering species, too.

The small area of moorland holds a colony of Arctic Skuas, and there is a chance of encountering Short-eared Owls in the vicinity.

KEY BIRDS

SPRING AND SUMMER: Tufted Duck, Teal, Wigeon, Shoveler, Red-breasted Merganser, Eider, Corncrake, Snipe, Dunlin, Redshank, Arctic Skua, Arctic Tern, Short-eared Owl, Corn Bunting. Migrants in spring.
AUTUMN AND WINTER: Whooper Swan, wintering wildfowl, waders. Autumn migrants.

ACCESS

OS MAP: 5

There is a daily ferry and flight service from Kirkwall.

14 EDAY

Breeding seabirds and moorland breeders such as Arctic and Great Skuas, Golden Plover and a few Whimbrel along with Red-throated Diver are the main birds of interest. During spring and autumn, migrants may be found, one of the best places to search are the two small woods near Carrick House, grid reference HY 567 384.

ACCESS

OS MAP: 5

Daily ferry service from Kirkwall.

15 STRONSAY

Wintering and breeding wildfowl, cliff-nesting seabird colonies, moorland breeding birds and above all migrants and rarities are big attractions.

KEY BIRDS

SPRING AND AUTUMN: Passage waders, and migrant passerines including rarities annually. Some outstanding vagrants have been recorded.
SUMMER: Red-throated Diver, Great and Arctic Skuas, Arctic Tern, various cliff-nesting seabirds, breeding wildfowl and waders, Corn Bunting.
WINTER: Whooper Swan, Greenland White-fronted Goose, various ducks.

ACCESS

OS MAP: 5

Accessible from Kirkwall by ferry and plane daily, except Sundays.

NORTH RONALDSAY

Perched on the north-eastern edge of the Orkney archipelago, North Ronaldsay is better placed to receive migrants than the other islands. That it does, and not just drift migrants from the near continent, but some outstanding vagrants make landfall here annually. The bird observatory opened in 1987 is the perfect base for a stay on the island.

North Ronaldsay is flat with fields, cultivated land and some important, albeit small, wetlands. The sheep on the island graze on seaweed and are retained on the shore by the 'Sheep Dyke', a 1.5-metre (5-foot) high wall that runs around the island's perimeter.

Passerine migrants can turn up just about anywhere on the island, however, many are concentrated in areas of cover, crofters crops and in sites such as the walled garden at Holland House, a site where many rarities have been found over the years. Impressive falls of migrants can occur in both spring and autumn, south-easterly winds are best, but any wind

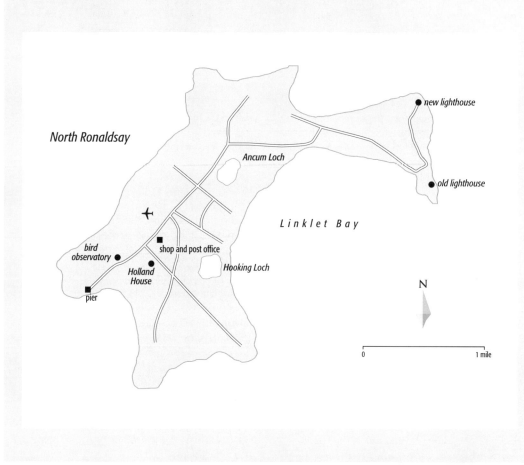

with an easterly bias can produce birds. Siberian Blue Robin, Pine Bunting and Spanish Sparrow are just three of the vagrants that have made landfall on the island in recent years.

The autumn arrival of thrushes can be spectacular when the weather conditions create a fall, and numbers, Redwings in particular, can be very impressive. Geese and Wild Swans are another autumnal feature from late September onwards.

The island is well situated for observing seabird passage, too. The old beacon in the north-east corner is the best site from which to watch. Sooty Shearwaters and Leach's Storm Petrels are two of the possibilities in autumn.

North Ronaldsay is, in fact, one of the best sites in Britain for views of Sooty Shearwaters, which often pass very close to the shore. Sabine's Gulls, Cory's and Great Shearwaters and Long-tailed Skuas are further possibilities when seawatching in autumn.

During the summer months, more than 30 species of bird breed annually. They include seabirds such as Arctic Terns and a large population of Black Guillemots, which are easily seen around the island's rocky shores. A colony of Cormorants nest on Seal Skerry, Orkney's most northerly point.

Various wildfowl, including Pintails and Shovelers, breed within the island's wetlands, while waders are also well represented.

🐦 KEY BIRDS
ALL YEAR: Teal, Oystercatcher, Ringed Plover, Snipe, Curlew, Redshank, Black Guillemot, Rock Dove, Twite, Hooded Crow, Raven.
SPRING: Apart from the commoner chats, pipits, warblers and flycatchers occurring as migrants; rare drift migrants annually include Bluethroat, Red-backed Shrike, Common Rosefinch.
SUMMER: Cormorant, Arctic Tern, Shelduck, Gadwall, Pintail.
AUTUMN: Migrants and drift migrants as for spring, plus vagrants likely. Passage waders and wildfowl; seabird passage offshore may include Sooty Shearwater, Leach's Storm Petrel, Sabine's Gull and Long-tailed Skua.

🗺 ACCESS
OS MAP: 5 REF: HY 750 522
There is a weekly ferry service from Kirkwall on Friday or Saturday, and on occasions on Sunday in summer. Contact Orkney Ferries Ltd on tel: 01856 872044. Loganair operate twice daily flights from Kirkwall from Monday to Saturday with an additional Sunday flight in summer.

🏠 FACILITIES
Comfortable accommodation available at the North Ronaldsay Bird Observatory, Twingness, North Ronaldsay, Orkney, KW17 2BE. Tel: 01857 633200.

Twite
Carduelis flavirostris

A drab-looking version of the Linnet is perhaps the best way to describe the Twite. Distinctive features include a pinkish rump on the male and streaky back and front. In winter, a large number move to our coasts, often favouring saltmarsh, where they feed on the seeds of salt-loving plants. They breed in our upland areas, especially moorland edges and upland farms.

The Twite feeds on the ground and can be seen perching on fence posts or low vegetation in summer. In some northern locations, it is a late breeder, often not laying eggs until late May or early June. The Twite has a life expectancy of between two to three years.

SHETLAND

Strung out for some 112 km (70 miles) and including around 100 islands, the Shetland Isles are closer to the Arctic Circle than to London. One amazing fact is that you are never more than 5 km (3 miles) from the sea when on Shetland.

There are many attractions, from searching for migrants to walking along cliffs, crowded with seabirds in summer – the islands have a year-round appeal. In the south, Fair Isle has a world famous bird observatory, mecca to students of bird migration and those that seek rarities. There is scarcely a better place in Britain than Fair Isle to 'find your own' birds. Dramatic cliff scenery here as with many other sites around the archipelago teem with auks, Kittiwakes, Gannets and Shags in summer.

Noss and Hermaness stand out as two other outstanding sites for cliff-nesting seabirds. The latter lies at Britain's northernmost extremity on Unst. A wild, remote place with few visitors the National Nature Reserve here ranks as one of the grandest in Britain. Noss has the famous Noup – a section of cliff that juts into the ocean and looks a bit like a nose, hence the name Noss, being Norse for nose.

Just to the south of Noss lies Mousa, rich in both birds and history. Its much visited landmark, the Iron Age Broch, comes alive at night as the air fills with European Storm Petrels, a species that breeds in the cracks and crevices of the Broch.

There are numerous other great birding sites scattered across these barren islands, and whilst good weather might not be guaranteed, memorable birding certainly is.

Whatever the time of year you go, there are both good sea and air links to the islands. Ferries run from Aberdeen to Lerwick. There are daily flights from Aberdeen to Sumburgh at the southern tip of the mainland, from where a hire car can be picked up. The islands are all connected by small roll-on/roll-off car ferries, and it is advisable to book some of these during busy periods in summer.

KEY

1) Fair Isle
2) Sumburgh
3) Loch Spiggie
4) Pool of Virkie
5) Lerwick Harbour
6) Kergord
7) Sullom Voe
8) Isle of Noss
9) Mousa
10) Fetlar
11) Foula
12) Yell
13) Outer Skerries
14) Whalsay
15) Hermaness

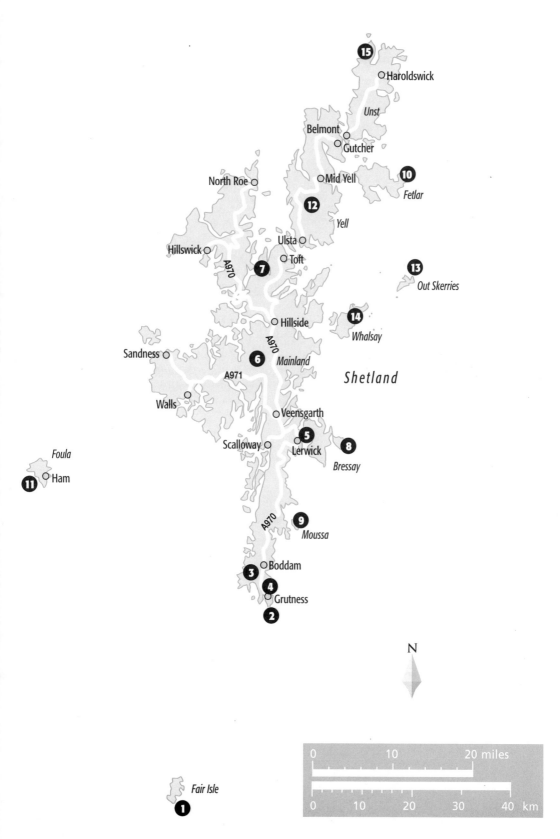

Haroldswick

⑮

Unst

Belmont

Gutcher

North Roe ⑩

Mid Yell

Fetlar

⑫

Yell

Hillswick

Ulsta

A970

Toft

⑦

⑬

Out Skerries

Hillside

⑭

A970

Whalsay

Sandness

⑥

Mainland

Shetland

A971

Walls

Veensgarth

⑤

⑧

Foula

Scalloway

Lerwick

⑪ Ham

Bressay

A970

⑨

Moussa

Boddam

③

④

Grutness

②

N

0   10   20 miles

0   10   20   30   40 km

Fair Isle

❶

FAIR ISLE

NATIONAL TRUST FOR SCOTLAND (765 ha/1,890 acres)

Fair Isle lies 38 km (24 miles) off the southern tip of mainland Shetland. It is owned by the National Trust for Scotland, and measures 5 km (3 miles) in length and 2.5 km (1½ miles) at its widest. A feature of the island are dramatic sea cliffs, which support large seabird colonies in summer. The island's interior consists of heather moorland, marshy areas and crofting land.

The Fair Isle Bird Observatory was established in 1948, and is where the majority of visitors stay. Whilst the breeding seabirds are impressive, it is the islands attraction to migrants and rarities that make it a popular destination. Indeed, during spring but particularly autumn, anything can turn up. Birds arrive from all points on the compass. However it is the migrants and particularly vagrants from the east that are most reliable. Such sought after rarities as Lanceolated Warbler are almost annual visitors in September. When an east wind blows and birds are arriving, Fair Isle is the place to be.

The last two weeks in September are reckoned to be the best time for rarities in autumn, but quite often better periods come before or after this period, and a stay in October can be

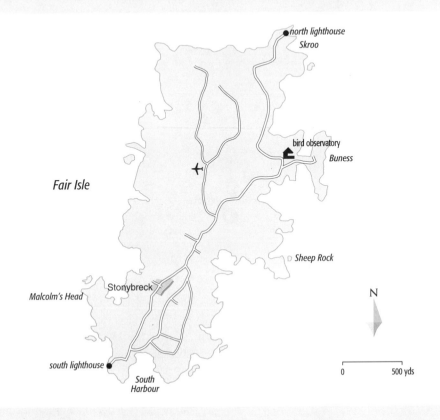

equally exciting. At this time, dramatic falls can occur, particularly of thrushes such as Robins. If the winds are right, geese can be watched overhead migrating south. Common and scarce drift migrants are a feature of spring, with April and May being best.

A visit in late May or early June gives the chance of a scattering of common and often scarce migrants, plus the chance of an outstanding vagrant. A Thick-billed Warbler was recorded in mid-May recently.

Fair Isle has some outstanding seabird colonies, notably on its north and west cliffs. On the moorland skuas and Arctic Terns breed, and there is a good population of Eiders. The cliffs, some of the most scenic in Britain, house all the expected species, whilst the island is a great place to enjoy close encounters with Puffins.

KEY BIRDS

ALL YEAR: Fulmar, Shag, Eider, Black Guillemot, Rock Dove, Twite, Raven.
SPRING: Easterly winds can bring Red-backed Shrike, Golden Oriole, Common Rosefinch, Wryneck, Bluethroat, Icterine and Marsh Warblers, with rarer species such as Thrush Nightingale possible. All the commoner flycatchers, chats, warbler, pipits and wagtails can be expected, with thrushes in March.
SUMMER: Breeding seabirds include European Storm Petrel, Puffin, Gannet, Kittiwake, Razorbill, Guillemot, Arctic and Common Terns, Arctic and Great Skuas, Wheatear.
AUTUMN: As for spring, plus Barred Warbler, Yellow-browed Warbler, and Red-breasted Flycatcher are all possible, in addition, annual vagrants include Lanceolated Warbler, chance of Yellow-breasted Bunting, Pechora Pipit and perhaps an American vagrant. Late autumn brings thrushes, finches and buntings and skeins of geese. Impressive falls can occur.

ACCESS

OS MAP: 4 REF: HZ 21 72
The *Good Shepherd*, the island's supply vessel, sails on Tuesday, Thursday and Saturday. However, there is often a swell, so if you are suceptible to seasickness, flying is the better option. Flights run from Tingwall or Sumburgh on Monday, Wednesday, Friday and Saturday.

FACILITIES

The bird observatory offers comfortable accommodation and excellent food; stays are on a full board basis. For bookings contact FIBO, Fair Isle, Shetland, ZE2 9JU. Tel: 01595 760258.

Lanceolated Warbler
Locustella lancedata

This species is a much sought after rarity in Britain, and Fair Isle offers the best chance of a sighting. They are almost annual on the isle in autumn, with September claiming the lion's share of records. They breed across Siberia, whilst their winter quarters are in southern Asia.

Lanceolated Warblers are known for their creeping, mouse-like behaviour, and often confiding nature. Indeed, vagrants on Fair Isle have famously perched on birders' feet, and walked between tripod legs. There is a good chance that this species turns up with regular frequency in autumn at other island and east coast sites, but that their secretive nature means they go undetected. The lack of cover, coupled with excellent birding coverage on Fair Isle in autumn, means the chances of discovery are far higher here.

They can be difficult to identify, with Grasshopper Warblers most easily confused with Lanceolated Warblers, so any possible find needs to be seen well, for identification to be confirmed.

2 | SUMBURGH HEAD

RSPB RESERVE

These seabird cliffs on the southernmost tip of the mainland are the haunt of various species of cliff-nesting seabird. The head attracts migrants and provides a good seawatching point.

One of the star attractions in summer are the Puffins which give close views. Skuas patrol the cliffs, while offshore passing seabirds including Gannets can be seen. Seawatching is best in early autumn during strong onshore winds.

An impressive number of vagrants have been found here, some of the best areas to search for migrants are in the stone quarries on the approach road, around the lighthouse and along the stone walls below the head. The nearby Sumburgh Hotel has a garden with stunted sycamores that are a regular haunt of both migrants and rarities in spring and autumn.

KEY BIRDS
SPRING AND SUMMER: Migrants. Breeding seabirds include Fulmar, Shag, Kittiwake, Guillemot, Black Guillemot, Razorbill, and Puffin. Passing offshore, both Great and Arctic Skuas, Gannet and Eider.
AUTUMN: Migrants and the chance of a rarity. Passage seabirds include European Storm Petrel and Sooty Shearwater, chance of Little Auk in late autumn and winter.

ACCESS
OS MAP: 4 REF: HU 407 079
The head is reached by taking the A970 south past Sumburgh Hotel and the airport to Grutness, where a single track road leads to a parking area below the lighthouse.

3 | LOCH SPIGGIE

RSPB RESERVE

115 ha (284 acres)
In the south of the mainland, this large loch attracts mostly wildfowl, a few waders and gulls. Of interest throughout the year, in autumn it becomes a staging post for migrating Whooper Swans and Greylag Geese, whilst in spring Long-tailed Ducks congregate before moving off north to their breeding grounds.

Marsh surrounding parts of the loch supports a few breeding wildfowl and waders. Skuas, gulls and terns come to bathe in the loch in summer, and during winter the occasional white-winged gull may be found.

KEY BIRDS
SPRING: Long-tailed Duck congregate, chance of migrant Osprey. Red-throated Diver in early spring. Passage waders may include Ruff and Black-tailed Godwit.
SUMMER: Visits to bathe by gulls, notably Kittiwake, skuas and Arctic Tern. A few species of wildfowl breed, as do waders that include Snipe, Redshank and Lapwing.
AUTUMN AND WINTER: Passage waders include Common, Green and Wood Sandpipers, chance of a rarer species. Passage Whooper Swan and Greylag Goose, wintering Long-tailed Duck, Wigeon, Teal, Pochard, Goldeneye, more rarely Scaup and Goosander. Both Glaucous and Iceland Gulls; offshore from the Bay of Scousborough Great Northern Diver and Long-tailed Duck can be located, and in the dunes, Snow Bunting.

ACCESS
OS MAP: 4 REF: HU 373 176
From the A970, take the B9122 at Boddam, turn left on to a minor road just before Scousburgh. The loch can be viewed fairly well from the roadside.

FACILITIES
For disabled visitors, it is possible to view the loch from a vehicle.

4 | POOL OF VIRKIE

A tidal pool on the northern edge of Sumburgh airport. Passage waders occur and vagrants are found annually. Wildfowl use the pool in winter, and during passage periods the small areas of cover notably the bordering gardens can harbour migrants.

KEY BIRDS
SPRING AND AUTUMN: Passage waders, rarities.
SUMMER: Shelduck, often a few waders.
WINTER: Estuarine waders, sometimes seaduck.

⛵ ACCESS

OS MAP: 4 REF: HU 393 113

The pool is easily viewed from a minor road off the A970.

⬛ FACILITIES

Disabled visitors can easily view from a vehicle.

5 | LERWICK HARBOUR

The haunt of Black Guillemot in summer, in winter divers, grebes and seaduck can be found, whilst the fish processing plants in Lerwick attract plenty of gulls, including Glaucous and Iceland Gulls.

🐦 KEY BIRDS

WINTER: Seaduck including Long-tailed Duck, Slavonian Grebe, Great Northern Diver, possible Little Auk, Glaucous and Iceland Gulls.

6 | KERGORD

Kergord is home to the longest established woodlands in Shetland. A few interesting species for Shetland breed, these include Rooks. This site is of most interest for the migrants and annual rarities it attracts.

🐦 KEY BIRDS

SPRING AND AUTUMN: Migrants and rarities. **SUMMER:** Goldcrest, Rook and other breeding woodland birds.

⛵ ACCESS

OS MAP: 3 REF: HU 395 542

Take the B9075 along the Weisdale valley. The plantations are on both sides of the road and cannot be missed. Please respect the privacy of the residents here.

7 | SULLOM VOE

Best know for its oil terminal, this large sea inlet is best in winter for divers, grebes and seaduck. In summer a large mixed tern colony, located next to the oil refinery, is of interest.

🐦 KEY BIRDS

AUTUMN AND WINTER: Divers, grebes and seaduck including Great Northern Diver, Slavonian Grebe, Long-tailed Duck and Velvet Scoter.

SPRING AND SUMMER: Breeding Common Gull, Arctic and Common Terns.

⛵ ACCESS

OS MAP: 3 REF: HU 380 740

The Voe can be viewed from the B9076 and from one or two minor roads on the north shore.

8 | ISLE OF NOSS

NNR

313 ha (773 acres)

Separated from the island of Bressay by a narrow sound, Noss can be visited in summer to experience its very impressive seabird colonies. A circular route can be taken around the island, taking in some of the most spectacular cliff scenery in Shetland at the Noup. Alternatively, daily boat trips from Lerwick allow the cliffs to be viewed from the sea, equally impressive.

🐦 KEY BIRDS

SPRING AND SUMMER: Fulmar, Shag, Gannet, Great and Arctic Skuas, Arctic Tern, Kittiwake, Great Black-backed Gull, Eider, Black Guillemot, Guillemot, Razorbill, Puffin.

⛵ ACCESS

OS MAP: 4 REF: HU 531 410

The island is open from 10am to 5pm from late May to late August on Tuesday, Wednesday, Friday, Saturday and Sunday. Take the ferry from Lerwick to Bressay, drive across the island, following the signs to Noss. Park at the end of the road, grid reference HU 542 405, and walk down to the 'wait here' sign. The wardens will come and pick you up in a zodiac.

⬛ FACILITIES

A small visitor centre.

9 MOUSA

NNR / RSPB RESERVE

182 ha (450 acres)

Mousa is a small uninhabited island lying off the south mainland coast. In summer the island teems with birdlife, both cliff nesting seabirds, breeding skuas, terns and in the Iron Age Broch a European Storm Petrel colony.

There are few more exciting birding experiences on offer in Shetland than a visit at night to view the Storm Petrels that nest along the boulder beach and nearby Broch. After dark hundreds of petrels can be buzzing around entering and leaving their nest chambers.

Visit in the day and a circular route can be taken around the island. Care should be taken not to approach the tern colonies or nesting skuas too closely as both are very suceptible to human disturbance.

KEY BIRDS

SPRING AND SUMMER: European Storm Petrel, Fulmar, Guillemot, Black Guillemot, Razorbill, Puffin, Arctic Tern, Great and Arctic Skuas, Ringed Plover.

ACCESS

OS MAP: 4 REF: HU 460 240

A ferry runs from Leebitton Pier in Sandwick. For times and details of Storm Petrel trips contact the boatman Tom Jamieson on 01950 431367. Alternatively, details are on his website at www.mousaboattrips.co.uk.

10 FETLAR

RSPB RESERVE

690 ha (1,705 acres)

'The garden of Shetland', Fetlar is a green, fertile island, incorporating a large area of serpentine heath important for breeding Whimbrel. The island is home to Loch Funzie and an adjacent mire, centre of the British breeding population of Red-necked Phalaropes.

These dainty and colourful waders are wonderfully confiding and when feeding around the shores of Loch Funzie, will approach the seated observer often to within a few inches. The phalaropes arrive around the third week in May

and are present to early August. Numbers vary from year to year, but there are normally no more than half a dozen on the loch at any one time. Still, sunny days are best as they feed on flies on the stones around the shore. Windy, cold days can make them elusive, and are then best searched for on the mire which is overlooked by a hide. The loch usually has a pair of Red-throated Divers present.

Access to the heath is closed during the breeding season, however, all the breeding birds including Golden Plovers and Whimbrels can be seen from the roadside.

Fetlar attracts its fair share of migrants, and rarities are found annually. Any area of cover is worth exploring. The area around Houbie, the gardens, Feal Burn by the interpretative centre and small fields with crops here are all potential havens for passerine migrants.

KEY BIRDS

SPRING AND SUMMER: Cliff-nesting seabirds, Red-throated Diver, Black-tailed Godwit, Dunlin, Snipe, Lapwing, Golden Plover, Whimbrel, Curlew, Red-necked Phalarope, Arctic and Great Skuas. Manx Shearwaters and European Storm Petrels breed in small numbers. Migrants and chance of a rarity.

AUTUMN: Migrants and rarities, especially in easterly winds.

ACCESS

OS MAP: 2 REF: HU 583 943

Ferries to Fetlar leave from Gutcher on Yell or Belmont on Unst, advance booking is often essential in summer.

11 FOULA

1,380 ha (3,410 acres)

Foula lies 22 km (14 miles) west of the Shetland mainland, its spectacular cliffs are visible on a clear day. Large numbers of seabird breed including a small number of Leach's Storm Petrel. The island also hosts a large great Skua colony. Migrants turn up during passage periods.

KEY BIRDS

SPRING AND AUTUMN: Migrants and occasional rarities.

SUMMER: Red-throated Diver, Gannet, Manx Shearwater, European Storm and Leach's Storm Petrels, Shag, Great and Arctic Skuas, Black Guillemot, Guillemot, Razorbill, Puffin.

⛴ ACCESS
OS MAP: 4 REF: HT 960 390
Flights operate throughout the year, and there is a boat service twice a week from Walls on West Mainland, weather permitting.

12 YELL

RSPB RESERVE
Lying between the mainland and Unst, Yell is clad in heather moorland and has many lochs favoured by breeding Red-throated Divers. The RSPB reserve at Lumbister, is on the western side of the island and supports the typical moorland breeding species.

⛴ KEY BIRDS
SPRING AND SUMMER: Red-throated Diver, Red-breasted Merganser, Eider, Merlin, Oystercatcher, Lapwing, Golden Plover, Snipe, Dunlin, Great and Arctic Skuas, Wheatear, Raven, Twite.
WINTER: Divers, grebes and seaduck in the voes and around the coast.

⛴ ACCESS
OS MAP: 1 REF: HU 509 974
The Lumbister reserve can be viewed from the A968. Many breeding birds are suceptible to disturbance here, particularly divers.

13 OUTER SKERRIES

A group of small low-lying islands which, due to their position as the most easterly point in Shetland, are good for migrants and particularly rarities, of which there have been some outstanding finds over the years.

⛴ KEY BIRDS
SPRING AND AUTUMN: Migrants and rarities.
SUMMER: Eider, Black Guillemot, breeding terns and gulls.

⛴ ACCESS
OS MAP: 2 REF: HU 688 715
Passenger ferry from Lerwick and from Vidlin in East Mainland, and there are weekly flights too.

14 WHALSAY

Situated off the mainland's east coast, the island attracts migrants and rarities. Anywhere with cover is worth checking. Productive areas include the crofts around the Skaw area in the north-east of the island. In the west, the seaward side of Ibister and Brough are also worth checking. Past rarities have included Ruppell's Warbler and Lesser Grey Shrike.

⛴ ACCESS
OS MAP: 2 REF: HU 539 627
Ferries run from Laxo on the mainland and there are flights from Tingwall.

HERMANESS

NNR (964 ha/2,382 acres)

Hermaness lies at the northern end of the island of Unst, and offshore a row of sea stacks with a lighthouse – Muckle Flugga – represents the most northerly point in Britain. Hermaness is scenically superb, with cliffs rising to 200 metres (650 feet) and huge seabird colonies. No visit to Shetland is complete without a visit here.

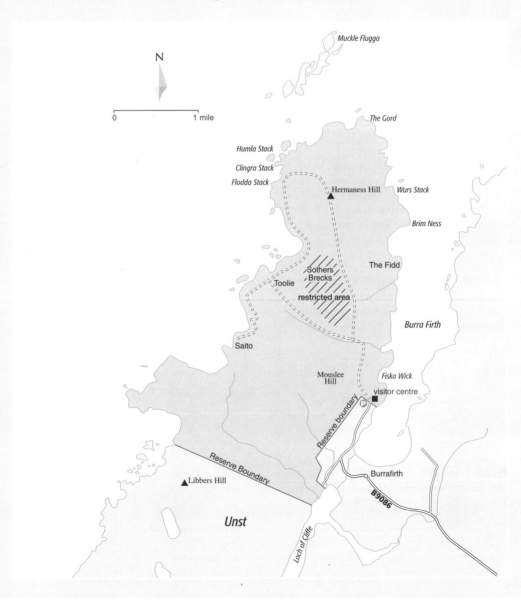

A path leads from the car park out on to blanket bog dotted with lochans and patches of cotton grass. The quickest route to the cliffs is to keep left on the path which climbs uphill to the cliffs. The bog supports populations of waders, notably Dunlins and Golden Plovers as well as Arctic Skuas, and one of the star attractions the Great Skua.

At the cliffs, turn left and walk for a few hundred metres and you will be confronted by a spectacular Gannet colony. Retracing your steps, you can walk along the cliff tops to the Muckle Flugga. Large numbers of Puffins nest along these cliffs, however, they can be largely absent during the middle of the day. A visit during the evening will guarantee close encounters. Razorbills and Guillemots cling to the cliff ledges, and on the sea stacks at the Muckle Flugga, more Gannets can be enjoyed. The path eventually turns up towards Hermaness Hill, past more nesting Great Skuas, then downhill back to the car park. The route will take half a day, or if taken at a leisurely pace with plenty of stops a full day to complete.

Burrafirth, the sea inlet bordering the eastern side of Hermaness, is always worth checking for seaduck, grebes and divers. In June 2002, it held a White-billed Diver. A bit further afield, the bay at Haroldswick is a good site for Great Northern Diver, whilst the roadside pools regularly attract passage waders, and occasional rarities. Anywhere with any cover on Unst is worth checking for migrants in spring and autumn.

KEY BIRDS
SPRING AND SUMMER: Gannet, Great Skua, Arctic Skua, Razorbill, Guillemot, Puffin, Fulmar, Kittiwake, Dunlin, Golden Plover, Snipe, Raven, Rock Pipit, Wheatear, Twite.

ACCESS
OS MAP: 1 REF: HP 60 16
Unst is reached by ferry from Yell. From the ferry terminal at Belmonst drive north to Burrafirth. Great care should be taken on the cliffs, especially in wet weather, as there are many steep, grassy slopes. There are no access restrictions, other than a restricted area in the middle of the reserve, but you should keep to the marked paths to minimize disturbance.

FACILITIES
There is a visitor centre at Burrafirth in the shore station, below the reserve car park, where the summer warden is based.

Great Skua
Stercorarus skua

This pirate of the skies nests across a wide area of blanket bog on Hermaness. Also known as the 'Bonxie', the Great Skua will let you know if it strays too close to its nest by rising to the air and dive-bombing you. At Hermaness this can be unavoidable as it often nests very close to the paths, therefore a stick or tripod leg held above the head will deter a bird from striking you on the head.

It preys on seabirds returning with food for their young, usually harrassing them until the catch is dropped. In Shetland in recent years, the Bonxie has also increased its predation of chicks, particularly Kittiwakes. This has had a detrimental affect on some colonies, particularly on Hermaness where there are just a few breeding pairs left.

IRELAND

Due to its geographic location, perched on the western edge of Europe, Ireland offers some exciting birding. South and west coast headlands can shine in autumn, attracting American vagrants and often offering some of the finest seawatching in Europe. Cape Clear is renowned throughout the world for its outstanding seabird passage, whilst during spring and autumn, the lure of rarities makes the island one of the most popular sites in the country.

Some of the most impressive seabird cliffs are found on Great Saltee in Wexford, in the south and, in the north, on Rathlin Island, where they teem with auks and Kittiwakes.

A mild climate means that many species are attracted to winter here, and during cold snaps in the rest of Europe, mass influxes of birds can occur. The country is blessed with numerous estuaries and large sea loughs, which are havens for wintering wildfowl and waders that pour into the country each autumn.

Fine examples of sea loughs include Strangford Lough, close to Belfast, and the large Lough Foyle. Strangford acts as a staging post for thousands of Light-bellied Brent Geese in autumn and early winter. Waders throng the loughs' vast mudflats, and at high tide divers and the rarer grebes may be discovered.

Ireland's south coast headlands, famed for their autumn attraction to vagrants, are interspersed by some top winter sites, including little visited estuaries that buzz with wildfowl and waders. North Bull, on the outskirts of Dublin, is hard to beat in winter for both the spectacle of numbers and often very close views. On Ireland's west coast, winter can produce sought after rare gulls. Glaucous and Iceland Gulls are sometimes joined by the occasional vagrant from farther afield. Key sites include Galway Bay.

Visitors to Ireland might be surprised to find that many species common to Britain are absent here – they include all three species of woodpecker, Nuthatch and Tawny Owl. This deficit more than compensated by the spectacular and varied birding Ireland has to offer at any season.

KEY

1) Rathlin Island	13) Carlingford Lough	27) Clonakilty and Inchydoney
2) Bann Estuary	14) Castlecaldwell	28) Galley Head
3) Lough Foyle	15) Dundalk Bay	29) Cork Harbour
4) Malin Head	16) Ireland's Eye	30) Dursey Island
5) Lough Swilly	17) North Bull	31) Cape Clear
6) Lough Beg	18) North Slob	32) Skelligs
7) Lough Neagh / Oxford Island	19) Lady's Island Lake	33) Akeragh Lough
8) Portmore Lough	20) Tacumshin	34) Castlemaine Harbour
9) Shanes Castle	21) Great Saltee Island	35) Loop Head and Bridges of Ross
10) Belfast Lough	22) Hook Head	36) Galway Bay
11) Strangford Lough	23) Ballymacoda	37) Lough Corrib
12) Copeland Island Bird Observatory	24) Knockadoon Head	38) Donegal Bay
	25) Ballycotton	
	26) Old Head of Kinsale	

1 RATHLIN ISLAND

RSPB RESERVE

1,416 ha (3,500 acres)
Shaped like an inverted letter L, Rathlin lies
5km (3 miles) off the picturesque North Antrim
coast. Rathlin has high cliffs, and is covered in
moorland, rough pasture, marsh and scattered
pools. Much of the western end is part of the
Kebble National Nature Reserve, with a stretch
of cliffs along the northern side.

These cliffs swarm with thousands of nesting
seabirds in summer, which can be viewed from
the West Lighthouse platform. Whilst it is the
cliff-nesting seabirds that tempt most birders to
Rathlin, the island has a good range of farmland
birds and in spring a fine display of orchids along
the roadside verges. Black Guillemots can be
found along the low chalk cliffs on the southern
side, and on summer evenings Manx Shearwaters
can often be seen congregating off the south-east
tip of the island before coming ashore under the
cover of darkness.

Very occasionally both Golden and White-
tailed Eagles have visited Rathlin.

⬛ KEY BIRDS

ALL YEAR: Little Grebe, Tufted Duck, Eider,
Buzzard, Peregrine, Oystercatcher, Ringed Plover,
Lapwing, Redshank, Snipe, Black Guillemot,
Rock Dove, Skylark, Raven, Stonechat,
occasional visits from Choughs.
SPRING AND SUMMER: Manx Shearwater, Shag,
Shelduck, Kittiwake, Razorbill, Guillemot,
Puffin, Wheatear, Whinchat, Sedge Warbler.
Chance of a few passerine migrants.
AUTUMN: A few migrants, whilst offshore chance
of passing seabirds.

⬛ ACCESS

DISCOVERY SERIES MAP: 5
A ferry service operated by Caledonian
MacBrayne runs daily during the summer months
from Ballycastle.

2 BANN ESTUARY

THE NATIONAL TRUST

This small estuary on the Antrim coast is of most
interest for waders, particularly in autumn, when
a typical visit will provide a good range of
species. A National Trust hide provides views

over the estuary. A visit a couple of hours before
high tide is likely to be most productive, as birds
are pushed closer to the shore.

Sand dunes protect the northern side of the
estuary and sometimes harbour Snow Buntings in
winter, whilst a pier along Castlerock Strand, just
up the coast, can be a good vantage point for
seawatching during onshore winds in autumn.

⬛ KEY BIRDS

SPRING AND SUMMER: Passage waders in spring
include often large numbers of Whimbrel. In
autumn Curlew Sandpiper, Little Stint, Spotted
Redshank, with at both seasons Oystercatcher,
Ringed Plover, Golden Plover, Lapwing, Knot,
Dunlin, Sanderling, Greenshank, chance of a
rarity. Offshore in autumn, skuas, terns, gulls
with the chance of shearwaters and Sabine's Gull
in strong onshore winds.
WINTER: Great Northern and Red-throated
Divers, and Great Crested Grebe offshore and in
estuary mouth. Eider, Teal, Wigeon, Goldeneye,
Oystercatcher, Ringed Plover, Golden Plover,
Lapwing, Dunlin, Sanderling, Curlew,
Greenshank, Snow Bunting.

⬛ ACCESS

DISCOVERY SERIES MAP: 4
Travel west from Coleraine on the A2, turn right
at Articlave and after 1.6 km (1 mile) turn left at
the T-junction. Cross a bridge and then turn
right, parking before the railway line. For
Castlerock Strand, continue on past Articlave
to Castlerock.

3 LOUGH FOYLE

RSPB RESERVE
Separating Co Londonderry from Co Donegal,
Lough Foyle stretches for almost 30 km (20
miles). It is relatively shallow and has extensive
mud flats on its eastern and southern shores. The
key birding areas lie in the south-east corner,
from Longfield Point to the Roe Estuary. Much of
this area is an RSPB reserve, and is best visited
from late autumn through winter, when
thousands of wildfowl and waders feed out on the
mud flats and salt marsh.

Wigeon can in some years be counted in their
thousands. Up to 4,000 Light-bellied Brent
Geese arrive to feast on the eel grass beds, also
numerous are Whooper Swans, with lesser

numbers of Bewick's. Wintering waders are equally numerous. At the mouth of the estuary Magilligan Point on the southern side is the tip of an extensive area of sand dunes, and a regular wintering site for Snow Buntings. The deep water off the point attracts divers and grebes, and in late summer and autumn it is a good site from which to view terns and often skuas.

To the south of the point lies the Roe Estuary. Best visited just before or at high tide, waders and wildfowl roost on the salt marsh here. The fields known as the Myroe Levels regularly hold wild swans and geese. Longfield Point located in the south-east corner of the lough is a good vantage point for viewing the lough, and the Longfield Levels – low-lying pasture behind the point which attracts swans, geese and hunting raptors.

KEY BIRDS

SPRING: Departing winter species and a few migrant waders, including Whimbrel.
SUMMER: Terns and skuas off Magilligan Point, waders start to return by mid July.
AUTUMN: Passage waders include Spotted Redshank, Ruff, Curlew Sandpiper, Little Stint. During strong onshore winds, seawatching from Magilligan Point.
WINTER: Great Northern Diver and Red-throated Diver, Great Crested Grebe and Slavonian Grebe, Whooper and Bewick's Swans, Light-bellied Brent Goose, Greylag and Greenland White-fronted Geese, Wigeon, Teal, Pintail, Peregrine, Merlin, Golden Plover, Lapwing, Dunlin, Sanderling, Knot, Curlew, Redshank, Snow Bunting and Twite.

ACCESS

DISCOVERY SERIES MAP: 4/7 REF: C 545 237
For Magilligan Point take the A2 from Limavady, turning off on to the B202 to the point. For the Roe Estuary, take the B69 north out of Limavady, after 1 km (1½ miles) take a left turn to Limavady Junction railway station. After a further 1 km (1½ miles) turn right at the T- junction to the estuary. From the car park walk along the river embankment, and over the railway line. The Myroe Levels are behind the sea wall. Longfield Point is reached by travelling west from Limavady along the A2 and turning right for signs to Donnybrewer; go over the railway line and follow the track.

4 MALIN HEAD

A familiar name to those that listen to the shipping forecast. Malin Head north of Londonderry and the most northerly point on mainland Ireland, is a superb seawatching site. Autumn north-west winds are best, often bringing with them Sabine's Gulls, Leach's Petrels, shearwaters, auks and skuas. Passerine migrants appear too, with south-easterly winds ideal for these. It is a great vantage point in autumn for watching the arrival of geese and swans from the north.

KEY BIRDS

SPRING AND AUTUMN: Passerine migrants, and arrival in autumn of Whooper Swans, Greylag Goose, Barnacle Goose and White-fronted Goose. During autumn seabirds may include Leach's Storm Petrel, Sooty Shearwater, Sabine's Gull, Grey Phalarope, Little Auk, skuas.

ACCESS

DISCOVERY SERIES MAP: 3
The head is reached from the R242 from Malin.

5 LOUGH SWILLY

This is a long deep sea lough just west of Londonderry. Most bird interest centres around Inch, where there is a lagoon attractive to waders and wildfowl. The lough itself is favoured by seaduck, divers and grebes in winter.

Wild swans and geese can occur in large numbers in autumn, before many disperse further south. The fields and shore at Inch and at the head of the estuary at Big Isle are favoured sites.

KEY BIRDS

ALL YEAR: Grebes, Shelduck, Tufted Duck, Oystercatcher, Ringed Plover, Lapwing, Curlew, Redshank, Stonechat.
SUMMER: Sandwich and Common Terns, Quail, potential for Corncrake.
AUTUMN AND WINTER: Red-throated Diver and Great Northern Diver, chance of Black-throated Diver, Slavonian Grebe, Whooper Swan and Bewick's Swan, Brent Goose, Greylag Goose, and Greenland White-fronted Goose, Wigeon, Teal, Pintail, Shoveler, Scaup, Pochard, Goldeneye, estuarine waders.

ACCESS

DISCOVERY SERIES MAP: 6/7
Viewing of much of the lough is possible from the roads running close to it. For Inch turn left off the Derry to Fahan road just after Burnfoot. The causeway here allows good views. For Big Isle view from the road from Manorcunningham to Newton Cunningham.

6 LOUGH BEG

NNR
Lough Beg is a shallow lough connected to Lough Neagh by the River Bann. Winter flooding of the meadows bordering the lough make the site attractive to wildfowl. During autumn passage, waders feed along the lough's shoreline. During spring there is less variety, however, Icelandic Black-tailed Godwits use the lough as a staging-post before migrating north.

The western side of the lough around Church Island is the best point of access.

KEY BIRDS

ALL YEAR: Great Crested Grebe, Teal, Shoveler, Tufted Duck, Pochard, Sparrowhawk, Kestrel, Lapwing, Snipe, Curlew, Redshank, Kingfisher, Raven, Reed Bunting.
SPRING: Passage waders include Whimbrel and Black-tailed Godwit, chance of Garganey.
SUMMER: Red-breasted Merganser, Shelduck, Black-headed Gull.
AUTUMN: Passage waders include Ruff, Black-tailed Godwit, Curlew Sandpiper, Little Stint, Greenshank, Common, Green and Wood Sandpipers. Chance of a vagrant wader, a number of American species have been recorded.
WINTER: Whooper Swan, Bewick's Swan, Wigeon, Pintail, Goldeneye, Peregrine, Hen Harrier, Merlin, Short-eared Owl, Golden and Grey Plovers and Greenshank.

ACCESS

DISCOVERY SERIES MAP: 14 REF: H 975 947
If travelling west on the A6 from Toome, after approximately 1.6 km (1 mile) turn right on to the B182 (Bellaghy Road), then right down Ballydermot Road towards the church. The church spire can be seen for some distance and is a good reference point. Head towards the church and the island.

7 LOUGH NEAGH/ OXFORD ISLAND

NNR
Lough Neagh is vast – the largest freshwater lake in the British Isles – and is one of the most important wintering sites for wildfowl in Europe. Birding over such a vast area can seem daunting, nevertheless, Oxford Island, a peninsula sticking into the lake along the south-east shore is an excellent site from which to view.

Winter is the best time to visit, diving ducks are numerous, with Smew visiting in some years. Wild swans feed in the surrounding fields. During passage periods waders use the site and in summer various waterbirds nest on the lake's islands.

Oxford Island offers good visitor facilities including hides and trails.

KEY BIRDS

ALL YEAR: Grebes, Gadwall, Pochard, Tufted Duck, Ruddy Duck, Water Rail, Kingfisher, Reed Bunting.
SPRING AND AUTUMN: Passage waders similar to Lough Beg, including Oystercatcher, Ruff, Black-tailed Godwit, Common Sandpiper and Whimbrel.
SUMMER: Black-headed Gull, Common Tern, warblers including Grasshopper Warbler.
WINTER: Large numbers of diving ducks, notably Tufted Duck, Pochard and Goldeneye, a few Scaup, Teal, occasional Smew and Goosander. Whooper and Bewick's Swans and Golden Plover on adjacent fields.

ACCESS

DISCOVERY SERIES MAP: 20 REF: J 047 618
The reserve is well signposted from junction 10 of the M1, 30 km (20 miles) west of Belfast.

FACILITIES

The Discovery Centre has displays, a restaurant and information desk. There are hides overlooking the lough, most of which are accessible to wheelchairs.

8   PORTMORE LOUGH

RSPB RESERVE

Lying at the south-east corner of Lough Neagh, Portmore Lough is primarily of interest for its wet meadows, reed beds fringing the lough, and the lough itself. Waders breed in summer, and in winter a good variety of wildfowl use the meadows and open water.

KEY BIRDS

SPRING AND SUMMER: Snipe Curlew, Water Rail, Grasshopper Warbler.
AUTUMN AND WINTER: Whooper Swan, Greylag Goose, Shoveler, Wigeon, Teal, Goldeneye, Tufted Duck, Pochard, Ruddy Duck.

ACCESS

DISCOVERY SERIES MAP: 20 REF: **J 107 685**
From Aghalee follow the Ballycairn Road to Gawley's Gate, and then turn right. Take George's Island Road which is 1.6 km (1 mile) further on, on the right.

FACILITIES

There is a shelter and hide.

9   SHANES CASTLE

NNR

This reserve lies within an estate overlooking Antrim Bay on the shores of Lough Neagh. Whilst Oxford Island is likely to be more productive for wildfowl in winter, this reserve is worth a visit in spring and summer for woodland birds, and species breeding along the streams such as Dipper and Grey Wagtail.

Rhododendron dominates much of the woodland with willow and alder scrub. The woodland and parkland consists of beech, lime and sycamore along with exotic evergreens.

KEY BIRDS

ALL YEAR: Waterfowl as for Oxford Island plus Buzzard, Water Rail, Long-eared Owl, Kingfisher, Grey Wagtail, Dipper, and common woodland birds.
SPRING AND SUMMER: Sedge Warbler, Blackcap, Willow Warbler, Chiffchaff, Spotted Flycatcher.
AUTUMN AND WINTER: Wildfowl as for Oxford Island, plus thrushes, Siskin.

ACCESS

DISCOVERY SERIES MAP: 20 REF: **J 115 878**
Reached from Belfast along the M2, turn off on to the A26 towards Antrim, and then Randalstown.

FACILITIES

Hides and nature trail, and the estate offers many family attractions including a funfair and steam railway.

10   BELFAST LOUGH

RSPB RESERVE

Located within the Belfast Harbour Estate, a large artificial lagoon lies at the centre of this reserve. The lagoon attracts wildfowl and waders from autumn through to spring. Passage waders include all the regular species expected in northern Europe, and the site has a respectable list of vagrant species to its name. Garganey are annual in spring, whilst in summer both Shoveler and Shelduck breed. Returning wildfowl in autumn include a small flock of Light-bellied Brent Geese.

KEY BIRDS

ALL YEAR: Grebes, Shoveler, Shelduck, Peregrine, Ringed Plover, Oystercatcher, Lapwing, Snipe, Redshank, gulls, Stonechat.
SPRING: Garganey, plus passage waders including Whimbrel, Common Sandpiper and Greenshank.
SUMMER: Passage waders start to appear from mid-July, various species of gull present.
AUTUMN: Passage waders include typical estuarine species plus Spotted Redshank, Greenshank, Little Stint, Curlew Sandpiper, Black-tailed Godwit, plus the chance of a vagrant North American species.
WINTER: On the deep water of the lough, divers, grebes and seaduck. Light-bellied Brent Goose, Wigeon, Teal, Golden Plover, Greenshank, Black-tailed Godwit and estuarine species. Chance of a rare gull such as Ring-billed.

ACCESS

DISCOVERY SERIES MAP: 15
The reserve is closed on Mondays. Access is from the A2 Belfast to Holywood road. If coming from Belfast, the Belfast Harbour Estate is signposted from the second set of traffic lights.

FACILITIES

There is a heated observation room and two hides.

STRANGFORD LOUGH

NNR / WWT

Stretching for over 29 km (18 miles) and at almost 6 km (4 miles) at its widest, this lough has vast areas of mudflat and salt marsh, and is surrounded by farmland, woods and marsh. Autumn and winter are the best times to visit, when thousands of wildfowl and waders are present. Some species such as Light-bellied Brent Geese use the lough as a staging post arriving in autumn, and stay for a few weeks before many disperse south to other wintering sites. The Brents can number close to 15,000 in October.

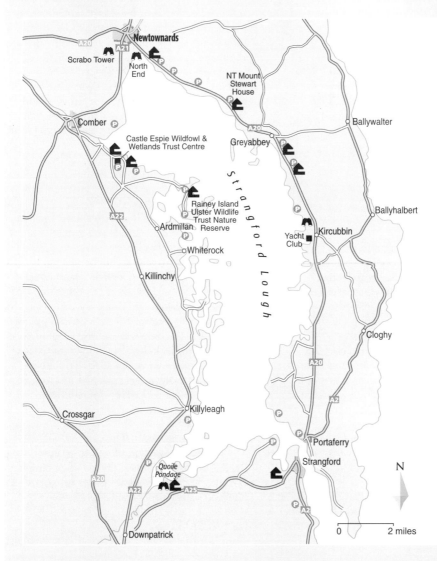

Over 40,000 waders can be present, which can be distant at low tide, so a visit on a rising tide is best. A few Whooper Swans winter, whilst other wintering waterfowl include Gadwall and Pintail. In the deeper water and particularly towards the Narrows – the narrow channel that separates the sea from the lough – divers, grebes and diving duck may be found along with auks such as Black Guillemot, which breed locally. Breeding birds include various species of waterfowl, a few waders and gulls, and terns that use some of the lough's islands to nest.

There are various points from which to view. At Castle Espie a Wildfowl & Wetlands Trust reserve, there is a captive collection of waterfowl. The site also has lagoons attractive to wild birds and hides overlooking the mudflats. Woodland birds can be seen here too. Not far from Castle Espie is Reagh Island which has a hide overlooking the mud flats.

In the south-west corner of the lough is Quoile Pondage, a National Nature Reserve. A freshwater lagoon here overlooked by hides, it is one of the best sites for finding passage waders, and is as good a site as any for finding a Garganey in spring. Various other viewing sites around the lough include Kircubbin, halfway along the east shore – park near the Yacht Club and walk north along the shore. It is a favourite site for grebes, divers and Black Guillemots. Further north between Greyabbey and Newtownards there are various laybys allowing good views.

KEY BIRDS

ALL YEAR: Grebes, Grey Heron, Shelduck, Gadwall, Shoveler, Tufted Duck, Pochard, Eider, Red-breasted Merganser, Peregrine, Ringed Plover, Lapwing, Snipe, Curlew, Redshank, Black Guillemot, Kingfisher.
SPRING: Passage waders such as Whimbrel, chance of Garganey.
SUMMER: Arctic, Common and Sandwich Terns, gull colonies, warblers, a few waders.
AUTUMN: Passage waders include Whimbrel, Common, Wood and Green Sandpipers, Spotted Redshank, Greenshank, Ruff.
WINTER: Slavonian Grebe, divers, Whooper Swan, Light-bellied Brent Goose, Wigeon, Pintail, Teal, Scaup, Goldeneye, Golden Plover, estuarine waders, Purple Sandpiper, Black-tailed Godwit, Snipe, Jack Snipe, Greenshank.

ACCESS

DISCOVERY SERIES MAP: 21 REF: J 50 70
Quoile Pondage is reached by taking the A22 south through Killyleagh and onto the Quoile Bridge. Turn left at the bridge and then left again towards Strangford. The reserve is signposted from here.

Castle Espie is south of Comber off the A22. Opening hours are 10.30am to 5pm.

FACILITIES

Castle Espie and Quoile Pondage have wheelchair accessible hides.

Light-bellied Brent Goose
Branta bernicla

The Light-bellied Brent Geese wintering in Ireland, remarkably breed in the Canadian Arctic and Greenland. Almost the entire Irish wintering population arrive on Strangford Lough in autumn, from September onwards, with a peak in October, before many disperse to other Irish sites to the south.

Eel grass is one of their favourite foods, and vast beds of this stringy plant grow on the mudflats of Strangford. Brent Geese are easily identifiable, being small, stocky and dark, with the Light-bellied Brent having distinctive whitish underparts. They have a life expectancy of up to 15 years.

12 COPELAND ISLAND BIRD OBSERVATORY

BIRD OBSERVATORY

16 ha (40 acres)

Sited on St John's, one of the three islands in the Copeland group, accommodation and facilities for ringers are available. There is a colony of Manx Shearwaters, which have been studied since the 1950s. Passerine migration is of interest, and although a bit hit and miss, spring is more productive than autumn. Autumn has in the past brought the occasional outstanding rarity, such as Fox Sparrow and Whites Thrush.

KEY BIRDS

SPRING: Chats, warblers, flycatchers and pipits.
SUMMER: Manx Shearwater, Storm Petrel, Fulmar, Eider, Black Guillemot.
AUTUMN: As for spring plus crests, Skylark, chance of scarce migrants.

ACCESS

DISCOVERY SERIES MAP: 15 REF: J 597 858
The island is private. Prior permission to stay is required. Contact Neville McKee, 67 Temple Rise, Remple Patrick, Co Atrim BT39 0AG. The boat departs from Donaghadee.

13 CARLINGFORD LOUGH

RSPB RESERVE

Incorporating Greencastle Point and Green Island reserves, this long, deep lough attracts seaduck and divers in winter; in summer terns breed. Rostrevor Bay at the head of the lough is best for wildfowl, including Scaup, whilst Greencastle is best for the terns in summer.

KEY BIRDS

SPRING AND SUMMER: Common, Sandwich and Arctic Terns.
WINTER: Red-throated and Great Northern Divers, grebes including Slavonian, Light-bellied Brent Goose, Shelduck, Wigeon, Teal, Long-tailed Duck, Scaup, Red-breasted Merganser, Goldeneye, waders.

ACCESS

DISCOVERY SERIES MAP: 29/36
Greencastle is reached from Kilkeel. Rostrevor is a village on the A2 Kilkeel to Newry road.

14 CASTLECALDWELL

RSPB RESERVE

This reserve on the shores of Lower Lough Erne, encompasses wooded islands and forest, part of an old estate. A good range of woodland birds occur here, and various species of wildfowl breed. This was once the heart of Ireland's population of breeding Common Scoters.

KEY BIRDS

ALL YEAR: Grebes, Red-breasted Merganser, Teal, Tufted Duck, Lapwing, Curlew, Redshank, Snipe, woodland residents, including Siskin and often Crossbill.
SPRING AND SUMMER: Red-breasted Merganser, breeding gulls and terns, Garden Warbler, Blackcap, Sedge Warbler.
AUTUMN AND WINTER: Whooper Swan, Wigeon, Tufted Duck, Pochard, Goldeneye.

ACCESS

DISCOVERY SERIES MAP: 17 REF: H 017 597
The reserve is reached off the A47, 6 km (4 miles) east of Belleek.

15 DUNDALK BAY

Of most interest for wildfowl and particularly waders, this large sandy bay is backed by salt marsh, best visited between autumn and spring.

There are various vantage points. For good views of the outer bay where grebes and divers are most likely, visit Giles Quay on the northern side. Dundalk Bay is one of the most productive estuaries in western Europe for waders. Vantage points for wader watching include a number of sites at the back of the estuary including South Marsh, Lurangreen and Annagassan. At low tide waders can be far in the distance, so a visit within a couple of hours of high tide is a must.

KEY BIRDS

AUTUMN: Passage waders including Curlew Sandpiper, possible Little Stint, Spotted Redshank and Ruff, plus estuarine waders.
WINTER: Red-throated and Great Northern Divers, grebes may include Slavonian, Greylag, White-fronted and Brent Geese, Whooper Swan, Shelduck, Teal, Pintail, Shoveler, Goldeneye, estuarine waders plus

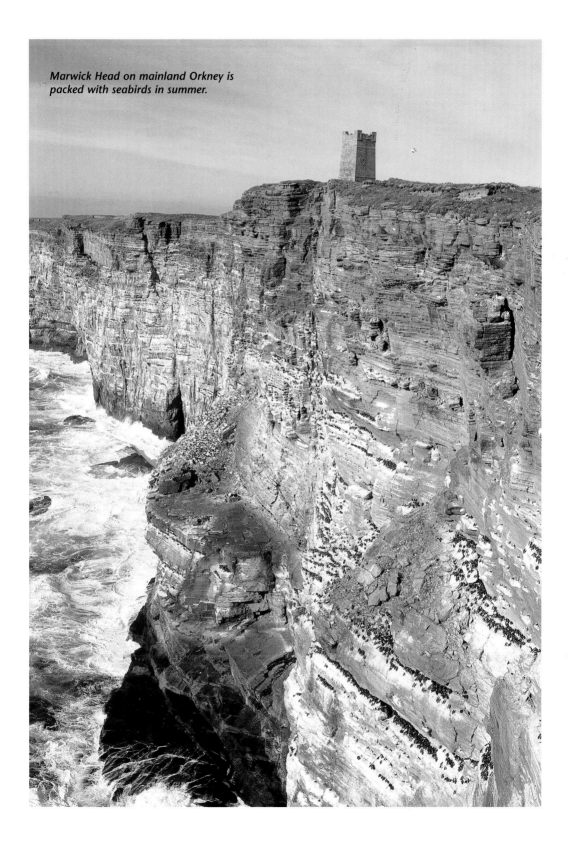

Marwick Head on mainland Orkney is packed with seabirds in summer.

Above: Cotton grass waving in the wind, a common plant on many of Orkney's moorland reserves.

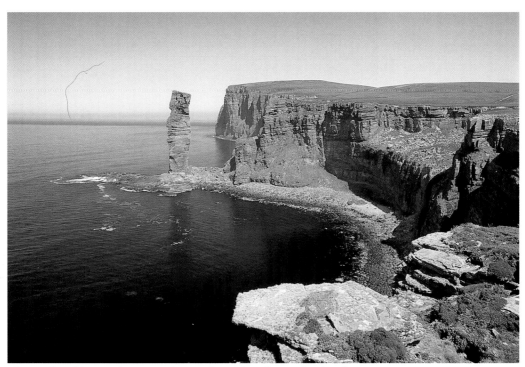

Above: The Old Man of Hoy is perhaps Orkney's best-known landmark.

Above: Kittiwakes crowd on to many of Orkney's cliffs, such as those on Westray.

Above: Slavonian Grebes winter around Orkney's shoreline.

Above: The Arctic Skua nests in scattered colonies on moorland in the Orkneys.

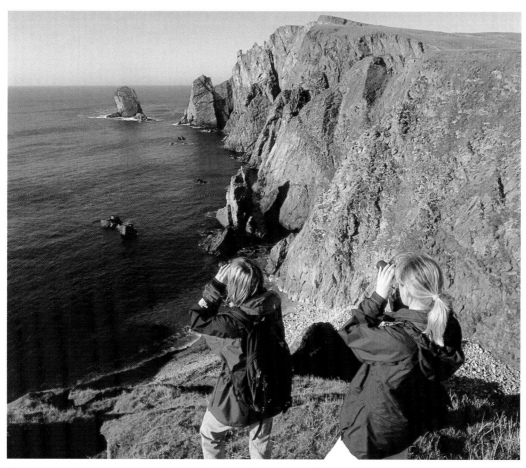
Above: Apart from outstanding birding, Fair Isle offers outstanding scenery, too.

Above: Muckle Flugga off Hermaness, Shetland, the most northerly point in Britain.

Above: A speciality of Shetland, Red-necked Phalaropes breed on the island of Fetlar.

Above: The plaintive call of the Golden Plover is a typical sound of the moors on both Orkney and Shetland in summer.

Left: Razorbills breed at many coastal cliffs around Ireland.

Right: Puffins rarely fail to bring a smile to the face. Often extremely tame, they nest in burrows on cliff tops at a variety of sites around Britain and Ireland. Some of the best places for close encounters include Hermaness in Shetland, the Farne Islands and Great Saltee in Ireland.

Below: Great Saltee Island, off the Wexford coast, boasts some impressive seabird colonies, none more so than the Gannet colony pictured here, located on the south-west tip of the island.

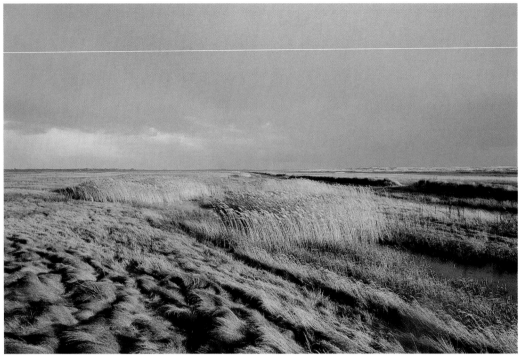

Above: Tacumshin, south-east Ireland, in autumn.

Above: Black Guillemots are resident at many sites throughout Ireland.

Above: The approach to Galley Head, near Clonakilty in southern Ireland.

Golden Plover and Greenshank.
SUMMER: Wildfowl and waders as above.

ACCESS
DISCOVERY SERIES MAP: 36 REF: **J 157 054**
The bay is just east of the town of Dundalk midway between Belfast and Dublin. Giles Quay is reached by turning off the R173 Carlingford road to Giles Quay. The Blackrock to Dundalk coastal road allows views across South Marsh and the bay. At Annagassan, in the south, the road runs alongside the bay.

16 IRELAND'S EYE
Close to Dublin, this small island has a thriving seabird colony including a Gannetry. Cliffs dominate the north-eastern side of the island, and there is a sea stack. A half-day visit is sufficient to cover the island.

KEY BIRDS
SPRING AND SUMMER: Manx Shearwater, Gannet, Fulmar, Cormorant, Shag, Guillemot and Black Guillemot, Puffin, Razorbill, Kittiwake and large gulls.
WINTER: Great Northern Diver offshore, Light-bellied Brent Goose and Purple Sandpiper in Howth Harbour.

ACCESS
DISCOVERY SERIES MAP: 50 REF: **O 288 413**
Boats run regularly from Howth Harbour during summer.

17 NORTH BULL
Lying on the northern side of Dublin Bay this 1 km (⅔ mile) wide sandbar, complete with two golf courses and long sandy beach, is attached to the mainland by a causeway. Either side of the causeway are mudflats and saltmarsh attractive to a wide range of wildfowl and waders.

Winter is the time to visit, and ideally on an incoming tide. Light-bellied Brent Geese feature with often very close views at high tide possible. All the other typical estuarine wildfowl and waders are present with the chance of seaduck, divers and grebes offshore. Snow Buntings are possible along the beach. During the summer months the beach is a popular recreational area, so birding is not that productive.

KEY BIRDS
SPRING AND AUTUMN: Passage waders include Curlew Sandpiper, Spotted Redshank, Ruff, Little Stint and sometimes rarities plus arriving and departing winter species.
SUMMER: Little Tern, Ringed Plover.
WINTER: Divers, grebes and seaduck possible offshore. Light-bellied Brent Goose, Shelduck, Wigeon, Teal, Pintail, Shoveler, Merlin, Peregrine, estuarine waders, Short-eared Owl, Snow Bunting. Sanderling on the beach and Purple Sandpiper on the Bull Wall.

ACCESS
DISCOVERY SERIES MAP: 50 REF: **O 234 370**
Easily reached from Dublin city centre by public transport. Take the coast road north from the docks towards Raheny and Howth. You can drive along the Bull Wall at the southern end. However, viewing is best from the causeway and road bordering the mudflats.

FACILITIES
There is an interpretative centre. Viewing for the disabled is good from the causeway, and it is possible to birdwatch from a car.

18 NORTH SLOB
IRISH WILDBIRD CONSERVANCY
1,012 ha (2,500 acres)
North Slob is best known for the geese attracted in winter to its low-lying fields bordering Wexford Harbour. The best time for a visit is from autumn to spring, with Greenland White-fronted Geese being the highlight in winter, smaller numbers of other species may be present with occasional Snow and small race Canada Geese.

A tower hide overlooks the slob and a wader scrape, the latter attracts a few passage waders and has hosted some major rarities.

KEY BIRDS
SPRING AND AUTUMN: Passage waders.
WINTER: Bewick's Swan, sometimes Whooper Swan, Greenland white-fronted Goose, Light-bellied Brent Goose, chance of a few Pink-footed Geese and vagrant Snow and Canada Geese, various ducks, Golden Plover, Black-tailed Godwit, Peregrine.

ACCESS

DISCOVERY SERIES MAP: 77 REF: T 077 238
From Wexford travel on the road to Gorey.
Two and a half kilometres (1½ miles) after the
bridge, take the right-hand turn to the reserve.
Opening times are 10am to 5pm daily from 1st
October to 15th April, and 9am to 6pm for the
rest of the year.

FACILITIES

There is a viewing tower and hide, plus a visitor
centre.

19 LADY'S ISLAND LAKE

Separated from the sea by a shingle beach, this
lake, technically known as a back-barrier lagoon,
is of most interest in summer for its tern
colonies. A small island attracts large numbers of
nesting Sandwich Terns along with a few
Common, Arctic and, of most interest, Roseate
Terns. The terns can be viewed from a path
leading around Lady's Island, attached to the
shore by a causeway. Another good vantage
point is at the shingle bank barrier where the
birds fly through a narrow cutting to the sea.

During winter a few wildfowl winter and at
passage periods the lake is worth checking for
waders.

KEY BIRDS

SPRING AND SUMMER: Passage waders, Sandwich,
Common, Arctic and Roseate Terns.
AUTUMN: Passage waders and always the chance
of an American vagrant.
WINTER: Occasionally Bewick's Swan and
Whooper Swan, Wigeon, Teal, Gadwall,
Shoveler, Pochard, Tufted Duck, Goldeneye,
Red-breasted Merganser, Golden Plover, and
Greenshank.

ACCESS

DISCOVERY SERIES MAP: 77 REF: T 090 050
The lake is reached by turning off the N25
Wexford to Rosslare road at Tagoat.

20 TACUMSHIN

Close to Lady's Island Lake, this too is a lagoon
separated from the sea by a shingle beach. Best
known as a site for waders and particularly
American vagrant waders in autumn. Aside from

this interest the lake attracts a good variety of
passage and wintering wildfowl, and is hunted
over by raptors in winter.

In the south-west corner a small marsh known
as White Hole often attracts geese and swans,
and good views of the lake and reed swamps can
be had from here. If looking for waders during
autumn, then any areas of shore are worth
investigating. A full day would be necessary to
cover the site thoroughly.

KEY BIRDS

SPRING: A few passage waders, terns and Little
Gull, chance of Garganey.
AUTUMN: Garganey; passage waders including
Curlew Sandpiper and Little Stint, Spotted
Redshank, chance of American species with
Pectoral Sandpiper and Buff-breasted Sandpiper
being two of the most regular.
WINTER: Bewick's and Whooper Swans, Light-
bellied Brent Goose, Shelduck, Wigeon, Teal,
Pintail, Shoveler, Scaup, Hen Harrier, Water
Rail, waders.

ACCESS

DISCOVERY SERIES MAP: 77 REF: T 040 060
Just 1.6 km (1 mile) west of Lady's Island Lake,
Tacumshin is reached along country lanes, and
there are a number of access points. The north-
east shore is reached by passing through
Tacumshin, over a crossroads and turn left by the
ruins of an old castle. Either fork along this road
reaches the shore. The north-west corner can be
reached by travelling towards Tacumshin from
Tomhaggard and turning right 0.8 km (½ mile)
from Tomhaggard to a cul-de-sac.

White Hole is reached by turning left 0.8 km
(½ mile) west of Tomhaggard. Follow this road to
a small parking area. The White Hole can be
covered from here, and by walking east you will
reach the lagoon. Nowhere is suitable for
disabled access.

21 GREAT SALTEE ISLAND

At approximately 1.6 km (1 mile) long, 0.8 km
(½ mile) wide, Great Saltee is the largest of the
two Saltee islands, and by far the more
interesting for birds. A visit in spring or summer
will reveal some impressive seabird colonies, and
close encounters can be enjoyed with Gannets,
Puffins, Razorbills and Guillemots. Choughs are

easily seen coasting along the cliff tops.

A visit in spring or autumn may produce a good variety of migrants, this is one of Ireland's best migrant hotspots. Spring can produce some impressive falls.

KEY BIRDS

ALL YEAR: Peregrine, Raven, Chough.
SPRING AND SUMMER: Passerine migrants, chance of rarities such as Hoopoe or Golden Oriole. Breeding seabirds include Manx Shearwater, Fulmar, Shag, Gannet, Guillemot, Razorbill, Puffin, gulls, Kittiwake. European Storm Petrel seen from boat crossing.
AUTUMN: Passerine migrants, chance of rarities, and seabird passage in southerly winds.

ACCESS

DISCOVERY SERIES MAP: 77 REF: X 950 970
Day trips are run during the summer from Kilmore Quay. Enquiries should be made at the quay. Permission from the owners is required if an overnight stay is desired.

22　HOOK HEAD

A long thin headland, Hook Head lies south-east of Waterford. Best in spring and autumn for migrants and seawatching. During May a good range of migrants make landfall here, with always the chance of a rarity. In autumn, too, although with fewer birds to find, they often make up for this with quality, and some outstanding vagrants have been found.

Seawatching in spring annually produces Pomarine Skuas. Autumn seawatching is more weather dependant, with south-westerly winds associated with poor weather being most productive. Seawatching is best from the lighthouse, whilst migrants should be searched for wherever there is suitable cover.

KEY BIRDS

SPRING: Passerine migrants include chats, warblers, flycatchers, Cuckoo, Turtle Dove, and the chance of rarities such as Hoopoe or Serin. Offshore Manx Shearwater, Gannet, Pomarine Skua.
AUTUMN: Offshore Sooty Shearwater, Manx Shearwater, Storm Petrel, Gannet, skuas Passerine migrants as for spring. Chance of Chough.

ACCESS

DISCOVERY SERIES MAP: 76 REF: X 733 974
Follow signs for Fethard, from here follow the road south to Churchtown and the lighthouse.

23　BALLYMACODA

Ballymacoda is a south-coast estuary with a large area of inter-tidal mud, fed by the Womanagh River. Thousands of waders winter in the area notably Black-tailed Godwits and Golden Plover, and there are normally good numbers of wildfowl, using both the estuary and surrounding fields.

KEY BIRDS

SPRING AND AUTUMN: Passage waders. In Autumn may include Ruff, Curlew Sandpiper, Green Sandpiper, Wood Sandpiper and Little Stint.
SUMMER: A few waders on mudflats, particularly from July.
WINTER: Light-bellied Brent Goose, Wigeon, Teal, Shelduck, Black-tailed Godwit, Golden Plover, estuarine waders, Peregrine, Merlin, Hen Harrier and Short-eared Owl.

ACCESS

DISCOVERY SERIES MAP: 81 REF: X 050 730
The estuary is east of Cork easily reached off the N25, close to Youghal. There are various access points, two of the best being from Clonpriest Graveyard, just east of Crompaun Bridge. Alternatively, park at the bridge on the road between Ballymacoda and Youghal, and walk south along the river to the estuary.

24　KNOCKADOON HEAD

Close to Ballymacoda this headland is best in autumn for migrants. Some excellent rarities have been found here, and there is much opportunity for finding good birds yourself as it is very underwatched. The hedgerows and any areas of cover are worth investigating, with the caravan park having been one of the more productive sites in recent years. Choughs are a year round feature.

KEY BIRDS

ALL YEAR: Peregrine, Chough.
SPRING: A few migrants.
AUTUMN: Migrants include warblers, chats,

flycatchers and crests, chance of a rarity. Past records have included Pied Wheatear and Woodchat Shrike.

ACCESS
DISCOVERY SERIES MAP: 81 REF: X 088 702
The head lies east of Ballymacoda.

25 BALLYCOTTON

Worthy of a visit at any time of year, Ballycotton comes into its own in autumn, attracting a wide range of waders and annually rarities, notably American vagrant waders.

Mudflats, lagoons and muddy pools attract both waders, and in winter wildfowl. The hedgerows and gardens in the town attract passerine migrants in autumn. During winter, there is a good variety of wildfowl.

KEY BIRDS
ALL YEAR: Shelduck, Redshank, Dunlin, Chough.
SPRING: Passage waders include Whimbrel, godwits and Sanderling.
SUMMER: Warblers, plus a few waders, autumn passage from mid-July.
AUTUMN: Estuarine waders, plus Little Stint, Curlew Sandpiper, Spotted Redshank, Wood Sandpiper, chance of American wader such as Pectoral, Baird's or White-rumped Sandpiper. Passerine migrants include chats and flycatchers.
WINTER: Estuarine wildfowl and waders, wild swans and chance of Glaucous and Iceland Gulls in bay.

ACCESS
DISCOVERY SERIES MAP: 81 REF: W 995 635
Ballycotton is south-east of Cork. Turn left to Ballynamona Strand about 0.8km (½ mile) from Shanagarry on the Ballycotton road. Park at the end and walk north for the pools. Go south for the mudflats and lake.

26 OLD HEAD OF KINSALE

This beautiful headland is second only to Cape Clear for seawatching off the south coast in autumn. Strong south westerlies are best, however, these are not always necessary for seeing passing auks, skuas, Gannets and Manx Shearwaters.

During summer seabirds breed along the cliffs on the western side, along with Choughs that are easily located. Migrants have little cover on the head, and so are often more conspicuous a little inland, where any patches of cover should be checked in autumn.

KEY BIRDS
ALL YEAR: Peregrine, Rock Dove, Chough, Raven.
SPRING: Passing seabirds include Manx Shearwater and Gannet, chance of Pomarine Skua in May. Passerine migrants.
SUMMER: Breeding seabirds include Fulmar, Shag, Kittiwake, Guillemot, Razorbill, Black Guillemot.
AUTUMN: Seabird passage in late summer includes Cory's Shearwater. Plus Sooty Great and Manx Shearwaters, Gannet, Great and Arctic Skuas, terns, auks, Kittiwake, European Storm Petrel, chance of a rarity such as Little Shearwater.

ACCESS
DISCOVERY SERIES MAP: 87 REF: W 631 392
A golf course sits on the end of the head, access is permitted for birdwatchers. The head is reached by leaving Kinsale west. Cross the bridge and follow signs for the Old Head of Kinsale. Care should be taken along these high cliffs.

27 CLONAKILTY AND INCHYDONEY

Picturesque and adjacent to each other these two estuaries attract passage and wintering waders. Clonakilty attracts the lions share of waders including a wintering flock of Icelandic Black-tailed Godwits.

Inchydoney has behind its causeway some freshwater pools attractive to passage waders and wildfowl. Out in Clonakilty Bay both Red-throated and Great Northern Divers can be located in winter.

KEY BIRDS
ALL YEAR: Shelduck, Oystercatcher, Ringed Plover, Sparrowhawk, Kingfisher.
SPRING AND AUTUMN: Passage waders notably in autumn include Little Stint, Curlew Sandpiper,

Ruff, Spotted Redshank, Wood Sandpiper, Greenshank, always the chance of an American wader. Skuas and terns in the bay in autumn.
SUMMER: Black-tailed Godwit and other passage waders start to reappear in July.
WINTER: Wigeon, Teal, Black-tailed Godwit, Golden Plover, Greenshank, Spotted Redshank and estuarine waders, Short-eared Owl, Hen Harrier, Peregrine, and gull roost in bay.

ACCESS
DISCOVERY SERIES MAP: 89
Best views of the bay are from Dunmore. The estuaries are reached from Clonakilty town, with good views from bordering roads. Freshwater pools can be viewed from the road running along the back of Inchydoney estuary.

FACILITIES
Disabled access is good here as all birdwatching is done from the roads.

28 GALLEY HEAD
Close to Clonakilty this headland is best in autumn for migrants and seawatching. Strong south-westerly winds can produce shearwaters, petrels and skuas in autumn, with the best place to view being the vicinity of the lighthouse; you will need to seek permission.

Migrants in autumn can be located anywhere on the head, and have in the past included some outstanding vagrants. The bays either side of the head are worth checking for divers in winter, and Kilkerran Lake on the west side holds a few wildfowl and is worth checking for migrants.

KEY BIRDS
ALL YEAR: Shag, Rock Dove, Chough, and Stonechat.
SPRING: Passing seabirds include Manx Shearwater and chance of Pomarine Skuas in May. Passerine migrants.
SUMMER: Little Grebe, Fulmar, Wheatear, offshore passing Manx Shearwater, European Storm Petrel, Gannet and terns.
AUTUMN: Warblers, flycatchers, chats and crests with possibility of scarce migrants such as Yellow-browed Warbler and vagrants. Offshore in right conditions Great and Sooty Shearwaters, skuas and petrels.

ACCESS
DISCOVERY SERIES MAP: 89 REF: W 340 313
From Clonakilty drive south past Inchydoney estuary and follow signs to the head.

29 CORK HARBOUR
This large harbour is at its best in winter when thousands of birds use the mudflats, lagoons and deep water channels. Waders include all the typical estuarine species, joined in spring and autumn by a few passage migrants. Gulls are another feature of winter with white-winged gulls recorded annually.

KEY BIRDS
SPRING AND AUTUMN: Passage waders include Whimbrel and Curlew Sandpiper.
WINTER: Diving and dabbling ducks including Red-breasted Merganser, Goldeneye, estuarine waders, gulls including Glaucous Gull, Iceland Gull, Mediterranean Gull and chance of Ring-billed Gull.

ACCESS
DISCOVERY SERIES MAP: 87
Various access points around the harbour. East of Carrigaline, Lough Beg is worth visiting in autumn for waders. Lough Mahon, on the south side of the city of Cork, is easily accessible.

30 DURSEY ISLAND
This island off the Beara Peninsula, is known for turning up scarce migrants and vagrants in autumn. Firkeel Glen is worth searching for birds, and is found 3 km (2 miles) from Dursey Sound.

KEY BIRDS
AUTUMN: Scarce migrants and vagrants. Seawatching produces similar species to other headlands on this coast, including Cape Clear.

ACCESS
DISCOVERY SERIES MAP: 84 REF: V 505 416
The island is reached by cable car.

CAPE CLEAR

BIRD OBSERVATORY (300 ha/741 acres)

The name Cape Clear has long been synonymous with legendary seawatches and autumn rarities. Home to a bird observatory since 1959, the island can offer some outstanding birding. Cape Clear is hilly with plenty of cover for migrants including well vegetated gardens, hedgerows, patches of gorse and bracken covered hillsides, and small copses.

As the southernmost point in Ireland, excepting the Fastnet Rock just offshore, the island is well placed for observing seabird passage. From July to September seabird passage can be spectacular – on some days Manx Shearwaters have been counted at up to 30,000 passing per hour. There are few better sites for seeing Great Shearwaters, and in July and August they can on some days pass in their hundreds. On occasions, thousands have been recorded in a single day. Cory's Shearwater are much more scarce, occurring between late

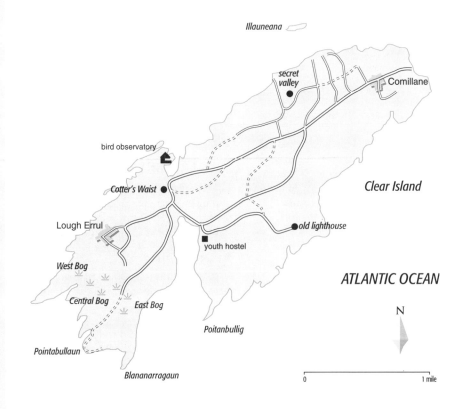

June and September. During September, in inclement weather and onshore winds, skuas, Leach's Storm Petrel and Sabine's Gull are likely, along with auks and shearwaters.

Spring migrants include the commoner chats, warblers and flycatchers, and although usually in relatively low numbers, a good variety of species are likely. The island annually attracts continental overshoots. Species such as Serin, Hoopoe and Woodchat Shrike are all possible. As with most spring migrants, the chances are they will not linger for long.

It is the autumn that brings great excitement to the island. Apart from the commoner migrants, annually both Red-breasted Flycatcher and Yellow-browed Warblers are found in the more sheltered parts of the island. However, the American landbirds, which occur almost annually, arouse the most interest. They have included, in past years, exciting rarities such as Yellow-bellied Sapsucker, Grey Catbird and, more recently, Europe's first Blue-winged Warbler.

Siberian vagrants occur, too – indeed the island is one of those sites where almost anything is possible. Vagrants from the east have included Siberian Thrush, Lesser Grey Shrike and Pallas's Grasshopper Warbler. There are various hotspots for searching for migrants and rarities, these include Cotter's Garden, just south of the observatory, and the Youth Hostel garden.

KEY BIRDS

ALL YEAR: Gannet, Shag, Black Guillemot, Peregrine, Rock Dove, Stonechat, Chough, Raven.
SPRING: Pomarine Skuas pass offshore in May, plus Manx Shearwater. Passerine migrants include chats, flycatchers, warblers, Turtle Dove, Cuckoo, chance of a rarity.
SUMMER: Breeding are Guillemot, Puffin, Razorbill, gulls, Wheatear. Offshore, Manx, Sooty and Great Shearwaters, chance of Cory's Shearwater, also Fulmar and Storm Petrel.
AUTUMN: Seabirds as for summer, plus skuas, auks, terns, Kittiwake, chance of Sabine's Gull and Leach's Storm Petrel. Passerine migrants as for spring, rarities annually include Red-breasted Flycatcher and Yellow-browed Warbler, chance of American or Siberian vagrants.
WINTER: Divers offshore.

ACCESS

DISCOVERY SERIES MAP: 88 REF: V 955 219
Ferries leave Baltimore daily, local tourist office has times. Baltimore is reached from Cork via the N71 and then R595. If time allows, good birding can be had from the car at Rosscarbery Bay, which is along the route.

FACILITIES

The bird observatory has accommodation, alternatively there are a number of bed and breakfast establishments on the island, and a youth hostel.

Great Shearwater
Puffinus gravis

This large shearwater is an annual passage migrant off the coast of Cape Clear, during late July and August. They breed in the southern oceans and migrate north during our summer. Great Shearwaters close-to are easily identified by their dark brown cap and narrow white collar. They also have a white patch over the tail. They can be confused with Cory's Shearwater at a distance. However, Cory's Shearwaters fly with their wings slightly bowed and have a more uniform look to their upperparts, lacking the cap and collar.

Great Shearwaters often bank steeply and glide at speed with a few flaps of their wings.

32 SKELLIGS

19 ha (47 acres) and 0.4 ha (1 acre)
Found 13 km (8 miles) off Valentia Island, these
red sandstone and slate islands tower out of the
Atlantic. Little Skellig has a thriving Gannet
colony, whilst Great Skellig is home to various
seabirds including Puffins and Manx Shearwaters.

KEY BIRDS
SPRING AND SUMMER: Manx Shearwater,
European Storm Petrel, Fulmar, Gannet, Puffin,
Razorbill, Guillemot, Kittiwake.

ACCESS
DISCOVERY SERIES MAP: 83
Boats run from Valentia Pier at 10am, and
Portmagee Pier at 11am during summer.

33 AKERAGH LOUGH

Although not attracting the number of birds it
once did, this site is still one of the best in Ireland
for American waders and wildfowl in autumn. A
brackish lake for much of the year, it often shrinks
in summer. If sufficient water remains in autumn,
both waders and waterfowl can be found.

The nearby beach should be checked for
waders. Pectoral Sandpiper has occurred almost
annually here, and the site has a long list of
Nearctic waders to its name. During winter wild
swans and wildfowl use the lough and
surrounding flood meadows.

KEY BIRDS
ALL YEAR: Oystercatcher, Ringed Plover,
Redshank, Hooded Crow, Chough.
SPRING: A few passage waders.
AUTUMN: Passage waders include Little Stint,
Wood Sandpiper, Spotted Redshank, Greenshank,
chance of Nearctic species such as Pectoral
Sandpiper, a Baird's Sandpiper or a White-rumped
Sandpiper. Nearctic wildfowl have included
American Wigeon.
WINTER: Bewick's and Whooper Swans, Wigeon,
Gadwall, Pintail, Teal, Shoveler, Pochard, Tufted
Duck, Red-breasted Merganser, Hen Harrier,
Merlin, Peregrine, Golden Plover, godwits,
Dunlin, Greenshank.

ACCESS
DISCOVERY SERIES MAP: 71 REF: Q 758 265
Located in the north of Kerry, the lough is
reached by taking a rough track south from the
centre of Ballyheigue, parallel with the sea and
past some caravans. The farmhouse at the end of
the track is strictly private. Alternatively,
viewing is possible from Route 105, with turnings
off this road allowing further views.

34 CASTLEMAINE HARBOUR

At the head of Dingle Bay is Castlemaine
Harbour. Winter is by far the best season to visit
for wildfowl and waders. There are various access
points allowing views, one of the best is Inch
Point, a sand dune promontory at the harbour
mouth.

KEY BIRDS
ALL YEAR: Oystercatcher, Ringed Plover,
Peregrine.
SPRING AND AUTUMN: A few passage waders, terns.
SUMMER: Terns in harbour.
WINTER: Great Northern Diver, Light-bellied
Brent Goose, Wigeon, Teal, Shoveler, Pintail,
Goldeneye, Scaup, Long-tailed Duck, Common
Scoter, Red-breasted Merganser, estuarine waders
plus Greenshank.

ACCESS
DISCOVERY SERIES MAP: 71/78
Access to the harbour from the N70 and R561.
Inch Point can be reached off the R561, park at
Inch Strand and walk out to the point.

35 LOOP HEAD AND BRIDGES OF ROSS

This headland is an outstanding seawatching
site in autumn. North-westerly winds are
needed for variety and numbers of birds. The
area around the head should be searched for
migrants in autumn, rarities have been found in
recent years.

KEY BIRDS
AUTUMN: Passerine migrants and the chance of a
rarity. Offshore, shearwaters, petrels, skuas, auks

and good chances of Sabine's Gull, Leach's Storm Petrel, Long-tailed Skua and Grey Phalarope.

⛴ ACCESS
DISCOVERY SERIES MAP: 63
Loop Head is reached off the R487 from Kilkee. The Bridges of Ross are on the north side of the head about 3km (2 miles) before the lighthouse, and is the best site for seawatching.

36 GALWAY BAY

Many birders know Galway Bay as a site for winter gull watching, for this it is one of the best. The outer bay attracts Great Northern Divers, but it is the inner bay that is most productive.

January to March is best for gulls, and is when wildfowl numbers peak. For gulls try Nimmo's Pier in the city's dock area. Tawin Island is productive for waders and wildfowl. Numerous other access points around the bay will produce birds.

⬛ KEY BIRDS
WINTER: Great Northern Diver, Light-bellied Brent Goose, Shelduck, Wigeon, Shoveler, Teal, Scaup, Long-tailed Duck, Red-breasted Merganser, Common Scoter, estuarine waders, and a large variety of gulls.

⛴ ACCESS
DISCOVERY SERIES MAP: 45/46/51
Tawin is reached off the Galway to Limerick road by turning off at Clarinbridge or near Oranmore. Nimmo's Pier is close to the mouth of the River Corrib, on the western side of the little harbour.

37 LOUGH CORRIB

Lough Corrib hosts large numbers of ducks in winter, notably Pochard. Various species of wildfowl breed and there are a few tern colonies. One of the best sites from which to view is Angilham on the eastern shore.

⬛ KEY BIRDS
ALL YEAR: Grebes, Tufted Duck, Pochard, Red-breasted Merganser.
SPRING AND SUMMER: Terns, Common Scoter, breeding gulls, Whimbrel on passage.

AUTUMN AND WINTER: Wigeon, Teal, Shoveler, Snipe, Curlew, Lapwing.

⛴ ACCESS
DISCOVERY SERIES MAP: 45
The lough can be reached from a few points. For Angilham take the road for Headford from Galway, at Ballindooly turn left for the lakeshore.

38 DONEGAL BAY

Donegal Bay is a winter site, incorporating vast areas of habitat attractive to wildfowl and waders. Seaduck are a feature of the deeper water, whilst all the typical estuarine wildfowl and waders can be expected. A key site to visit is Killybegs, which attracts large numbers of gulls. As a result this is one of Britain and Ireland's top winter sites for white-winged and vagrant gulls.

⬛ KEY BIRDS
WINTER: Red-throated, Black-throated and Great Northern Divers, Whooper and Bewick's Swans, Light-bellied Brent Goose, Wigeon, Teal, Pochard, Tufted Duck, Scaup, Common Scoter, Long-tailed Duck, estuarine waders, Greenshank, Purple Sandpiper, Glaucous and Iceland Gulls.

⛴ ACCESS
DISCOVERY SERIES MAPS: 10/11/16
Lots of points to view the estuary from surrounding roads. Killybegs is a port on the north side.

GLOSSARY

Auk Family of seabirds that include Razorbill, Guillemot and Puffin.

Drift migrant A migrant that loses its course by being drifted by winds or inclement weather.

Estaurine wader Collective term for species commonly seen on estuaries. Birds include Oystercatcher, Curlew, Dunlin, Knot and Redshank.

Fall A mass arrival of birds, usually grounded by adverse weather.

Fleet An inlet or creek by the coast.

Flood Normally an area of grassland that has been flooded to a shallow depth to attract wildfowl and waders.

Hirundine Collective term for martins and swallows.

Large gull Collective term for Herring and Great and Lesser Black-backed Gulls.

Nearctic Collective term for species originating from the Americas.

Passage migrant A migrant passing through an area, where it does not remain, to either winter or breed.

Passerine A perching bird.

Raptor A bird of prey.

Saltmarsh Inter-tidal mudflats colonized by salt-loving plants.

Sawbill Collective term for fish-eating birds that have serrated edges to their bills. They include Smew, Red-breasted Merganser and Goosander.

Seaduck Ducks commonly found on the sea in winter and include scoters, Eider, Long-tailed Duck, Red-breasted Merganser and Scaup.

Scrape Shallow excavation designed to attract wildfowl and waders.

Vagrant A rare visitor not native to the country.

White-winged gull Collective term for Glaucous and Iceland Gulls.

Wild swan Collective term for Whooper and Bewick's Swans.

USEFUL ADDRESSES

The Wildlife Trusts
The Kiln, Waterside, Mather Road, Newark, Nottinghamshire BG24 1WT
Tel: 0870 0367711
www.wildlifetrusts.org

Birdwatch Ireland
Ruttledge House, 8 Longford Place, Monkstown, Co Dublin, Ireland
Tel: (353) (01) 280 4322
www.birdwatchireland.ie

English Nature
Northminster House,
Peterborough PE1 1UA
Tel: 01733 455101
www.english-nature.org.uk

Field Studies Council
Montford Bridge, Preston Montford,
Shrewsbury SY4 1HW
Tel: 01743 852100
www.field-studies-council.org

Royal Society for the Protection of Birds (RSPB)
The Lodge, Sandy,
Bedfordshire SG19 2DL
Tel: 01767 680551
www.rspb.org.uk

Scottish Natural Heritage
12 Hope Terrace, Edinburgh EH9 2AS
Tel: 0131 447 4784
www.snh.org.uk

The Wildfowl & Wetlands Trust
Slimbridge, Gloucestershire GL2 7BT
Tel: 01453 890333
www.wwt.org.uk

INDEX

SPECIES INDEX